The
Great
Uranium
Cartel

The
Great
Uranium
Cartel

Earle Gray

McClelland and Stewart

McClelland and Stewart Limited
The Canadian Publishers
25 Hollinger Road
Toronto, Ontario
M4B 3G2

Canadian Cataloguing in Publication Data

Gray, Earle, 1931-
   The great uranium cartel

Bibliography: p.
ISBN 0-7710-3537-3

1. Uranium industry. 2. Uranium industry – Canada.
3. Uranium industry – United States. 4. Trusts,
Industrial. I. Title.

HD9539.U7G72   338.8 '87   C82-094121-2

Printed and bound in Canada

Contents

CHAPTER ONE

The Bomb
From Australia

The existence of an international uranium cartel, involving the governments and uranium mining companies of Canada, Australia, France, and South Africa, as well as an international mining firm with headquarters in England, was first brought to public attention in 1976 by some 200 pages of confidential documents stolen from the files of an Australian company.

The documents stolen from Mary Kathleeen Uranium Ltd. revealed that the cartel had been established in 1972. Its purpose was the classical purpose of a cartel: to control supply and increase price. In four years following the formation of the cartel, the world price of uranium increased more than 700 per cent.

The Mary Kathleen documents, as they soon became known, triggered a nuclear chain reaction that sent tremors through corporate headquarters, government offices, embassies, legislatures, and court houses around the world.

A whole series of events was unleashed by the disclosure of the cartel. In the United States, a flagging investigation of uranium prices by the Department of Justice was quickly revived. A more sensational investigation was launched by a Congressional committee, acting in concert with a committee of the New York State Legislature. A score of law suits, with billions of dollars at stake, were launched. Canada, Australia, France, England, and South Africa took steps to protect their uranium producing companies from prosecution under U.S. laws. Diplomatic relations were strained as U.S. courts and legislators accused these governments of a cover-up, while the governments in turn accused the United States of heavy-

7

handed attempts to extend its laws outside of its own borders, in violation of the sovereignty of other nations. The government of Canada went so far to protect Canadian uranium producers from prosecution under U.S. law as to pass a law which made it illegal for any Canadian to talk about the cartel. Having taken that step, Ottawa later charged the Canadian uranium producers with a criminal price conspiracy under Canadian law; this despite the fact that Ottawa had been instrumental in establishing the cartel in the first place.

Public and political attitudes on energy pricing matters had been made sensitive by actions of the Organization of Petroleum Exporting Countries. In late 1973, Arab members of OPEC embargoed oil shipments to many nations of the western world, resulting in gasoline and fuel oil shortages and rationing. Oil prices quadrupled within three months, marking the start of skyrocketing energy prices, which were still being blamed seven years later as a principal cause of the world's economic ills. With the revelations contained in the Mary Kathleen documents, it seemed that another group of world energy producers were following in the footsteps of OPEC.

THE GREAT AUSTRALIAN DEBATE

The Mary Kathleen documents had surfaced in Australia in the midst of what the *Encyclopaedia Britannica* yearbook has called "potentially the most divisive issue in Australian society."

The issue was whether or not to permit development in northern Australia of large reserves of uranium, among the richest in the world. It had been a divisive issue for nearly half a dozen years, with conflicting views among both politicians and the public. All the public opinion polls in late-1975 ranked uranium mining as the number one political issue, and even the government and Labor Party of Prime Minister Gough Whitlam were sharply divided. The cabinet was in favour of proceeding, largely under government ownership of the mines, but the Labor caucus was opposed, as were most of the rank and file party members of the trade unions.

Comparatively small uranium deposits had been discovered

in Australia in the early-1950's, and had helped provide material for the nuclear arms build-up in both the United States and Great Britain. The last operating uranium mine in Australia, owned by Mary Kathleen and located in Queensland, had been shut down since the mid-1960's.

The much larger uranium discoveries in Australia's Northern Territory were not made until 1970, however. The U.S. Industrial Atomic Forum estimated that each ton of ore in the most spectacular of these finds contained up to one hundred times as much uranium as the ore being mined in the United States. The Australian Atomic Energy Commission predicted that Australia's annual uranium exports by 1985 could equal the entire world production of 1971.

Plans to develop this latent source of energy ground to a halt following the election of the Labor government of Prime Minister Whitlam in 1972. It was not that Whitlam's government opposed the development of uranium resources and nuclear power. Energy Minister Reginald Connor, in fact, promised that Labor would stimulate the growth of nuclear technology, establish a multi-billion dollar plant to enrich the uranium, and build power plants to produce electricity from the uranium.

But there were problems. Labor was determined that this development would take place mainly under government ownership, and the mining tax laws were drastically revised. There was concern that the low prevailing prices for uranium would yield inadequate public revenues, unless the pace of planned development was slowed down to avoid swamping the markets. There was concern about the effects of the mining activity on the lives of the Aborigines in the Northern Territory, and the possible effects on a wilderness environment. There was mounting opposition by anti-nuclear organizations and the trade unions. And there was sharply divided opinion within the cabinet.

While Energy Minister Connor foresaw large revenues and employment from the development of Australian uranium and nuclear energy, Environment Minister Dr. Moss Cass came to a different conclusion. Nuclear energy, he declared, created "the most dangerous, insidious and persistent waste products ever experienced on the planet." He said it was "futile to seek salvation from the energy crisis through development of nuclear energy."

Faced with these conflicts, the government called a halt to any new uranium export contracts, and in April, 1975, appointed Justice Russell W. Fox to head a commission of inquiry. Fox and the two other members of the commission undertook a wide-ranging examination of all the nuclear issues, including safety, environmental factors, health, implications for native people and their unresolved land rights in the prospective mining areas, nuclear proliferation, and the alleged threat of terrorist activities.

The Labor government was defeated at the general election late in 1975, and the new Liberal-Country government of Prime Minister Malcolm Fraser soon made it known that it favoured development of the uranium resources, and by private industry. That, however, would have to await completion of the inquiry by the Fox commission.

As the Fox inquiry proceeded, the anti-nuclear forces intensified the emotion-charged debate, with marches, demonstrations, sit-ins, and a barrage of doomsday literature. Prime Minister Fraser was hanged in effigy on the streets of Melbourne.

Leading the parade of the anti-nuclear forces was the Australian chapter of the Friends of the Earth, an international organization with headquarters in San Francisco. Uranium mining, argued the Friends, would "destroy the physical environment" on which the Aborigines "depend for the survival of their culture," cause miners to die of lung cancer, and create dangers of nuclear explosions, contamination by radioactive wastes, "a rapid spread of nuclear weapons," and "expanded police powers."

"The use of commercial nuclear power dramatically increases the fragility of human civilization," according to a booklet published by the Australian Friends of the Earth. "Acceptance of nuclear technology amounts to acceptance of the inevitable spread of nuclear weapons from nation to nation, and the near-certainty that some nuclear bombs will end up in terrorists' hands."

In August, 1976, the Fox commission was completing public

hearings on the first of the two phases of its inquiry. The day before the public hearings were to close, the Friends of the Earth obtained the original documents from the files of Mary Kathleen Uranium.

The documents had been sent anonymously to FOE's Melbourne office, according to G. D. Woods, a senior lecturer in law at the University of Sydney, and counsel for FOE at the Fox commission hearings. "As soon as they came to my notice I took steps to put them in the right hands," Woods was later quoted as telling reporters. "You can draw your own conclusions by reading them."

The Friends reportedly spent a feverish night duplicating copies of the more relevant documents, and the next day tabled the original documents with the Fox commission. Others might have drawn some conclusions by reading the stolen documents, but not the commission. It ruled that the documents were received "too late" for inclusion in the record, were "not relevant" (presumably because they dealt primarily with uranium pricing, which was not what the commission was examining), and turned them over to the police.

The Mary Kathleen documents failed to generate much stir in Australia, but two weeks later duplicates were in the United States, where the interest was far more pronounced. They had been sent from Australia to Jim Harding, a staff member of the California Energy Commission, and the former energy projects director of the Friends of the Earth in the United States.

The documents were released to reporters on Sunday, August 29, 1976, at a news conference in Sacramento, California. The conference was held by Ronald Docter, a California energy commissioner, Leonard Ross, a member of the state Public Utilities Commission, and Jim Harding. "There is a single uranium market world-wide and the existence of a cartel and its success suggests we are at least at the financial mercy and we may be putting ourselves completely at the mercy of another foreign cartel like OPEC," Ross told reporters, according to the *Washington Post*.

Copies of the documents were sent by the California officials to U.S. Attorney General Edward Levi and to Senator Frank Church, chairman of the Senate Committee on Multinational Corporations. The California officials wrote Levi as well:

It is impossible to tell from these documents whether the cartel was responsible for the seven-fold increase in world prices, but it is apparent that the U.S. domestic price of uranium has moved upward in parallel with world prices, and that an effective world-wide cartel would cost American consumers billions of dollars. . . . If the foreign cartel continues and America's nuclear commitment increases as planned, we will be at the mercy of a uranium OPEC.

While the documents had been sent to Senator Church, the Congressman from Sacramento, John E. Moss, was off the mark first with a Congressional investigation of the cartel. Moss, who was chairman of the House Sub-committee on Oversight and Investigation of the Interstate and Foreign Commerce Committee, first learned about the Mary Kathleen documents from a small item that appeared in the *Sacramento Bee* following the August 29 news conference. Moss convened his committee in Sacramento on November 4 for the first of a series of public hearings on the cartel, held intermittently throughout the following thirteen months.

At the Sacramento hearings, John Atkisson, general counsel for the Moss committee, questioned Jim Harding about how he came into possession of copies of the stolen Mary Kathleen documents. Harding replied:

'They arrived at the Friends of the Earth . . . in a plain brown wrapper. They were sent to me by a Friends of the Earth employee who was at that time travelling to Britain, who stopped in San Francisco and delivered them to my office.'

Atkisson: 'Did the Friends of the Earth employee write to you a note of any sort, a letter, along with that?'

Harding: 'There was no note. In fact, I was not present when she arrived.'

Atkisson: 'But as far as you are concerned, any knowledge of their source is speculative?'

Harding: 'That is correct.'

The speculation alluded to by Atkisson was that the Westinghouse Electric Corporation may have been involved in the disclosure of the Mary Kathleen documents. Westinghouse was being sued for failure to deliver uranium that it had contracted to supply to electric power utilities at fixed prices that were much lower than prevailed in 1976. Westinghouse did not have the uranium, and would suffer a loss of billions of dollars if it purchased it at the 1976 prices. Westinghouse, in turn, was then preparing to sue uranium producers, based on the allegation that the high prices had been caused by an illegal conspiracy.

> Atkisson: '[I]t has been suggested by certain cynical people that the timing of the leak of these documents is less than casual.'
> Harding: 'What would it have been timed for?'
> Atkisson: 'There is some serious litigation going on concerning the affairs of Westinghouse Electric Corporation, and how the cartel may have affected their lot in life. As I said, certain cynical people have suggested that the timing is something other than casual.'
> Harding: 'That may be correct, but I wouldn't have any control over that. They were released in Australia a week and a half before they were released in this country.'

In the book, *Yellowcake: The International Uranium Cartel*, authors June Taylor and Michael Yokell reported that immediately after the release of the documents in Australia,

> Friends of the Earth in Australia was telephoned by a United States public interest group indicating it was interested in seeing the cartel documents. Something made the FOE staffers suspicious of the request, and they checked up on the 'public interest group,' only to discover it did not exist. Since the call was from Chicago [where the law firm handling Westinghouse's uranium litigation was located], FOE assumed, rightly or wrongly, it was really Westinghouse's attorneys trying to get the materials. They did not supply the documents. A few days after this incident, FOE's Melbourne office was burgled and there was some suspicion on the part of the staff that Westinghouse was behind it. However, others had motives and it was neither the first time nor the last that the office was broken into.

The Friends of the Earth apparently did not have time to duplicate all of the stolen documents they had obtained from the files of Mary Kathleen before submitting them to the Fox commission. The Australian cabinet quickly passed a regulation making it illegal to disclose information about the cartel. (The regulations were later succeeded by legislation – the Foreign Proceedings (Prohibition of Certain Evidence) Act of 1976 – which had the same effect.) Thus, if FOE did have more incriminating documents, divulging them would be a criminal offence.

As late as 1978, Westinghouse was still trying to secure additional documents thought to be held by the Friends of the Earth, according to Taylor and Yokell. The San Francisco headquarters of FOE "was contacted by Canadians with environmental and political interests in the matter," the authors claimed.

> They suggested sending someone from FOE San Francisco to Australia to bring back the unpublished documents that remained hidden there. It sounded like a good plan, but somewhat expensive. One of the Canadians had a donor who would be willing to finance the scheme. FOE said it would need $3,000. The Canadian said the needed money and plane tickets would be there in two days, but FOE got suspicious. Inquiries were made and FOE got a clear indication that the money was being funnelled by Westinghouse. The FOE was not willing to break Australian law if it were to be primarily for Westinghouse's benefit. The trip was never made.

Whether or not the Friends of the Earth really had any more documents, or even if they existed, whether they contained anything of great interest, is a moot point. If Westinghouse really was very interested in seeing them, presumably it would have deposed FOE spokesmen for testimony, and obtained subpoenas to try and get at the additional documents. Unless, of course, Westinghouse wanted to avoid disclosure of how the initial documents had been obtained in the first place.

Regardless of how they arrived on the scene, the Mary Kathleen documents were the first strike of lightning in the storm over the cartel. Throughout the storm, politicians and others in the United States loudly denounced the dire threat posed by this new foreign cartel. In the other uranium producing nations, however, the matter was seen in a different light. The way they saw it, the most devastating uranium monopoly had been established long ago, by the government of the United States, for the benefit of American producers.

CHAPTER TWO

The History of Uranium B.C.
– Before Cartel

Commercial mining of uranium-bearing ores had been taking place for some seventy years before the international uranium cartel was organized in 1972.

The controversy created by the cartel is only the latest chapter in a long history of international intrigue and conflict surrounding the most powerful atom that man has yet harnessed.

At first, radioactive ores were mined for radium, used for medical purposes; uranium was a by-product with limited use and less value.

But after scientists learned how to use the enormous energy released by uranium – either for destruction or for the generation of electricity – it was never again marketed like any other product. It has been the subject of tight controls and disagreements by the governments of the world ever since.

Control of world uranium supplies was seen as essential to the survival of democracy during the Second World War, when scientists raced to build the first atomic bomb, and a matter of dispute between the United States and its war-time allies, Great Britain and Canada. The United States first sought to monopolize world uranium supplies, and when that failed, joined with Great Britain in a similar ill-fated effort that extended into the postwar nuclear arms race. International machinations over the control of uranium sprang not only from military considerations but also from early perceptions of its possible importance in global industrial strategy. Atomic secrets and uranium supplies were viewed – mistakenly – as the keys to industrial supremacy in the postwar era. Finally, the cartel itself sprang up as a response to a market monopoly established by the U.S. government for the benefit of American uranium producers.

THE FIRST URANIUM PRODUCERS

In an experiment in 1896, French scientist Henri Becquerel carefully wrapped some photographic plates in heavy, black paper, which he placed beside a chunk of pitchblende, an ore containing radium and uranium. When Becquerel developed the photographic plates, they turned black, as though they had been exposed to light. Becquerel had discovered radioactivity.

One of the first to foresee the full potential of "radioactivity" was Ernest Rutherford, a New Zealand physicist who was to make Montreal's McGill University one of the world centres for research on the structure of the atom and radioactivity.

In 1904, Rutherford published his book, *Radio-activity*, in which he announced that the energy released through the process of radioactivity was a million times greater than energy released in other chemical changes. "If it were ever found possible to control at will the rate of disintegration of the radio-elements, an enormous amount of energy could be obtained from a small quantity of matter," Rutherford concluded. It would take forty years before men learned how to release at will the enormous amounts of energy that Rutherford had said existed in the radioactive elements.

Meanwhile, radium was much in demand, for research laboratories, and for medical purposes. Contained in the same ore as uranium, radium was found in only trace amounts: more than 30,000 ounces of uranium for every ounce of radium.

Until about 1912, the Joachymsthal mines in Czechoslovakia were the only sources of uranium and radium bearing ores. Radium sold for a price equivalent to $6 million an ounce. Then, a second source of supply, produced as a by-product of vanadium mines in Colorado and Utah, brought the price down to a rate equivalent to $3.5 million an ounce. A third major source of uranium and radium supply was to emerge in the Katanga region of the Congo, where Belgian prospectors found a large deposit of ore, along with copper, in 1915. The First World War prevented the development of this deposit until 1921, when Union Minière du Haut Katanga placed its big Shinkolobwe mine into production, driving the price of radium down, to about $2 million an ounce. A little more than a decade later another mine was brought into production, at the edge of the arctic circle in Canada, and again the price of radium was driven down, to as low as $600,000 an ounce. In a little more than two decades, new supply sources cut the price of radium by 90 per cent.

THE MINE AT GREAT BEAR LAKE

March 28, 1930. The snow lay heavily on the granite rocks of the Precambrian shield in the Canadian sub-arctic. A single-engine aircraft, equipped with skis – a fly speck in an infinity of space – landed on the frozen surface of Great Bear Lake, and deposited two passengers and their gear on the rock-strewn shore: tent, sled, canoe, provisions. The men, Gilbert LaBine, a veteran prospector and promoter, and his assistant, Charles St. Paul, came to seek their fortune, hidden in the frozen rocks.

A farm boy from the Ottawa valley, Gilbert LaBine had left home at the age of fifteen to join his older brother, Charles, at the booming mine centre at Cobalt in northern Ontario, where Gilbert worked as a boiler fireman at a silver mine. The LaBines had spent two decades prospecting and staking claims in northern Ontario and Manitoba, forming Eldorado Gold Mines Limited in 1925 to develop claims on a gold mining prospect in southeastern Manitoba. With Charles as president and Gilbert as managing director, Eldorado had little difficulty in raising half a million dollars during the Roaring Twenties; but by 1929, drilling had failed to find commercial grade ore on the property.

There were still enough funds left in the Eldorado treasury to stake another prospecting venture, and in the summer of 1929, Gilbert LaBine flew to the eastern shore of Great Bear Lake where he spent three weeks prospecting, finding evidence of copper, bismuth, and cobalt, and staking three claims. Gilbert spent the following months studying government geologic reports of the area, before returning in 1930 with St. Paul for more extensive prospecting. During a period of nearly five months, LaBine and St. Paul explored outcroppings along 500 miles of shoreline on Great Bear Lake.

18

In mid-May, St. Paul was struck by snow-blindness and forced to remain in camp for several days, while LaBine continued on his own. LaBine later recalled the discovery, as reported in W. Eggleston's *Canada's Nuclear Story*:

> On the morning of the 16th of May, about half a mile from where we were camped, I was following around the shore of an island and I discovered what I considered a beautiful looking vein.
>
> As I looked over to the shore, a distance of about 300 or possibly 400 feet, I noticed a great wall there that was stained with cobalt bloom and copper green. I walked over to this place and investigated it thoroughly, and found all the associated ores of cobalt, including silver. Following along, I found a tiny piece of dark ore, probably the size of a large plum. Looking more closely, I found the vein. I chipped it off with my hammer, and there it was – pitchblende.

The plum that LaBine found was the richest radium and uranium bearing ore that had then been discovered. It contained one gram of radium per six and one-half tons of ore, five times as rich as the ore then being produced at the Shinkolobwe mine in the Belgian Congo, and twenty times as rich as the concentrates in the United States.

Putting the Canadian property into production was a monumental achievement. It involved digging what was then the most northerly mine in the world; building a mill to reduce the ore to concentrates containing about 60 per cent uranium; shipping the concentrates 5,000 miles; and building a refinery at a former seed-cleaning plant in Port Hope, Ontario, to extract the radium and uranium. The ore also contained modest quantities of copper and silver.

A remote arctic community of 200 people was established to operate the mine and mill. From the new town of Port Radium, the concentrates were shipped during the summer months by a 1,400-mile water route, including several portages, to the nearest railway at Fort Smith, on the northern tip of Alberta, and another 3,000 miles to Port Hope. The water route lay across Great Bear Lake, the fourth largest lake in North America, bisected by the arctic circle; down the Great Bear River; up the Mackenzie River, across Great Slave Lake, and up the Slave River to Fort Smith. The movement by tug and barge was handled by an Eldorado subsidiary, Northern Transportation Company. Charles LaBine became president of Northern Transportation, and Gilbert succeeded his elder brother as president of Eldorado.

The price of Eldorado shares, which had been selling for pennies before LaBine discovered the Great Bear Lake deposit, soared to $8 by 1933. Prospectors flooded into the area, staking thousands of claims; but Eldorado was to remain the only producer in the area.

By mid-1934, 4 years after the discovery, the mine had shipped 65 tons of concentrate to Port Hope. The refinery had processed 58 tons of these concentrates, recovering 5½ grams of radium, 30,000 ounces of silver, and nearly 18 tons of uranium. It was late 1936 before Eldorado had produced a total of one ounce of radium.

By mid-1940, Eldorado's sales totalled less than $8 million, and its prospects were not encouraging. The sharply reduced prices for radium had failed to enlarge a limited demand. The market for uranium was even worse, with few buyers at prices as low as $1.50 per pound of uranium oxide, the untreated uranium recovered at the refinery. A stockpile of several hundred tons of concentrates had accumulated at the Port Hope refinery. In July, the mine was shut down and allowed to fill with water. Two years later, it was to be re-opened, to produce uranium for atomic bombs.

URANIUM MIGHT BE NEEDED

Washington, January 26, 1939. Niels Bohr had come from Denmark to give the opening address to the Fifth Washington Conference on Theoretical Physics. He made a startling announcement for his American audience. The uranium atom had been split. Scientists at the Kaiser Wilhelm Institute for Theoretical Physics in Berlin and at Bohr's own Institute of Theoretical Physics in Copenhagen, had achieved the first induced fission – or splitting – of the uranium atom by bombardment with neutrons. As the uranium atoms split, more neutrons are released. If the released neutrons could be induced to split more uranium atoms, the result would be a self-sustaining nuclear chain reaction. Enormous amounts of energy might be released, for use in peace time to produce electricity, or in war to create a greater explosive force than man had ever dreamed of. Rutherford's prophecy some thirty-five years earlier had been taken one step closer to reality.

The scientists at the conference were aware of the importance of Bohr's announcement. Even before he had finished speaking, several had 'phoned their laboratories to relay the news. Before the end of 1939, close to one hundred papers were produced on research related to nuclear fission.

To a small group of scientists who had fled to the United States from the fascist forces in Europe, Bohr's news was a matter of the gravest concern. Among these émigré scientists were Albert Einstein from Germany; Leo Szilard, a Hungarian who taught for ten years at the University of Berlin where he worked with Einstein; Edward Teller and Eugene Wigner, both from Hungary; and Enrico Fermi from Italy.

The émigré scientists were concerned that if Nazi forces were the first to develop an atomic bomb, the flame of democracy could be snuffed out, not only across Europe, but in North America. Later that year, Szilard and Wigner composed a note of warning for President Franklin Roosevelt. To carry added weight, they persuaded Einstein to sign the letter. The famous letter from Einstein and an accompanying memorandum from Szilard were delivered to Roosevelt by Alexander Sachs, a Russian émigré and economist, who had access to the White House.

"Early this year it became known that the element uranium can be split by neutron bombardment," Szilard stated in the memorandum accompanying the letter from Einstein. "There is some reason to believe that if fast neutrons could be used, it would be easy to construct extremely dangerous bombs. The destructive power of these bombs can only be roughly estimated, but there is no doubt that it would go far beyond all military conceptions."

Progress on the development of an atomic bomb during the following three years was slow. The first U.S. government research contract, to Columbia University, was not awarded until November, 1940, and then amounted to only $40,000.

Almost until the day that the first atomic bomb was exploded, there was widespread scepticism that one could be built, especially in time to be of use during the war. It was given such low priority that the research work was assigned to the émigré scientists from Hungary, Poland, France, Italy, and Germany, because they did not have the security to work on what were considered more vital projects. A war-time laboratory in Boston was called a "radiation laboratory" because the scientists hoped to fool the Germans into thinking "that instead of our working on something important and practical like radar, . . . we were wasting our time on something impractical and useless like an atomic bomb." As late as January, 1945, President Truman's Chief of Staff, Admiral William Leahy, declared the atomic bomb program to be "the biggest fool thing we have ever done. The bomb will never go off, and I speak as an expert on explosives."

After Einstein and the other scientists had sounded their warning to President Roosevelt in 1939, the initial U.S. atomic program, little more than a watching brief, was assigned to a "Uranium Committee," headed by Dr. Lyman Briggs of the National Bureau of Standards. In late 1940, a somewhat expanded research program was taken over by the Office of Scientific Research and Development, Section S-1, headed by Vannevar Bush, former chairman of the Carnegie Institute. Bush's right-hand-man was former Harvard University president James Conant, as chairman of the National Defense Research Committee. Finally, the U.S. Corps of Army Engineers took command of what was then called the Manhattan Project, in September, 1942.

In July, 1941, Bush informed Roosevelt that his committee believed that the "possibility of a successful outcome was very remote" and had therefore not felt justified "in diverting to the work the efforts of scientists in considerable numbers, in view of the scarcity of highly qualified physicists for its other important work."

Bush, at that time, had not seen the report of an English group known as the MAUD committee. (The committee's name arose from a request from Niels Bohr in Nazi-occupied Denmark to pass along a message to "Maud Ray Kent." Maud Ray was a former governess for the Bohr household who had moved to Kent, but the English thought the message contained some sort of secret code.) The MAUD committee had concluded that an atomic bomb could be built within two years.

The English, at this stage, were further ahead in their research than the Americans. The Americans, at the urging of Bush and Conant, proposed that the two countries should undertake the development of an atomic bomb as a joint project, even though the United States was still not yet at war. But Britain determined to go ahead with its own program, which it dubbed Tube Alloys. It proved to be an effort beyond the war-time capacity of embattled Britain. Later that year, Roosevelt wrote to Churchill that the two should "converse concerning the subject which is under study by your MAUD committee, and by Dr. Bush's organization in this country, in order that any extended efforts may be co-ordinated or even jointly conducted." Instead of a joint effort, the two Allies agreed to "collaborate" on their separate programs, by exchanging information and other assistance and co-operation. It did not, however, turn out to be the smoothest of collaboration, especially when it came to sharing uranium supplies.

PROBLEMS OVER URANIUM

One of the great mysteries about the epic Manhattan Project that produced the first atomic bomb involves the story that those in charge of the project knew nothing about a supply of 1,200 tons of Belgian Congo uranium ore that was stockpiled for nearly two years in a warehouse on Staten Island, New York.

The story of the Belgian Congo ore was told by Lieutenant General Leslie R. Groves, the U.S. Army engineer in charge of the Manhattan Project. "[B]ut for a chance meeting between a Belgian and an Englishman a few months before the outbreak of the war, the Allies might not have been the first with the atomic bomb," General Groves wrote in his book, *Now It Can Be Told*, his history of the Manhattan Project.

According to Groves's account, in May, 1939, Edgar Sengier, managing director of Union Minière, was approached in London by the British government with a request for an option on the entire uranium production from the Shinkolobwe mine, the world's largest source of uranium. "Naturally, Sengier refused," Groves reported. Sir Henry Tizard, head of a British committee engaged in military research under the shadow of the gathering war clouds, then reportedly told Sengier: "Never forget that you have in your hands something which may mean catastrophe to your country and mine if this material were to fall in the hands of a possible enemy."

In October that year, Sengier moved to New York, where he spent the rest of the war managing the distant affairs of Union Minière.

"Toward the end of 1940, fearing a possible German invasion of the Belgian Congo, Sengier directed his representatives in Africa to ship discreetly to New York . . . the very large supply of previously mined uranium ore, then in storage at the Shinkolobwe mine," Groves continued in his account. Some 1,200 tons of ore, containing 65 per cent uranium, were moved 1,400 miles by river and rail to the seaport of Lobito, in Portuguese Angola, and from there by ship to the warehouse on Staten Island. And there it sat for nearly two years.

According to Groves, the bomb makers knew nothing about the presence of this uranium. Three times, Sengier contacted the Department of State to see if anyone wanted his ore. But the Department of State reportedly did not know about the highly secret project to build atomic bombs, and no one seemed interested in Sengier's ore.

"The first intimation" of the existence of this ore came to the attention of the Manhattan Engineering District on September 10, 1942, just one week before the Army was due to take over the project from the civilian research group. The Army was alerted, Groves reported, by a 'phone call from the Department of State concerning the shipment of 500 tons of this ore to Canada for processing in the Port Hope, Ontario refinery of Eldorado Gold Mines Ltd.

On September 18, the day after the Manhattan Engineering District was officially in business, Colonel K. D. Nichols, the man in charge of acquiring the materials to build the bomb, met with Sengier in New York.

"Colonel, will you tell me first if you have come here merely to talk, or to do business," Sengier asked, according to the account reported by Groves. The Colonel had arrived to do business. Within an hour, Nichols had "a sheet of yellow scratch paper on which were written the essentials of an agreement to turn over to us at once all the ore in the Staten Island warehouse and to ship to the United States all the richer uranium ore above ground in the Belgian Congo." The price was $1.60 a pound, nearly $4 million for the ore in the 2,000 steel drums at Staten Island, with a much greater quantity awaiting shipment from the Belgian Congo.

Groves's account of how this uranium came to sit so long in a warehouse makes good reading, but omits a few fascinating details. If the Army was unaware of this supply of bomb making material, it was only because of an enormous gap in communication with the civilian research group from which the Army had taken over. The scientists had been eyeing the Belgian Congo ore for three years before the Army completed its deal with Sengier; had been in contact with Sengier long before the Army; and were probably responsible for Sengier's decision to ship the ore on its perilous war-time journey from Africa to New York. None of this was reported by Groves.

In the memorandum that accompanied Einstein's letter to Roosevelt in 1939, Leo Szilard had first raised the importance of securing a supply of uranium. The Hungarian scientist suggested "the possibility of bringing over from Belgium or the Belgian Congo a large stock of pitchblende . . . and to keep this here for possible future use. Perhaps a large quantity of this ore might be obtained as a token reparation payment from the Belgian government."

After Roosevelt appointed the Uranium Committee to "study the possible relationship to national defense of recent discoveries in the field of atomistics," Szilard wrote to the committee chairman, Dr. Lyman Briggs on October 26, 1939, and again urged that a supply of uranium be sought as a gift from Union Minière, or purchased from Eldorado. "It would be of particular value to enlist the assistance of this Belgian corporation which is to some extent controlled by the Belgian government," Szilard wrote. He also reported that Eldorado "might be able to supply uranium oxide for our purposes at the rate of one ton per week. If the uranium oxide were to be bought rather than obtained as a gift or a loan, it might be secured from Canada just as easily as from Belgium. On the other hand, the Canadian corporation is rather small and can

25

hardly be asked to give away large quantities of material without financial compensation."

In mid-1940, the Briggs committee was still talking about the need to secure a supply of uranium. Alexander Sachs was delegated to approach Edgar Sengier of Union Minière with the suggestion that the company ship some of its Congo ore to the United States where it could be stored. The company would retain ownership of the ore, but would be committed not to re-export it without special permission. Sengier was reportedly cool to the suggestion that his company should, at its own expense, ship millions of dollars worth of ore from Africa to the United States where it might, some day, perhaps be sold. But several months later, that is exactly what Union Minière did – the 1,200 tons of ore concentrates arriving at Staten Island in late 1940.

The first uranium used for research on development of an atomic bomb was purchased from Eldorado's stockpile at Port Hope, while the Belgian Congo ore continued to sit in the warehouse on Staten Island.

In December, 1941, the British purchased two tons of uranium oxide from Eldorado for shipment to Britain. In April, 1942, the Americans purchased sixty tons from Eldorado, for $342,000. This was delivered to the University of Chicago where, on December 2, the team of scientists headed by Enrico Fermi achieved the world's first self-sustaining nuclear chain reaction. The atomic pile that Fermi built in the squash court underneath Stagg Field at the university contained 400 tons of graphite, 6 tons of uranium metal, and 50 tons of uranium oxide. News of Fermi's success was flashed to Washington by coded telegram: "The Italian navigator has landed in the new world."

Eldorado had no sooner contracted to supply this sixty tons of uranium to the Americans than Gilbert LaBine was called into the office of C. D. Howe, Canada's ram-rod Minister of Munitions and Supply. Howe did not want to interrupt Eldorado's contract with the Americans – he just wanted to make sure that there would be enough to supply the requirements of both of Canada's war-time allies. How long would it take Eldorado to re-open its mine at Great Bear Lake? LaBine promised to have it back in production that summer. The first work party arrived at the site before the end of April, to start pumping out the twelve million gallons of water that had flooded the mine. By August, the mine was back in production. Where earlier, the concentrates had been shipped out only during the summer by barge and rail, now they were flown out by air.

While Eldorado was busy delivering the sixty tons of uranium to the University of Chicago in early 1941, the British were also seeking a further order of twenty tons. On June 15, the United Kingdom High Commissioner to Canada and two British scientists called on Prime Minister Mackenzie King, to suggest that the Canadian government should acquire control of Eldorado. This, they argued, would ensure that the company's uranium supplies were allocated to meet British and American needs without further driving up the price of uranium. The prime minister called in C. D. Howe, who said he thought he could arrange to buy control through LaBine, a personal friend.

The British, according to the authorized history of Britain's war-time atomic program, felt that their uranium supplies were assured and felt "secure in the knowledge the Canadians were looking after them." The British reportedly even "stood aside," while their twenty-ton order was temporarily diverted to meet the more urgent needs of the larger American program.

Four days after the British had met with the Canadian prime minister, Chalmers Mackenzie, head of the National Research Council in Ottawa, met in Washington with Vannevar Bush of the Office of Scientific Research and Development to keep the Americans informed. Mackenzie later wrote: "Bush thinks we should proceed with the acquisitioning of the property, and appreciated very much Mr. Howe's offer. He thinks there should be an international arrangement as between the United States, the United Kingdom and Canada for post-war control. He is going to England shortly to discuss the matter."

On July 15, Bush wrote to Chalmers Mackenzie that the proposal to acquire government control of Eldorado and allocate production among the Allies had been discussed with President Roosevelt, who "agrees we should encourage the Canadians to go ahead . . . this, which is of course entirely a Canadian matter, nevertheless has been considered a wise step on this side of the line."

Howe quickly negotiated a deal with LaBine to buy a million

shares of Eldorado, only to find that this represented substantially less than control of the company. It was nearly two years later before the government moved to buy all the Eldorado shares.

One obvious reason for the great interest in the Eldorado supplies and the apparent lack of interest in Union Minière's ore is that what was required was not ore, but uranium oxide. There were then only two refineries in the world that could process the ore into uranium oxide. One was Union Minière's plant in Nazi-occupied Belgium. The other was Eldorado's plant at Port Hope, Ontario.

It was likely because of this that the first buyer to turn up for Union Minière's 1,200 tons of ore was not Colonel Nichols of the U.S. Army, as General Groves has reported. It was Eldorado. In August, 1941, Eldorado contracted to purchase 500 tons of the Congo ore, apparently with an option on the remaining 700. The contract was made, with C. D. Howe's approval, with the intent of processing the ore at Eldorado's Port Hope refinery, and as a back-up supply to production from the distant mine at Great Bear Lake.

This action by Eldorado finally prompted the Americans to buy Union Minière's stockpiled ore.

Sengier checked with the Department of State about obtaining approval to ship the ore to Canada. The Department of State checked with Bush. Bush checked with the Army.

"The general problem of supply of uranium ore is now, I believe, to be handled directly by the Army in all of its respects," Bush wrote to Brigadier General Wilhelm Styer on September 11, just six days before General Groves was scheduled to assume command of the Manhattan Project. Bush wrote that he had been informed of the Eldorado purchase of the Belgian Congo ore by Chalmers Mackenzie of Canada's National Research Council. "The reason for the purchase is to protect orders which Afrimet [a subsidiary of Union Minière] now has from Allied governments, and I judge that this includes England," Bush wrote in his letter to General Styer. "A further 700 tons of the same ore is also available in the United States from the same source, and apparently the Canadians wish to have this transferred to Canada for treatment and for control of the matter." Bush concluded: "It seems to me highly desirable that this matter be placed entirely in the hands of one Army officer."

That one Army officer turned out to be Colonel Kenneth D. Nichols. On September 17, Bush wrote to James Conant at the National Defense Research Committee that "The question of ore supply has become very complicated and involved with some international relations. I discussed it with Styer and the whole matter is in the hands of Colonel Nichols . . . Nichols is now getting it into order."

On the following day, Colonel Nichols, according to General Groves's account, walked into Sengier's New York office and arranged to purchase Union Minière's entire stockpile, including the ore at Staten Island and the stockpile at the Shinkolobwe mine site in Africa, for several million dollars.

After the Americans had acquired the African ore, it was shipped to Eldorado's expanded plant at Port Hope for processing, then returned to the United States.

Having acquired all the African ore, the U.S. Army Corps of Engineers then proceeded to acquire all the Canadian uranium. In September, the U.S. contract with Eldorado was stepped up from 60 tons to 350 tons, and in December to 850 tons (which was about equal to the amount of uranium in the 1,200 tons of African ore that had been stockpiled on Staten Island). The U.S. contracts committed Eldorado's entire production until nearly the end of 1945.

By this time, the British were moving their nuclear program to Montreal, where the work would continue as a joint project with Canada. When the British learned that all of Eldorado's production had been contracted by the Americans, they were furious. They could not even get their hands on their twenty tons of uranium that had been "temporarily diverted" to the Americans. According to author Margaret Gowing in *Britain and Atomic Energy*, "Mr. Churchill had told the Prime Minister of Canada that Mr. Howe 'had sold the British Empire down the river.' This was repeated to Mr. Howe who was not amused."

"I am beginning to feel," wrote Wallace Akers, head of Tube Alloys, "that the whole uranium and radium business is such a murky one that we will have to deal with the people in it, although they may not have the best of reputations."

The worst was yet to come.

In January, 1943, James Conant wrote to Chalmers Macken-zie at the National Research Council in Ottawa, to report that the terms of Anglo-American collaboration on atomic research had been changed, as a result of orders that he and Vennevar Bush had received from President Roosevelt. From now on, wrote Bush, information will be exchanged "only if the reci-pient of the information is in a position to take advantage of it in this war . . . Since it is clear that neither your government nor the English can produce elements '49' or '25' [the code names for plutonium and uranium 235] on a time schedule which will permit their use in this conflict we have been directed to limit the interchange correspondingly."

What Conant did not tell Mackenzie was that orders to implement this drastic change in the terms of nuclear collabor-ation between the Allies came as a result of strong recom-mendations that Bush and Conant had made to Roosevelt. Their concern was that the United States was spending 90 per cent of the money, and should therefore be able to retain for itself the resulting technology, which they believed would be of great industrial importance after the war.

"There can no longer be any question that atomic energy may be released under controlled conditions and used as power," Conant wrote to Bush in late 1942. The British, he declared, were showing an inordinate interest in "information which appeared to be of value to them solely for post-war in-dustrial purposes."

Later, Conant stressed that it was "of the greatest impor-tance to be sure that the President understands the basic issue. The question is whether or not British representatives shall have full access to plans for the design and construction of the manufacturing plants which we are now building and full knowledge of their operation."

Conant concluded that "The major consideration must be that of national security and post-war strategic significance."

Conant's arguments were incorporated into a report to Roosevelt prepared by Bush.

While the Americans had valid reasons for staking a claim to the perceived postwar benefits of nuclear technology, the change in the terms of collaboration posed a serious risk of delay in developing the atomic bomb. The biggest risk was that the British and Canadians might try to go it alone, and end all collaboration with the Americans.

If this were to happen, the Americans stood to lose their supply of Canadian uranium; the heavy water technology developed by the British-Canadian research team at Montreal; and vital supplies of heavy water. The Montreal group had focused its effort on the use of deuterium, or heavy water, as the moderator needed to achieve a nuclear chain reaction. The American effort focused more on the use of graphite, a less efficient but more readily available moderator, although the heavy water method was still of vital importance to the Americans. The world's entire supply of heavy water consisted of 180 litres that had been shipped ahead of the advancing German army from Norway to France to England and finally to Montreal; plus small production from a single plant at Trail, British Columbia.

Harold Urey, head of the atomic research team at the University of Columbia, wrote to Conant to warn that "our failure to establish satisfactory co-operation with the British . . . has certainly resulted in a delay of six months, or perhaps a year or more, in establishing the feasibility of the homogenous heavy water pile." This failure to co-operate, wrote Urey, "had no justification on scientific or technical grounds . . . If the decision not to co-operate fully with our principal ally was made on nationalistic grounds by the highest authority, I hope this authority was advised of the possible delay that might result from our not being able to use the only considerable supply of heavy water available anywhere."

"This Development has come as a bombshell," Sir John Anderson, the British cabinet minister responsible for the Tube Alloys project, advised Churchill. Churchill, in turn, pleaded with Roosevelt to reconsider this change in policy.

The new policy "limits drastically interchange of technical information and entirely destroys the original conception of 'a co-ordinated or even jointly conducted effort between the two countries,' " Churchill wrote to the American president. "That we should each work separately," he warned, "would be a sombre decision."

Despite the advice of Bush and Conant, Churchill did persuade Roosevelt to re-establish full co-operation and exchange of information. From Washington he cabled Sir John Anderson on May 26: "The President agreed that the exchange of information on Tube Alloys should be resumed and that the enterprise should be considered a joint one, to which both countries would contribute their best endeavours."

A secret agreement covering the resumed atomic co-operation was signed by Roosevelt and Churchill at the Anglo-American summit conference at Quebec City in August, "governing collaboration between the authorities of the U.S.A. and the U.K. in the matter of Tube Alloys." Among other things, the agreement provided that

> . . . in view of the heavy burden of production falling upon the United States as the result of a wise division of war effort, the British government recognize that any post-war advantages of an industrial or commercial character shall be dealt with as between the United States and Great Britain on terms to be specified by the President of the United States to the Prime Minister of Great Britain. The Prime Minister expressly disclaims any interest in those industrial and commercial aspects beyond what may be considered by the President of the United States to be fair and just and in harmony with the economic welfare of the world.

With the resumption of full collaboration, C. D. Howe continued to pursue government control of Eldorado.

"As a necessary means for the more effective prosecution of the war, the government of Canada has acquired all properties and assets of Eldorado Mining and Refining Limited by expropriating all the capital shares of the company," Howe announced in the House of Commons on January 28, 1944. The government paid the shareholders $5 million for the shares it had expropriated, just slightly more than the market value. "In the interest of military secrecy I hope that no questions about this matter will be asked," Howe stated.

Building the first atomic bomb was fundamentally an American accomplishment, with help from the émigré scientists (who were then American citizens), and collaboration with Britain and Canada. The British-Canadian research team based in Montreal did, however, build a small atomic energy pile at Chalk River, 125 miles northwest of Ottawa. Placed in operation in September, 1945, it was the first outside of the U.S. plant at Hanford, Washington, to produce energy by nuclear fission, but too late to be of value during the war. The most lasting legacy of the scientists at Montreal was the development of the Candu nuclear power reactor, which, by using heavy water as the moderator, permits the use of natural uranium in achieving nuclear fission, eliminating the need for the costly uranium enrichment required by most other nuclear power plants.

Exactly how much uranium Eldorado's Great Bear mine supplied during the war has never been revealed, but it appears to have been in the order of about 1,000 tons. The mine continued to produce until 1960, when the ore finally gave out. It was not the world's largest uranium mine, but one of the first, and one of the richest.

The struggle over control of uranium supplies that strained Anglo-American relations during the war years was to continue after the war.

CHAPTER THREE

Fuel For
The Arms Race

THE FIRST CARTEL

Uranium seldom has been bought or sold in quite the same manner as anything else.

Perhaps the best example of this was the arrangement set up less than a year before the end of the Second World War, which provided a United States Brigadier General with a personal and secret bank acount of $37 million.

This arrangement was part of a secret agreement set up by the United States and Great Britain in an attempt to control the world supply of uranium, not only during the war, but after as well.

The United States had already secured enough uranium for the Manhattan Project when its efforts in late 1943 to secure even more supplies by re-opening the Shinkolobwe mine led to the establishment of the Combined Development Trust, in effect, the first international uranium cartel.

As early as August, 1943, General Leslie Groves had assured President Roosevelt that the uranium supplies then lined up would be adequate to meet the needs of the Manhattan Project. These included about 2,500 tons of uranium that had been shipped from the Congo, about another 1,000 tons from Eldorado's mine at Great Bear Lake, and the small U.S. supplies recovered from the vanadium ores on the Colorado plateau.

General Groves, however, had wanted all the uranium he could get. He kept Roosevelt informed of his efforts to gain for the United States as "complete control as possible" over the uranium resources of the world. The key to this control then

34

appeared to lie in Union Minière's great Shinkolobwe mine.

The U.S. Army began negotiations in the fall of 1943 with Edgar Sengier for a contract for an additional 1,720 tons of uranium, to be produced by re-opening the mine. When these talks failed, negotiations shifted to London. The British were brought in because the exiled war-time government of Belgium was located in London, and partly because British interests owned some 30 per cent of Union Minière. These negotiations led to the Combined Development Trust, and the effort to control all the world's uranium resources.

The trust also proceeded from that earlier secret agreement "governing collaboration between the authorities of the U.S. and the U.K. in the matter of Tube Alloys," which Churchill and Roosevelt had signed at Quebec City on August 19, 1943. The Quebec agreement re-established American, British, and Canadian collaboration and information exchange on development of the bomb, to be effected by the new Combined Policy Committee in Washington. The committee included three Americans, two British, and one Canadian. (Details of the Quebec agreement were kept secret for twelve years, until the document was tabled in the House of Commons in London.)

The approach decided upon for the negotiations with the Belgium government was to set up another agency, funded 50-50 by the American and British governments. Uranium purchased by this agency would be allocated between the United States and the United Kingdom. Although Canada was represented on the Combined Policy Committee, it did not participate in this new uranium agency.

In his history of the Manhattan Project, *Now It Can Be Told*, General Groves wrote that the purpose of the Combined Development Trust "was to supervise the acquisition of raw materials outside of American and British territory."

This plan was given effect by the "agreement and declaration of trust" signed on June 13, 1944, by Roosevelt and Churchill. The agreement noted "the intention of the two governments to control to the fullest extent practicable the supplies of uranium and thorium ores within the boundaries of such areas as come under their respective jurisdictions." More importantly, "it has been decided to establish a joint organization for the purpose of gaining control of uranium and thorium supplies in certain areas outside the control of the two governments and of the governments of the Dominions and of India and Burma." To gain this control, "There shall be established in the City of Washington . . . a Trust to be known as 'The Combined Development Trust.' " Six trustees appointed by the Combined Policy Committee were charged with the responsibility of administering the trust. The intention to continue the arrangement after the war was made explicit in the final clause of the agreement:

> The signatories of this Agreement and Declaration of Trust will, as soon as practicable after the conclusion of hostilities, recommend to their respective governments the extension and revision of this war-time emergency agreement to cover post war conditions and its formalization by treaty or other proper method.

The functions outlined for the Combined Development Trust were sweeping. It would, among other things:

> Explore and survey sources of uranium and thorium supplies. Develop the production of uranium and thorium by the acquisition of mines and ore deposits, mining concessions or otherwise. Provide with equipment any mines or mining works for the production of uranium and thorium. Survey and improve the methods of production . . . Acquire and undertake the treatment and disposal of uranium and thorium . . . Provide storage and other facilities.

The United States and Great Britain saw compelling reasons for trying to control the world's uranium supplies, for both military and industrial purposes. Churchill saw atomic power as essential to Britain's postwar military defence. Britain had to have the atomic bomb, he told U.S. Secretary of War Henry Stimson in 1943, "because this will be necessary for Britain's independence in the future as well as for success during the war . . . It would never do to have Germany or Russia win the race for something which might be used for international blackmail."

The future peace and prosperity of the world would depend upon the United States and Great Britain, in the view of both Roosevelt and Churchill. To assure that peace and prosperity, it would be necessary to control the world's known supplies of uranium, some 90 per cent of which were then in the Belgian Congo.

The first business of the trust was to complete negotiations with the exiled Belgium government and Union Minière, which was achieved in September, 1944. It included a contract to purchase, 1,720 tons of uranium, and an option on all additional production from the Belgian Congo for ten years following completion of the initial contract. In fact, the trust, which was later called the Combined Development Agency, purchased all of the output of the Shinkolobwe mine until it was finally shut down in 1961.

"With the signing of the purchase agreement with the Union Minière the American trustees were confronted with a serious problem," General Groves later wrote in *Now It Can Be Told.* "The contract was for so long a term that appropriated funds could not be counted on from War Department sources. The Constitution would not permit it. Any such long-term commitment . . . would require prior authorization from Congress" – obviously impossible with the war-time secrecy that shrouded the Manhattan Project. He added:

> Under the terms of the contract the trustees would be personally responsible for the payments, and none of us had the necessary number of millions to take care of the obligation.
>
> Our dilemma was solved by arranging for me to be paid by the United States $37,500,000, a sum sufficient to cover the expected obligations. I then deposited this money in a personal account at the U.S. Treasury. From this I made withdrawals as necessary and deposited the money with the Bankers Trust Company of New York. Payments for ore were made from this account.

Aside from the members of the Combined Development Trust, the only other people aware of this unique arrangement were the president of the Bankers Trust Company and two other bank officials.

It was only the start for the first uranium cartel.

In the seven years following the war, to 1953, more than 85 per cent of the total U.S. uranium supplies came from this one mine in the former Belgian Congo, now the Republic of Zaire.

After that, rapidly soaring uranium production in both the United States and Canada far surpassed the Congo production, although a large part of this Canadian and U.S. output wound up in surplus government stockpiles rather than in atomic bombs. By the time the Shinkolobwe mine was finally closed down in 1961, it had produced some 26,000 tons of uranium, more than 10 per cent of the total non-Communist world production to that time. It was a volume of uranium worth, at 1980 prices, nearly $2 billion.

In addition to procuring the production from Shinkolobwe, the Combined Development Agency invested a quarter of a billion dollars to develop the next large source of uranium supply. This was for the plants, which, starting in 1952, extracted uranium as a by-product of the gold produced in South Africa. In the first four years of operation, these plants provided more than a third of the free world's uranium supplies. Finally, it was also the Combined Development Agency that arranged for the initial development of uranium production in Australia, in 1954.

But history was quickly demonstrating the futility of attempting to maintain an atomic monopoly, for either war or peace.

IN THE HEAT OF THE COLD WAR

The world in 1945 stood trembling before the might of atomic power, and began the uneasy and unending quest to ensure that it would never be used to destroy civilization.

Connecticut Senator Brien McMahon, who sponsored the U.S. Atomic Energy Act, voiced universal apprehension when he spoke in Congress three months after the bombs had destroyed Hiroshima and Nagasaki.

> [W]hen the bomb bay doors of the B-29 opened, there occurred . . . the most momentous development in the 2,000 years of the world's history since the birth of Jesus Christ.
>
> Eve tempted Adam, and Adam succumbed and partook of the fruit of the tree of knowledge, and as a result Adam and Eve were banished from Paradise. Man today has tasted of the secret of energy; he has finally discovered the

secret of matter, and I say that unless this momentous development is handled wisely and judiciously, unless it leads to peace and righteousness among men and among nations, all mankind will be banished from the face of the earth.

A major instrument in maintaining the peace, by means of the precarious balance of terror, was the U.S. Atomic Energy Commission, created by the Atomic Energy Act of 1946. Its five-man civilian board eventually took over the Manhattan Project from the U.S. Army Corps of Engineers. The Act gave the AEC unprecedented powers. It would procure and control the required uranium supplies. It would create a domestic uranium producing industry. It would build the nuclear weapons. It would develop the nuclear power industry. And it would regulate the industry that it built.

It was, said the sponsors of the Act,

> a radical piece of legislation . . . never before in the peacetime history of the United States has Congress established an administrative agency vested with such sweeping authority and entrusted with such portentous responsibilities . . . The Act creates a government monopoly of the sources of atomic energy and buttresses this position with a variety of broad governmental powers and prohibitions on private activity. The field of atomic energy is made an island of socialism in the midst of a free enterprise economy.

The inherent conflict involved in regulating the very product that it was promoting became increasingly clear. "[T]he very difficult job facing the Commissioners is compounded by the fact that the AEC . . . is subject to a strain on its objectivity for, in many instances, it is both the promoter and the regulator of the atomic energy project in question," the Congressional Joint Committee on Atomic Energy observed in 1956.

The same charge was later to be applied to the Joint Congressional Committee itself. The act that created the AEC also created the Joint Committee, comprised of nine Senators and nine Congressmen, as the Congressional watchdog. But like the commission itself, the joint committee was given unprecedented powers. It was the only arm of Congress ever given the power to use the "services, information, facilities and personnel" of the executive branch, including, for example, such powers as the ability to order the files or investigations by such departments as the Central Intelligence Agency and the Federal Bureau of Investigation. The AEC was charged with the responsibility of keeping the committee "fully and currently informed," which soon led the Joint Committee to include itself in the decision-making process of this executive branch of government, including the establishment and administration of multi-billion dollar budgets.

When the Atomic Energy Commission held its first meeting on January 2, 1947, in cramped quarters on the sixth floor of the new War Department Building in Washington, to take over from the Army, it acquired, according to its chairman, "properties and an organization which, in magnitude, are comparable to the largest business enterprises of the country." It took over 37 installations in 19 states and Canada, 254 military officers, 1,688 enlisted men, 3,950 government workers, and nearly 38,000 contractor employees, the total representing an investment of $2.2 billion. It took another $300 million to run this organization in the first year of its administration by the AEC, but that was only a fraction of what the annual expenditures would quickly reach.

In 1946, the world's "super powers" – the United States, Britain, and the Soviet Union – sought agreement for effective international control of nuclear arms. When the talks failed, the nuclear arms race began. Its progress was swift. August, 1949: the Soviet Union became the second nation to explode an atomic bomb. October, 1952: Britain joined the atomic club with the explosion of a nuclear bomb at Monte Bello, Australia. November, 1952: the era of the hydrogen bomb arrived with the first explosion of a thermonuclear device, by the United States at Eniwetok. August, 1953: the Soviet Union demonstrated that it, too, had the H bomb secret. March, 1954: the United States dropped an even bigger H bomb on Bikini, a thousand times more powerful than the bomb that fell on Hiroshima, ten times more powerful than all the bombs dropped on Germany during the Second World War.

Parallel efforts were being made to harness the energy of uranium for peaceful uses. December, 1951: the first experimental production of electricity by a nuclear reactor was achieved by the U.S. Atomic Energy Commission. June, 1954: the Soviet Union placed the world's first nuclear power station in operation near Moscow. May, 1956: Britain started producing electricity at a nuclear power plant. December, 1957: the AEC and Duquesne Light and Power started up the first commercial U.S. nuclear power reactor at Shippingport, Pennsylvania.

The costs were enormous. "The doors of the treasury swung open," said the AEC's first chairman, David Lilienthal, "and the money poured out." Annual expenditures by the AEC increased from $300 million in 1947 to $1 billion in 1951, $2 billion in 1952, and $4 billion in 1953. In 1956, the enormous spawling plants of the AEC were consuming 10 per cent of the electricity produced in the United States, to separate fissile U 235 – the fuel for atomic bombs and power reactors – from natural uranium.

In 1974, the U.S. Atomic Energy Commission was terminated, most of its functions taken over by a new agency, the Energy Research Development Administration, which itself later became the Department of Energy. The job of regulating the nuclear power industry was assumed by a separate agency, the Nuclear Regulatory Commission. The Congressional Joint Committee on Atomic Energy came to its end in 1977. By the time the AEC was wound up, it had spent some $60 billion – $40 billion to build nuclear bombs, and $20 billion to help develop a nuclear power industry. Shortly before it wound up its operations, the AEC was employing the services of 538 companies, 223 colleges and universities, and 125,000 contractor employees in all.

The last uranium purchased by the Atomic Energy Commission was in 1971. By that time it had bought 190,000 tons of uranium, more than half of all the uranium produced throughout the free world to that date. Some 50,000 tons of uranium purchased by the AEC wound up in the government's surplus stockpile.

DEVELOPING THE URANIUM SUPPLY

One of the first and most pressing problems confronting the

new Atomic Energy Commission when it was set up in 1947 was finding an adequate supply of uranium.

The AEC's first director of raw materials, responsible for the acquisition of uranium, was John K. Gustafson, mining engineer and business executive.

To Gustafson, the outlook in 1947 was not encouraging. The entire multi-billion dollar investment inherited by the AEC depended on one mine deep in the Belgian Congo that might be able to produce 2,000 tons a year, a smaller mine at the edge of the arctic circle in Canada, and a trickle of U.S. production. Moreover, Gustafson could not even count on all the output of the Shinkolobwe mine, because production was allocated jointly to the United States and Great Britain by the Combined Development Agency.

General Groves told Gustafson that when he had run the Manhattan Project, it had been his policy to exploit foreign uranium in order to save what few domestic resources the U.S. had. In 1947, Gustafson had been able to secure only 67 tons of U.S. uranium, another 137 tons from Canada, and more than 1,400 tons from the Belgian Congo. The immediate problem was resolved when the Combined Development Agency agreed to allocate all of the Belgian Congo production in 1948 and 1949 to the United States, but that did little to look after the longer term needs. The problem would take nearly a decade to solve.

Gustafson recognized that the discovery and development of significant U.S. uranium reserves was not a job that could be done entirely by one agency, no matter how large. The best hope lay in a program that would encourage prospectors and mining companies by the hundreds, even thousands, to scour the land in search of uranium. The difficulty was in creating the incentive. Gustafson calculated that uranium from the low grade ores in the Colorado plateau would cost $20 or more per pound. The price of Belgian Congo yellowcake, delivered in the United States, was only $3.40 per pound.

The plan developed by Gustafson to meet this problem was announced by the AEC in April, 1948. Explorers were offered a base price of $3.50 a pound, plus a bonus of $10,000 for the first 20 tons of yellowcake from a new high-grade deposit, plus transportation allowances to move the ore to AEC buying stations. Subsequent announcements added to the incentives. A prospecting rush slowly gathered momentum, and in the early 1950's became, if briefly, the biggest U.S. mining rush ever. *Fortune* magazine called it "the first government-promoted, government-sponsored and government-controlled mineral rush in American history."

Prospectors focused on the 120,000 square-mile Colorado plateau covering parts of Utah, Arizona, New Mexico, and Colorado, where the first U.S. uranium had been produced as a by-product of vanadium. In addition to the search by private prospectors, the government undertook its own program, building more than 1,000 miles of road across the plateau, drilling thousands of exploratory holes, and completing more than 12,000 square miles of topographical and geological mapping. Government aircraft fitted with radiation meters to detect hot prospects skimmed across the plateau, flying as low as 100 feet off the ground. Results were posted twice a month in the nearest post office, and prospectors rushed to see the results. Some tried to get a jump on these posted results by watching the "rim flyers" and noting areas where they made repeated passes.

In addition to scouring the plateau, AEC geologists were sent in search of uranium to Australia, Argentina, Brazil, Chile, Colombia, Peru, Portugal, Spain, and South Africa, working for the Combined Development Trust. The biggest foreign program was in developing the methods and building the plants to recover uranium from the South African gold production, which, starting in 1952, briefly made South Africa the world's largest uranium producer.

While the rush was slowly getting started in the United States, even quicker results had been obtained in northern Canada.

Canada's Atomic Energy Control Act, passed in 1946, gave the federal government exclusive control over uranium resources, in contrast with other mineral resources, which are controlled by the provinces. The newly established Atomic Energy Control Board was empowered to control exploration, mining, refining, production, possession, importing, exporting, purchase, and sale of uranium and uranium products. In addition, initially only the federally expropriated Eldorado Mining and Refining Limited was allowed to hold permits for uranium exploration or production.

As early as 1944, Eldorado prospecting teams were out looking for more uranium in the Great Bear Lake area, but to little avail. By 1946, the search had extended 500 miles south to the region of Lake Athabasca in the northwest tip of Saskatchewan. Veteran prospectors, working in pairs, were hired by Eldorado on a salary plus discovery bonus arrangement to search for uranium during the brief, sub-arctic summer months. That year, for the first time, the prospectors were equipped with a portable instrument developed in Ottawa by the National Research Council, which soon became the most indispensable tool for uranium exploration everywhere. It was called the Geiger-Muller counter, and was later sold by the thousands to amateur and weekend prospectors. At the height of the great uranium rush, Geiger counters were advertised on the pages of comic books at prices as low as $60.

North of Lake Athabasca is a land of rugged Precambrian rock, spattered with lakes, boulder-strewn muskeg, and ridges rising as high as 800 feet. Working here for Eldorado in the summer of 1946, prospectors Einar Larum and Phillip St. Louis were the first to discover a uranium ore deposit with the aid of a Geiger counter, at Beaverlodge Lake. By mid-1950, Eldorado had spent $2.5 million drilling some 200 claims at Beaverlodge and digging a pair of 300-foot mining shafts. "We think this is the hottest thing on the continent," Eldorado president William J. Bennett told *Time* magazine in 1950. The mine and mill were brought into production in 1953.

Eldorado's monopoly on uranium claims was lifted in 1948 and prospectors and mining companies flocked to the Beaverlodge area. A new community of 2,000 sprang up on the isolated north shore of Lake Athabasca, called Uranium City.

Among those who flocked to the area was Gilbert LaBine, come to repeat at Lake Athabasca his earlier achievements at Great Bear Lake. When the government had expropriated Eldorado in 1944, LaBine remained as president until 1947, and continued as a director of the company for another two years. Now he was again in business for himself. LaBine staked claims, hired prospectors, found uranium, brought in another dormant Manitoba gold mining company, Gunnar Gold Mines, raised more than $20 million, and in a little more than three years from the time the ground was staked, had a producing mine and mill, with a seven-year contract to sell uranium to Eldorado for a total of $76,950,000. Eldorado, in turn, sold it to the U.S. Atomic Energy Commission.

Activity, meanwhile, was picking up on the Colorado plateau. The first discovery of high grade uranium ore here was made in 1951 by Paddy Martinez, a Navajo sheepherder who came across some unusually coloured rocks on Santa Fe Railroad land near Grants, New Mexico. The next big strike was made the following year 100 miles west of Moab, a sleepy Mormon village in Utah, by a retired electrical contractor. Vernon Pick had spent nine months trudging through the remote hills of the plateau on foot, and was ill from drinking arsenic-laden stream water when the needle of his Geiger counter began registering very high radiation readings. Seriously ill, Pick barely managed to survive the trek out of the hills to record his claims. He recovered from the arsenic poisoning, and sold his Hidden Splendor Mine to the Atlas Corporation for $9 million. He retired to an 830-acre estate in the Santa Cruz Mountains south of San Francisco, where he taught himself chess, French, Spanish, and Greek, struggling through the Greek classics. "I have found that making money is uninteresting," he said.

Two weeks after Pick's discovery, Charles Steen found the even more spectacular MiVida mine, sixty miles southeast of Moab. Steen had quit his job as an oil company geologist, and spent two-and-a-half years searching for uranium. He lived with his wife and four children in a series of one-room shacks. His mother had mortgaged her home in Texas to help keep him going, but he was deep in debt and his credit exhausted when his drill found the MiVida vein at a depth of less than 200 feet.

The Martinez, Pick, and Steen discoveries increased the uranium rush to a fever pitch. Thousands of amateur and weekend prospectors – mechanics, lawyers, businessmen, doctors – loaded Geiger counters onto pick-up trucks and headed into the hills to find their fortunes. Many of them abandoned their jobs for the search. A few actually found their fortunes. There were stories about the new millionaires of Moab who took off for evening flights in their private aircraft in order to enjoy better television reception. But most of them wound up poorer than they had started.

Not all of those who did find their fortunes, managed to hang on to them. Steen was one who did not. Twelve years after the MiVida discovery, Steen was reported to have a net worth of more than $16 million in ranching and real estate, gold and silver claims, a marble quarry, an aircraft company, and a dozen other business interests. But Steen was a lavish spender, and not all of his investments turned out well. In 1968, the Internal Revenue Service seized much of his diminished properties, claiming he owed $3.5 million in back taxes, and a series of law suits and bankruptcy proceedings continued into the 1970's.

Sharp promoters again demonstrated that it is not always necessary to discover any minerals in order to become wealthy. The "rash of penny stocks that has broken out in Salt Lake City is a gambler's delight," *Fortune* reported. Shares issued by the new penny mining companies rapidly rose to ten, twenty, even eighty times their initial selling prices, before falling just as fast, but not before the smart promoters had sold out. "Rarely do any investors know whether a company has found any ore, or whether its officers know anything at all about the uranium business," said *Fortune*.

One of the more "relatively sound" deals involved a public issue of 1,430,000 shares at $1.25 issued by Standard Uranium Corporation, which had obtained some of the claims filed by Steen. The demand was so great that the shares traded at up to $3 on the day that the stock was issued. While the public paid a minimum of $1.25 a share, insiders had bought shares at a price of 1¢ each, and one of the promoters made a quick million dollar profit on a $6,000 investment.

Large mining and oil companies joined the weekend prospectors, and the great rush soon started providing the uranium supplies that the government sought. U.S. uranium output soared from 67 tons in 1947 to an annual rate of 13,000 tons by the end of the 1950's, enough to make the United States the world's largest uranium producer and more than enough to meet the needs of the Atomic Energy Commission for nuclear weapons.

But even as U.S. output was climbing rapidly, far greater reserves of uranium ore – enormously surpassing the strikes on the Colorado plateau, Great Bear Lake, Beaverlodge, and even the mighty Shinkolobwe – were uncovered by geologists in a remote corner of northwest Ontario.

JOE HIRSHHORN AND THE URANIUM ART TREASURE

Somewhere in the midst of the 6,000 paintings and sculptures that constitute one of the world's most treasured art collections, there ought to be a chunk of uranium ore from the Elliot Lake area of northern Ontario. For it was the discovery of uranium at Elliot Lake that made it possible. Spread over four and one-half acres of the Washington Mall – midway betweeen the U.S. Capitol and the Washington Monument – the Joseph H. Hirshhorn Museum and Sculpture Garden was completed in 1974, a circular four-storey structure that has been called "the biggest marble doughnut in the world." It was built by the U.S. government to house an art collection valued, in 1965, at some $50 million, and donated to the United States by Joseph Herman Hirshhorn, once described by *Fortune* as the bilingual "uranium king" who spoke "adequate English and fluent Brooklynese."

The twelfth of thirteen children of a Jewish family in Latvia, Hirshhorn was seven when he arrived in the United States in 1906 to join his widowed mother and her brood in a Brooklyn tenement.

Hirshhorn started work at fourteen as an office boy for a man who, as a sideline, edited *The Magazine of Wall Street*. By the time he was seventeen he was on his own, with $255 in capital, a broker on the New York Curb Market, which dealt in unlisted shares. Within a year he had made his first fortune: $168,000. Two years later he had lost all his savings, then started over again. Three months before the fatal stock market crash of 1929, Hirshhorn sold all his investments and brokerage business, netting $4 million. In 1933, he set up shop in Toronto as J. H. Hirshhorn and Co. Ltd., wheeling and dealing in stocks and gold mines.

"I'm a speculator, not an investor," Hirshhorn is reported to have once said. "I've always wanted the sort of proposition that costs a dime and pays ten dollars." He found it in the gold fields in Ontario.

Hirshhorn's first uranium play had been at Beaverlodge, on the heels of Eldorado's discovery. He bought up some leases at Beaverlodge and, with consulting mining engineer Franc R. Joubin, organized Rix-Athabasca Uranium Mines Limited, which brought a small mine into production in 1954.

Before the Rix-Athabasca mine was in production, Joubin was already on the trail of the largest uranium strike in history.

One of the regions well tramped by prospectors and geologists in search of uranium was the Algoma basin, a logged-over land of rock and small lakes that lay north of Lake Huron and 250 miles northwest of Toronto. Geiger counters had given exciting readings in this region, but assays showed no uranium. Joubin had checked prospects in the Algoma basin as early as 1949, with the same results. Joubin first thought that the Geiger kicks may have come from another radioactive material, thorium, potentially a source of fuel for nuclear reactors, for which there was and still is no commercial market. Joubin had some samples checked for thorium, and the results showed only minute traces.

Joubin then speculated that rain, snow, and sulphur in the earth had leached away the radioactive material in the surface outcrops and that the Geiger counters told the truth about a uranium ore body that lay beneath the surface.

Certain that he had solved the riddle, Joubin approached Hirshhorn who put up $30,000 to test the theory by drilling. Drilling started in April, 1953, and within a month the first cores were on the way to the assayers. Of fifty-six assays made, fifty showed good uranium prospects.

From a study of a government geological map of the area, Joubin figured that the uranium lay in a rock formation that stretched like a gigantic Z across 90 miles of wilderness.

The trick was to stake claims along the big Z as quickly and quietly as possible before word got out and the area was swamped with prospectors. Ontario mining laws of the time allowed anyone with a prospector's licence to stake up to nine 40-acre claims. Thirty-one days were allowed from the time the claims were staked until they had to be registered. Hirshhorn and Joubin organized a small army to conduct a staking bee, people drawn mostly from Hirshhorn's Preston East Dome, whose gold mine was then shut down by a strike. There were some eighty people involved – cooks, accountants, clerks, lawyers, wives, secretaries. Equipped with tents, bed-rolls, and Geiger counters, they were flown into Elliot Lake and other lakes in the area as unobtrusively as possible, and feverishly started staking along the big Z. By flying the staking party in from the north, rather than entering the area from the south off the Trans-Canada highway, Joubin hoped that the activity would go undetected. It became known as the "backdoor staking bee."

Lawyers were on hand to execute documents transferring ownership in the individual claims to Hirshhorn companies. On July 11, 1953, they marched into mining registry offices in Toronto, Timmins, Sault Ste. Marie, and other points, to simultaneously register 1,400 claims to 56,000 acres. In the following weeks, a stampede of prospectors flocked into the area to register an additional 8,000 claims.

The Hirshhorn claims were transferred to Preston East Dome and a number of quickly organized Hirshhorn companies with exotic names: Pronto Uranium Mines Limited, Peach Uranium and Metal Mining Limited, Algom Uranium Mines, Milliken Lake Uranium Mines, Spanish American Mines, Lake Nordic Uranium Mines, and Panel Consolidated Uranium Mines Limited.

The first hole was drilled on claims held by Peach Uranium, and in three months shares of this company climbed from $1.00 to $145.00.

As further drilling outlined the enormous amount of ore under these leases, Hirshhorn decided that he would need some outside help to bring this property into production. He made a deal with the Rio Tinto Company of London (later merged with Consolidated Zinc Corporation to form Rio Tinto-Zinc) and a new company was organized, The Rio Tinto Mining Company of Canada Limited, in 1955. The London firm provided the money for Rio Tinto Canada to develop the Elliot Lake properties. Hirshhorn contributed his holdings in forty-six mining companies across Canada, for which he acquired 55 per cent of the Rio Tinto Canada shares and wound up chairman of the board. In 1960, Hirshhorn sold his interest in Rio Tinto Canada to the London company for $46 million, devoting the rest of his life to a perpetual frenzy of investments, and the buying of art. All the far flung mining companies controlled by Rio Tinto Canada were eventually consolidated into one firm, Rio Algom Limited, which in 1981 was still one of the world's largest uranium producers, and more than 50 per cent owned by Rio Tinto-Zinc of London.

Hirshhorn returned to New York a far wealthier man than when he had arrived in Toronto in 1935 with $4 million to speculate in Canadian mines. By far the most profitable speculation of all was the $30,000 that Hirshhorn provided for the first test hole drilled by Franc Joubin.

STEPHEN ROMAN – A SLAV AMONG THE WASPS

Despite their elaborate precautions and frantic efforts, the biggest plum along the 90-mile big Z in the Algoma basin somehow managed to elude the back-door staking bee organized by Joubin and Hirshhorn. This plum fell instead into the hands of another Horatio Alger type, Stephen Boleslav Roman, who had emigrated from his native Slovakia to work as a tomato picker in southern Ontario.

"To understand how I operate, you must understand my philosophy," Roman once told a reporter. "Which is farmer's philosophy."

A man with a stocky, powerful build and a face like a beefstake tomato, Roman looks like a well-fed peasant disguised in a blue-striped business suit. He sometimes lapses from his impeccable English into a leaden Slovak accent, omitting the word "the." "I think I am here to do best thing I can and build best company I can," the *New York Times* has quoted Roman as stating.

Born in Velky Ruskov, Slovakia, Roman dropped out of agricultural school after one year, arriving in Canada with his brother in 1937, a sixteen-year-old immigrant who first found work in the farm fields of southern Ontario. He enlisted in the Canadian Army during the Second World War, was soon invalided out, and spent the rest of the war years as a munitions worker.

Roman's first fling in the stock market, in 1942, wiped out

his entire hard-earned savings of $2,000. After the war he worked as editor of the *Slovak Voice*, a small Slovakian language newspaper published in Oshawa; moonlighted for a local brokerage firm, and saved his money. "I realized that if I'm going to be a Slovak newspaperman, I'd just be poor the rest of my life," Roman has said. In 1946 he helped organize the Concord Mining Syndicate, which pooled $10,000 in savings to acquire seven claims on a gold mining prospect, later sold for $15,000 cash and 200,000 shares of Concord Mines Limited. The venture failed to find any gold, and in 1952 it was reorganized as the New Concord Development Corporation Limited. With Roman as president, New Concord speculated more profitably in oil leases in Alberta and Montana. Roman sold his interest in New Concord, and in 1953 paid 8.5 cents each for 900,000 shares of North Denison Mines Ltd., a firm with a history of 17 unsuccessful years in trying to develop nickel and copper production in northern Ontario. "I tell you how to make lots of money," Roman was later quoted by *Forbes* magazine as stating. "You buy into a company that nobody else wants." Nobody else had wanted Denison, but for Roman it was a vehicle to ride in search of a fortune.

Having acquired control of Denison, Roman needed to get the company into a mining play that would be attractive to potential investors. That opportunity came from another Toronto mining consultant, Art Stollery, together with a little unwitting help from Russia.

Stollery, who had earlier worked with Joubin, had somehow found out about the staking activity organized by Joubin and Hirshhorn in the Algoma basin. Whether he was tipped off, or whether the flights of the Hirshhorn staking party into the Algoma basin were detected, leading Stollery to make some shrewd deductions, are matters of speculation. In any event, Stollery and two associates were in the Elliot Lake area staking claims two weeks before the Hirshhorn claims were registered.

Stollery and his associates first offered their eighty-three claims to Hirshhorn, and when they failed to reach an agreement, began looking for another buyer. Stollery had figured the claims should be worth at least a million dollars, but with the best acreage seemingly acquired by the Hirshhorn group, there were no buyers at that price.

While Stollery was looking for a buyer for his claims,

Moscow announced, on August 20, 1953, that it had exploded a hydrogen bomb. Suddenly, the United States wanted all the uranium it could get for its mounting arms race. In December that year, the U.S. Atomic Energy Commission made a deal with Eldorado whereby it undertook to purchase all of the uranium that Eldorado could acquire from Canadian mines. Canadian miners were assured of sales of their uranium, as fast as they could produce it, for at least a few years. And the largest known uranium reserves in the world were in the Algoma basin.

In February, 1954 – two months after the United States had asked for all the Canadian uranium it could get – Steve Roman purchased from Stollery the claims that Hirshhorn had earlier rejected. The price was $30,000 cash, and 500,000 shares of North Denison.

The first hole drilled by Denison failed to find any uranium, and for awhile it seemed as though the Stollery claims might be worthless. But before the end of the year, further drilling had disclosed a main ore body a mile and a half long with a width of 3,000 feet, and a second, smaller, ore body.

To finance development of a mine, Denison shares were sold at a public offering for ten times the price that Roman had paid less than two years before; and $36 million was borrowed in the form of debentures.

By 1957, mines in the Elliot Lake area had found commercially mineable ore reserves estimated to contain some 365,000 tons of uranium, nearly twice as much as the 186,000 tons which the U.S. Atomic Energy Commission estimated had been found in the United States by that time. Through Denison, Roman controlled more uranium than all the mines in the United States.

As fast as they could find new ore bodies, the miners contracted for sales to Eldorado. By early 1956, the contracts totalled more than $1.6 billion for uranium to be delivered prior to April 1, 1963, with options for later additional deliveries. Of this, some $200 millions worth was contracted for sale to Great Britain, and the balance to the United States. More than $1 billions worth was to come from the mines in the Elliot Lake area.

Despite the obstacle of operating in rugged, remote wilderness, the new mines were brought in on schedule. In less than six years, a new town of 27,000 people had sprung up on the rocky slopes above Elliot Lake. Uranium City, on the northern shore of Lake Athabasca, continued to thrive. By 1959 there were 22 uranium mines operating in Canada, directly employing some 14,000 people, at Elliot Lake and Bancroft in Ontario, Beaverlodge in the far northwest corner of Saskatchewan, and on Great Bear Lake in the Northwest Territories. A brand new industry had matured in less than a decade, its impact rippling throughout the economy, generating a total of some 100,000 jobs. Production by 1959 reached 15,892 tons, more than one-third of the total free world output. Sales of $331 million ranked uranium as the nation's most valuable source of mineral production, and accounted for 7 per cent of the value of all Canadian exports.

It was all accomplished with a great sense of urgency, to protect the world peace by building the most destructive weapons that have ever threatened civilization.

"Until 1955, the Commission's problem had been to get enough uranium for the expanding program," Jesse G. Johnson, AEC's director of raw materials, later recalled. "We had been buying all that was available from foreign sources as well as domestic sources and seeking to find new sources everywhere."

The boom days were short lived. The year 1959 marked the apex of uranium production for atomic bombs; and a depressed uranium industry – hardest hit in Canada – would mark time, its product a glut on the market, awaiting the event of widespread use of nuclear energy for peaceful purposes.

An indication of the coming glut and the uranium depression emerged on February 21, 1957, before the Congressional Joint Committee on Atomic Energy in Washington.

Gordon A. Weller, vice-president of the Uranium Institute of America, with headquarters in Grand Junction, Colorado, informed the committee that "some small operators are experiencing difficulty in marketing their ore in sufficient quantity to meet current operating expenses. This is particularly true in newly developed areas."

"This is a problem, Mr. Weller, which to my knowledge has not come before this committee before," responded Senator Albert Gore. "I thought there was a ready market for all uranium ores . . ."

It was not the last word that Senator Gore and other members of the joint committee were to hear about the problems of marketing uranium.

CHAPTER FOUR

The Boom
and Bust Town

Elliot Lake was a roaring, brawling, booming mining town that burst overnight on the quiet solitude of the Algoma basin. The Atomic Energy Commission wanted the uranium in a hurry. Men, money, and machinery drove in on a narrow, twisting road, quickly pushed through in 1954, snaking its way beside the Serpentine River to the claims along the big Z, running nearly 100 miles north of the Trans-Canada highway. Someone calculated that in 1955 the big trucks and tractor-trailers that carried in machinery and construction material rumbled along the new road at the rate of one every seventy-two seconds. Those that did not make the hair-pin bends wound up in the ditch. The road was a sheet of ice in winter, a sea of mud in the spring; drivers swore that it was punched through by a catskinner chasing a jackrabbit. It was not uncommon to require a full day to drive the 30 miles to Elliot Lake.

"Along this stretch of road," said Ontario Mines Minister Philip Kelly, "we have the world's greatest source of a magic mineral with the potential power to change the entire world's standard of living." Along this stretch of road there were also, on any given winter's day, as many as fifty vehicles in the ditch. The ditched vehicles were often stripped by thieves. "One miner broke an axle and when he came back with a tow truck he found his tires were gone," *Maclean's* reported. "When he came back with new tires, his wheels were gone."

The impact of the mining boom was first felt by Blind River, a depressed logging town that had sunk $400,000 into debt when the lumber mills closed during the Depression of the 1930's. After the uranium claims were staked, the population of Blind River jumped from 2,400 to 3,200 in less than a year. It seemed that everyone in town – housewives, taxi drivers, high school students – was speculating in shares of the nearly one hundred companies that had staked claims, often earning paper profits in the five figures, even though most of the claims eventually turned out worthless.

The scene soon shifted 40 miles away to Elliot Lake, intended, said the *Canadian Geographical Journal*, as "one of Canada's most completely modern, wholly-planned and most thoroughly liveable communities." From the site of the new town you could see the headframes of most of the dozen mines that were being sunk to dig the ore of the big Z. Planners laid out a horseshoe-shaped business district. Fanning out from this were rows of neat new homes, strips of pleasant green belts, with fine beaches and wooded shorelines reserved for public parkland. With loans backed by the mining companies and the federal government, miners could buy new $11,000 houses with downpayments of less than $600.

Until the new houses were built, however, thousands of miners and construction workers lived in bunkhouses, trailers, log cabins, tar-paper shacks, and tents, quickly stuck up wherever space could be found. Businessmen bunked in their offices, the only bank in town operated out of a house, the dentist and hairdresser from trailers, and in 1957 a sign outside a cabin proclaimed "Elliot Lake Laundry. Established since 1956." The first public school opened with 6 students, and a year later had 450. The Communist-led Mine, Mill and Smelter Workers waged a bitter war with the rival Steel Workers union for control of the mines. (In the end, the Steel Workers won.) The town's six-man provincial police force was hard-pressed to keep up with crime and liquor problems. Joan Kuriski, who later chronicled the epic in the form of a novel, slept with a revolver under her pillow.

"We have temporary bunkhouses, temporary churches, temporary stores, temporary girl friends," Dick West, a civil engineer who helped build the town, was quoted as stating. "Everything's temporary. Everything but the mines. And some say that they're temporary, too."

West's words were more prophetic than he perhaps had realized.

THE FIVE-YEAR PHOBIA

The hopes for a sustained, viable industry held by the dozen mines that were producing in the Elliot Lake area by 1958 rested on two developments: the exercise by the U.S. Atomic Energy Commission of its options to extend beyond 1963 its contract to purchase yellowcake, and the then-promising development of a large, world-wide nuclear power industry.

Both seemed reasonable hopes. The mines at Elliot Lake represented the bulk of the world's then-known uranium reserves, and they were brought into production on a crash program to meet the AEC requirements. It seemed reasonable to anticipate that the AEC would continue to require them. The nuclear power industry was said to be on the verge of fantastic growth. The first U.S. commercial nuclear power plant was placed in operation in 1957, and *Maclean's* reflected the optimism that was felt that year. The magazine reported:

> The world is on the threshold of a revolution in power – electricity supplied by atomic reactors. Twenty-one are being built or planned in the U.S. Europe is even farther advanced. Atomic-powered merchant ships and planes are on the drawing boards and six more U.S. atomic submarines are under construction. The revolution revealed by the U.S. Atomic Energy Commission report has come farther and faster than anyone had realized.

Franc Joubin derided the fear that the mines would close down and Elliot Lake would become a ghost town after the AEC contracts ran out in 1963. He called it "the five-year phobia."

The AEC, however, was building up a stockpile of uranium that would soon be far in excess of any military requirements, while the development of the hydrogen bomb meant "a bigger bang for every buck," requiring less uranium for the same destructive power.

The production of cheap energy from nuclear power reactors, meanwhile, proved more elusive than anticipated, especially in light of a steady decline in the cost of energy supplied by crude oil and natural gas. In the late 1950's and 1960's, the world was swimming in a rising tide of low-cost oil, with oil wells in the Persian Gulf each producing several hundred times as much as the oil wells in the United States. Prices in the world market dropped to less than $1.50 per barrel. Natural gas was a burgeoning, low-cost source of energy in the United States, on its way to supplying one-third of the total energy requirements, at government-regulated prices that later proved to be below replacement costs. In Canada, the world's longest natural gas pipeline grid was under construction before the end of the 1950's, and would stretch from Vancouver to Montreal. In western Europe, the world's second largest natural gas field was discovered offshore from the Netherlands, and the North Sea was soon providing a large, new low-cost source of energy. In the Soviet Union, large reserves were being discovered, which would soon make it the world's leading oil and gas producer, with substantial exports to western Europe. Everywhere, it seemed, the promise of low-cost nuclear energy was bumping up against the reality of even lower cost oil and gas energy.

But the things that spelled disaster for Canada's uranium industry were the growing uranium ore reserves being found in the United States, and the preferential treatment of a solicitous AEC, eager to nurture and protect the U.S. uranium mining industry.

The first limitation in the AEC's uranium purchases was in 1955, when it called a halt to contracting for additional supplies from Canada. AEC director of raw materials, Jesse C. Johnson, in 1958, told the Congressional Joint Committee how it happened.

> [A]t the beginning of 1955 we got a picture of the development and the extent of the Blind River deposits. Up to that time Canadian production had been relatively small in comparison with our requirements, and it then looked as if we should limit our Canadian commitment.
>
> So we called the Canadians and said, 'You have been working with us for a number of years and we have been interested in taking all of the uranium you produced. You have agreed to sell it to us. We have reached the point now where we think we must place a limit on our purchase arrangement. How much uranium will be developed in the Blind River area on the basis of your present knowledge of the developments now going on?' They came back with an

estimate of the production that would be available from the developments then in progress. It was agreed, after discussions, that the AEC commitment would be limited to proposals for milling contracts that were submitted not later than March 31, 1956, and there should be assurance that production would commence at a reasonable date beyond that time.

On August 3, 1955, Trade Minister C. D. Howe announced in the House of Commons that no new contracts would be made to supply the United States with yellowcake after the following March 31. After Howe's announcement, exploration for new uranium deposits in Canada ground to an abrupt halt, which lasted for nearly a decade. With exploration stopped in Canada, it was only a matter of time before the continuing search in the United States provided that country with discovered resources larger even than those in Canada.

With its buying program in Canada and elsewhere limited to contracts already in hand, the AEC continued for the next couple of years to contract for the purchase of all the additional U.S. uranium supplies it could procure. The first hint that it might slow down even its domestic purchases came from Jesse Johnson in a speech to the Western Mining Conference at Denver, Colorado, on February 9, 1957. "We have now reached the position where the uranium supply from existing contracts and from estimated increased domestic production will provide for the Commission's requirements as now established," Johnson told the miners. "We no longer are concerned over the possibility of a uranium shortage for the government's military and power development programs as projected for the next ten years." Johnson said that the U.S. uranium mining industry "should now study the potential commercial market and look to that market for its main support after 1966." He painted a glowing picture of the prospects which the nuclear power industry would afford. "Once atomic power has been demonstrated to be practical and even economic in a commercial operation, this new industry should be headed for rapid growth."

Just twelve days after Johnson's Denver speech, Senator Albert Gore and other members of the Joint Congressional

Committee learned that some U.S. miners were starting to experience problems in selling all the uranium as fast as they could produce it.

"Do you mean to say that at the present time some individual who is digging ore out of the ground cannot dispose of it?" Senator Carl T. Dunham of North Carolina asked Gordon Weller of the Uranium Institute of America.

"Yes, there are those individuals," Weller acknowledged.

Weller had a few other complaints to air to the committee. While the AEC had provided U.S. producers with a guaranteed market until 1967 at a price of $8 a pound, Weller complained that the latest AEC announcement "eliminates haulage allowances, production bonuses, and other incentives which the industry is enjoying at the present moment."

It was all very well for Johnson to say that the miners would have to look to the commercial market after 1966, but there were still a lot of unanswered questions about just exactly what the needs of that market would be, and whether or not government stockpiles might pre-empt a part of it, according to Weller. "The business of uranium ore production and processing is fast growing to be a $300 million business in the west," Weller told the Congressmen. "[T]he industry is willing and ready to follow a course of well-planned transition to a commercial market, but such a transition is impossible without adequate answers to these and related questions."

The hint first sounded by Johnson in the speech in Denver on February 9, was translated into action eight months later when he, in another speech, to the Atomic Industrial Forum at New York, October 28, 1957, announced that the AEC would limit "production to the approximate level which will be reached as a result of existing commitments."

Mines then in operation would continue to have an assured market until 1967 for essentially all the uranium they could produce. But the development of additional production would be limited. The mines in Canada faced a different situation. They could all be shut down in 1962 and 1963, without any further sales, if the U.S. chose not to exercise its options to extend the contracts.

"[W]e have arrived at the point where it no longer is in the interest of the government to expand production of uranium concentrate," Johnson said in his New York speech. "It would be undesirable . . . to expand the uranium production rate beyond currently projected requirements and then be faced with a major curtailment at some later day."

Johnson once again told the U.S. miners they would have to rely on the commercial nuclear power industry for their long-term market, predicting that this could amount to an annual requirement of as much as 50,000 tons by 1975. (As it turned out, the free world demand for uranium in 1975 was only 20,000 tons.)

Johnson outlined how, in the previous ten years, purchases by the U.S. government had

> been almost entirely responsible for the development of the uranium industry outside Russia and its satellites. This market was for military requirements for the common defense. Had it not been for these military requirements . . . there would be little basis for the broad atomic-power development now underway [in the United States and Europe], because the limited resources of ten years ago would not have justified these projects.

Johnson described how the U.S. program had brought South African uranium into production, developed large reserves and production in Canada, and increased U.S. reserves from 2,000 to 175,000 tons, so that "we now lead the world in uranium production." He did not mention that twice as much uranium had been found in Canada, even though production was less.

The action announced by Jesse Johnson to limit purchases of U.S. uranium brought howls of protest from the miners. These protests led Senator Albert Gore to hold four days of hearings in February, 1958, before the Joint Congressional Committee on Atomic Energy dealing with "AEC uranium ore procurement policies, both domestic and foreign."

Senator Gore set the tone for these hearings in a speech at Denver two weeks earlier. "In uranium procurement, as in other matters, we have problems with our Canadian neighbors," Gore told the Western Mining Conference in Denver. "At our request, they joined with us in the quest for uranium in 1948." The principal problem seemed to be that the quest in Canada had been too successful. Canadian uranium produc-

61

tion was expected to reach a level of about "14,000 tons per year until most of the contracts expire on March 31, 1962. The Canadians, I am informed, could produce twice that amount per year except for the brakes that were placed upon the Canadian program by the AEC two and one-half years ago."

Another problem pointed out by Gore in his Denver speech was that, under its complex cost-plus method of setting prices, the AEC was actually paying higher prices to foreign uranium producers than to U.S. producers. In 1958, foreign producers were paid an average of $11.15 per pound, compared with $9.60 per pound paid to American mines. (The U.S. price, however, did not reflect the discovery bonuses, transportation allowances, and other incentives that the U.S. producers had received.)

"I can well understand the unhappiness of the domestic uranium miner in seeing his government pay a higher price for processed ores in Canada," Senator Gore said in his Denver speech.

> On the other hand, speaking as a lawyer, it seems clear to me that, both legally and morally, our contract commitments with our Canadian friends until March 31, 1962, are binding and should be honored. Thereafter, I surely see no justification for paying a premium for Canadian ore or any other foreign ore.

Senator Gore did not point out that previously the AEC had purchased foreign uranium at substantially less than it paid U.S. producers. Nor did he mention that under the options held by the AEC, the price for Canadian uranium after 1963 would drop nearly 50 per cent to $8 per pound.

Prompted by Senator Gore's remarks, a long parade of producers lined up to have their say when the Joint Committee opened its hearings in Washington on February 19. What they had to say was sometimes a bit contradictory. The Canadians were being unfairly subsidized and could not compete in any normal, commercial market, the producers complained. Under no circumstances should purchases of Canadian uranium be extended beyond the present contracts. At the same time, they argued that the AEC had overestimated the discovered reserves in the United States, and that there would not be enough supply to meet demand unless U.S. producers were paid higher prices. They extolled the virtues of the free enterprise system; then demanded that the government continue to spend billions of dollars to buy all the uranium they could produce.

Richard D. Bokum, II, president of Sabre-Pinion Corporation, described the higher prices paid for Canadian and South African uranium as a "disguised form of foreign aid." He urged the AEC to cease buying foreign uranium "at much higher prices than exist in this country," as soon as the existing contracts ran out, ignoring the fact that the foreign prices would then drop to $8 under the AEC options. (A few years later, Bokum was to be back before the Joint Committee, complaining about the threat of imports of low-cost foreign uranium.) Bokum also called for greater guaranteed markets for U.S. producers, and criticized the AEC estimates that the U.S. had 70 million tons of uranium ore. "I do not believe that we have 70 million tons of mineable ore in this country today proved out," Bokum said. "And if we do not have it, we are playing with the security of this country in stopping exploration and development."

André Senutovitch of Reserve Oil and Minerals Corporation claimed that

> it is a well-known fact in our industry that some mills are going to run out of ore before 1966 and that, therefore, the Atomic Energy Commission's projected yellowcake production statistics are bureaucratically fanciful and optimistic . . . We believe that the safety and welfare of our country demands and requires the discovery of additional uranium reserves . . . The very existence of our nation is dependent upon accomplishment of this objective.

Gordon Weller of the Uranium Institute complained that "at the very threshold" of the nuclear industrial revolution, when "we now have established an active uranium industry producing steadily increasing amounts of fissionable material," the miners had been told "that such production increases must now be curtailed." He said the uranium industry "could not accept this," and called on the government to proceed "with the same determination which characterized the inception of the atomic program."

63

Representative Joseph Montoya of New Mexico said he sincerely hoped that "this committee will analyse the impact of imports and the ruinous consequences that might follow unless procurement policies are geared to encourage further exploration and development."

Congressman Montoya was followed by Gordon E. McMeen of Rosewell, New Mexico, president of Lutah Uranium and Oil Inc., who heaped glowing praises on "the gifted members of our New Mexico congressional delegation" for their support of the state's uranium industry, including Representatives Montoya and John Dempsey, and Senators Dennis Chavez and Clinton Anderson. Senator Anderson was chairman of the Joint Committee.

Oblivious to any irony, McMeen said he spoke as a "third generation of a banking family . . . interested in the American investor . . . who has made our free-enterprise system possible, workable and profitable." He said the recent AEC announcements

> had the effect of casting adrift an industry dedicated to the principles of national security and common defense . . . I say to you, gentlemen, that the time has come for action and direction if we are to preserve the industrial complex we have brought together . . . it lies within the power of the federal government to get us pointed in a more favorable direction.

Against this background, the U.S. Atomic Energy Commission, on November 6, 1959, finally announced its decision on future purchases of Canadian uranium, and the fate of Canada's largest mineral industry.

A BLEAK CHRISTMAS AT ELLIOT LAKE

It will be a bleak Christmas at Canada's three uranium mining communities – Elliot Lake and Bancroft in Ontario, and Uranium City in Saskatchewan – warned the *Toronto Star* on November 7, 1959. More than half of Canada's 14,000 uranium workers would be laid off before Christmas, the *Star* predicted, as a result of the announcements made the previous day by Ottawa's Eldorado Mining and Refining Limited, and the U.S. Atomic Energy Commission.

The announcements, of course, were that the U.S. Atomic Energy Commission, as well as Great Britain's Atomic Energy Authority, would not exercise options to purchase additional Canadian uranium beyond that already contracted for. A billion dollars' worth of uranium remained to be delivered under the contracts, of which 80 per cent was to be taken up by the United States.

The three governments, however, worked out a deal to cushion the blow. Instead of the mines facing a total closure when the contracts ran out in early 1962 and 1963, an arrangement was made to stretch out the deliveries until November, 1966. The effect would be to cut the production rates from the mines in half, but to keep them going twice as long. As an inducement, the mines were to receive advance payments for the uranium that had been deferred for later production.

Eldorado vice-president R. E. Barrett said that the intent of the arrangement was to keep the uranium industry and communities alive until 1967, when the situation "should be much brighter."

The miners were not pleased. Steve Roman said that the arrangements were "strictly for the benefit of the U.S. government and U.S. producers." Robert Winters, president of Rio Tinto Mining Company of Canada, said the decision has "cut us in two."

As a long-time Liberal politician, Winters may not have found it too difficult to criticize John Diefenbaker's Conservative government over the uranium marketing arrangements. An engineer by training, Winters had served in the engineering corps during the war, followed by twelve years as a Liberal Member of Parliament, including ten years as a cabinet minister. In 1958, Winters joined Rio Tinto Canada as president (Hirshhorn was then chairman), and in addition served on the boards of more than a dozen of Canada's largest and most prestigious corporations. When Lester Pearson, former diplomat and Nobel peace prize winner, became Prime Minister in 1963, the fact that he represented the Elliot Lake area in Parliament did nothing to diminish the political sensitivity of Canada's troubled uranium industry.

"I feel that it is discriminatory against Canada," Winters reacted to the decision. "I just didn't believe the Canadian government could let this happen to us."

The Steel Workers union fired off a telegram to Ottawa demanding an "immediate meeting with responsible government ministers," protesting the government's announcement "without prior consultation" with the workers. "Employees' investments in homes, schools and churches is just as important as investments of financial syndicates now underwritten by government guarantees," Larry Sefton, director of district six of the United Steel Workers of America, declared in the telegram.

Within weeks of the announcement, 135 housewives from Elliot Lake had organized a motorcade for a 400-mile drive to Ottawa to petition the government to save their city from extinction. They met with Prime Minister Diefenbaker and Trade Minister Gordon Churchill, but did not manage to sell any uranium.

Two months after the announcements, Representative Chet Holifield, a member of the Congressional Joint Committee on Atomic Energy since its inception, travelled to Toronto to attend "the first Canadian conference on uranium and atomic energy," sponsored by the Ontario government.

Holifield lauded the "co-operation between Canada and the United States in the nuclear field," but did not have any encouragement to offer the Canadian miners. "I am aware that some Canadian producers believe that the United States should have exercised its options even though there was doubt of its need for additional material," Holifield said. "This could have created more problems than it solved, particulary when one considers the large sums involved, and the fact that large stockpiles are not always a blessing."

Rio Tinto Canada vice-president Dr. D. R. Derry, for one, was not mollified. Derry said that the simultaneous announcements in Ottawa and Washington on November 6 "came as a severe blow to the Canadian producers," particularly since Ottawa "had not kept the producers informed about their negotiations with the United States until the final decision was reached." He said that it was the U.S. Atomic Energy Commission that

insisted on the inclusion in all but the first few Canadian contracts, of options on production beyond the contract amounts. In this atmosphere it seemed almost sure that at least part of the production rate of Canadian mines would be taken after 1963 and, indeed, that the U.S. would feel some moral obligation to support the Canadian as well as the U.S. uranium industry.

Derry laid the blame on "pressure from the U.S. uranium producers on their government to make no further foreign commitments."

Not everyone in Canada, however, was critical of the U.S. action. "I would like to point out here that we were adequately warned that a condition of over-supply was certain to develop," Eldorado president Bill Gilchrist told the Toronto conference.

The Toronto *Globe and Mail* editorialized that the United States and Great Britain were "under no obligation" to purchase additional Canadian uranium, and that to do so

> would have been a gratuitous act of charity . . . Had the Canadian government convinced these buyers to take even more uranium, it would have been a most singular piece of diplomacy. Considering the circumstances, Ottawa has made the best of an unfortunate situation. Rather than merely accepting the inevitable negative answer from our two biggest customers, it has negotiated a delivery stretch-out which will cushion the blow to the producers and get them well through the critical period of the mid-1960's.

The *Globe and Mail* urged a joint effort by industry and government to meet that ever elusive hope of a coming commercial market by selling to foreign buyers both Canadian nuclear power reactors and Canadian uranium. "It is not only the future of the industry which is at stake," said the *Globe*, "but Canada's opportunity to play a leading world role in a field in which this country has become expert."

Whatever the arguments at the time, the fact is that in its purchasing programs, the United States government accorded preferential treatment to its own domestic producers. In the eight years following the 1959 announcement, all but three of Canada's uranium mines were shut down, production declined to less than 24 per cent of its 1959 peak, and even that was sustained only by a Canadian government stockpiling program. In contrast, U.S. uranium production during the same period was maintained at 57 per cent of its 1959 peak production.

Elliot Lake, the one-time boom town that was supposed to turn into a planned model community, was meanwhile rapidly becoming a ghost town. Before all the new houses were even finished, more than half of them were boarded up and left empty. Ten of the twelve mines were shut down. From a population of zero in 1954 to 27,000 in 1959, Elliot Lake was riding a roller-coaster that took it to a population of 6,000 by 1964.

Criticism of the U.S. action, however, was muted. Even if the effects for Canada were disastrous, still the United States did not have any contractual commitments to buy more Canadian uranium, and since it was U.S. tax dollars that were involved, it was not too surprising that the U.S. producers were given preferential treatment.

Many thought that the uranium mining industry was in the bottom of the valley. No additional supplies of uranium were needed to make nuclear bombs, but surely uranium would soon be in big demand to make electricity. It was a time for waiting, apprehensively.

CHAPTER FIVE

Surviving

With the annual production volumes slashed by the 1959 stretch-out of the sales contracts, it was immediately apparent that the only chance the industry had to survive was to shut down most of the mines, and transfer the sales contracts held by the shut-down mines to the few that continued in business. When all of the companies in the Rio Tinto group were merged, the resulting organization, Rio Algom Limited, wound up with one mine to produce the remaining portion of contracts totalling $631 million. Consolidated Denison, Can-Met Exploration, and Stanrock Uranium Mines, comprising the rest of the Elliot Lake mines, were merged into Denison Mines Limited, with sales contracts totalling $282 million. Rio Algom, Denison and the government-owned Eldorado, were the only surviving uranium producers in Canada.

There was some question how long even these three could stay in business. After the contracts ran out in 1966, it was a matter of awaiting the arrival of the promising but ever-elusive commercial market. During that waiting period, prices for non-American uranium were slashed by nearly two-thirds, to as low as $4 a pound.

When the world finally turned to nuclear reactors to meet its needs for electrical energy, Canada's large resources of uranium could be in big demand. But would the mines still be in business? When the world discovered it needed uranium, would it find that in Canada the mining companies were out of business, the miners gone, the boom towns boarded up, the mines abandoned and flooded with water?

That was a risk that seemed to be viewed in the United States with considerable equanimity by the miners, the Atomic Energy Commission, and the Congress. In 1964, Congress heard predictions that within a few years, only one uranium mine would be left in operation in Canada, and that chances of reviving the Canadian industry were slight.

No one had more at stake in the survival of the uranium mines than Steve Roman. His Denison Mines owned half the uranium ore in Canada. It had contracts to sell 13,000 tons of uranium to the U.S. Atomic Energy Commission, but unless more buyers could be found, that would still leave it with 200,000 tons of uranium in the ground. And with the cut-back rate of production, Denison's profits fell from $30 million in 1961 to $1.3 million six years later, and the slide did not seem over.

In trying to find new buyers for his enormous pile of uranium, Roman soon found himself caught in the web of international nuclear politics.

NO ATOMS FOR DE GAULLE

Long before the nuclear debate became a hot political issue, there was an ambivalence in Canada's attitude toward atomic energy. Canada's development of the Candu nuclear power reactor was seen as the basis for a new, high-technology industry, with uranium production providing a natural resource industry of considerable importance to the national economy. Against this hope was apprehension about the spread of nuclear arms, a concern that has constrained Canada's exports of both nuclear reactors and uranium. While the primary motivation of U.S. policies has been to curb the spread of nuclear arms, there have also been suggestions that these policies were designed in ways that would also enhance U.S. commercial interests, at the expense of competitors. Perhaps the best example of this is the tangled tale of the abortive attempts to sell Canadian uranium to France.

No one was more aware of Canada's ambivalent atomic attitude than Lester Bowles Pearson, the diplomat turned politician who in 1957 was head of the Liberal party, and became Leader of Her Majesty's Loyal Opposition in the House of Commons. As such, Pearson stood opposed to the use of uranium for bombs. As the Member of Parliament for Algoma East, which embraced the Elliot Lake mines, he stood for sales of as much uranium as Canada could capture – for peaceful uses, of course. Pearson told the House in 1957:

> [T]he great bulk of this product is now going into military use, . . . perhaps I was in a somewhat incongruous position when I was Secretary of State for External Affairs, inasmuch as in that capacity it was my duty and desire . . . to do everything I could . . . to make the use of uranium for destructive purposes unnecessary and impossible, . . . at the same time, as the honourable member for Algoma East, I was doing everything I could to encourage and develop the use of that production.

As the solution to that dilemma, Pearson urged the government to "do everything it can . . . to promote the search for markets for this product for civilian reactors."

One of the beckoning markets was France, already well launched on an aggressive nuclear development program, for both civilian and military purposes. It was the dual character of the French nuclear program that was to give Pearson and the Canadian government a fair-sized headache, as well as some pressure from Washington, over the opportunities to sell uranium to France.

The first indication that Canada had been talking with France about a possible sale of uranium was on December 21, 1957, when Secretary of State for External Affairs Sidney Smith told the House that Canada had completed an agreement with West Germany "for co-operation in the peaceful uses of atomic energy."

The agreement paved the way for the sale of 500 tons of uranium to West Germany over a five-year period, arranged by Eldorado. It was a small sale, but a vital door-opener. It was the first sale of Canadian uranium for strictly non-military purposes, and the first to anyone other than the United States or Great Britain.

Smith told the House that any transactions under the terms of the bilateral agreement "must be directed solely to peaceful ends, and there is provision for adequate safeguards to ensure that materials such as uranium . . . shall not be diverted to any military use." He said that the safeguards were "modelled closely upon those of the International Atomic Energy Agency of the United Nations." The agreement called for Canada to send inspectors to West Germany to ensure that none of the uranium was diverted to military purposes.

Paul Martin wanted to know "whether requests have come in from at least three other friendly countries" for the purchase of Canadian uranium. Smith responded that negotiations were underway with two other countries, which he said he could not publicly identify. "I can state, however, that there was hope that such an agreement might be negotiated with France, but they informed us that they were not interested in obtaining Canadian uranium on this basis."

Full details of the negotiations with France were never disclosed, but they involved a considerably greater amount than the sale to West Germany. Canada, in fact, was using a double standard in its safeguard policy. It was selling uranium for military purposes to both the United States and Great Britain, but not to anyone else. France had its ambitions for an "independent nuclear deterrent," and resented being treated as a third-class citizen of the world, like a "naughty child," according to Bertrand Goldschmidt of France's atomic energy authority.

Goldschmidt later wrote that the failure of these negotiations in 1957 led to the development of France's own uranium producing industry, and thus, ultimately, to France's participation in the uranium cartel. Goldschmidt should know. He participated in the discussions in 1957, and later in the meetings at which the cartel was organized. He had been involved in nuclear research right from the start. During the war, Goldschmidt was one of the scientists who played an active role in the development of the atomic bomb, working in the United States, and then as a member of the Canadian-British team of scientists working in Montreal and at Chalk River. When Charles de Gaulle established France's Commissariat à l'Energie Atomique in 1946, Goldschmidt was one of the first members of the commission, later headed the CEA's international relations, and eventually served as chairman of the United Nation's International Atomic Energy Agency.

Goldschmidt's account of the failure of the 1957 negotiations is contained in his book, *The Atomic Adventure*, published in 1962. In it, he reveals that France was seeking an initial order for 1,000 tons of Canadian uranium. He claims that the negotiations failed not because France was unwilling to limit the use of the uranium to civilian reactors, but because of a failure to agree on price, and because of U.S. pressures.

President Eisenhower's "Atoms for Peace" program was two years old in 1957. The essence of the program was to make nuclear technology and materials available to "friendly countries" for use in producing electricity, while seeking to preclude their use for weapons. This would also, of course, provide export opportunities for U.S. industry.

The key to controlling the use of uranium for nuclear weapons was the monopoly the United States then had on the ability to enrich natural uranium into fuel-grade material for use in nuclear power reactors. In addition to this, according to Goldschmidt, the United States also sought to apply other controls. "In particular," Goldschmidt wrote, the United States "attempted to obtain understandings from her suppliers of natural uranium not to sell to other countries without arrangements for control of the materials used. The uranium producers, anxious to see their contracts with the United States and Britain renewed, agreed to this request." Two years later, of course, the contracts were not renewed.

The situation that faced France in 1957, according to Goldschmidt, involved "a choice between opening a new mine in France and building the corresponding extraction mill – an expensive investment – or signing a substantial contract with Canada, covering a thousand tons of uranium and open to renewal."

Goldschmidt continued his account of the 1957 events:

The negotiations opened satisfactorily for the Canadians; the clause providing for peaceful use verified by Canadian control, which was suggested to France, was acceptable because this was uranium needed for the French power production program. However, when the financial terms were discussed the Canadians suggested the average price paid by the United States. The French delegation [of which Goldschmidt was a member] caused some surprise by replying that it could only pay the same price for the same goods, and the material sold to the United States was free from any restrictions as to use, whereas that offered to the French would not be free. It was felt by the French that this justified a substantially lower price. The negotiations broke down over this point, to the great regret of the Canadians, who were prevented by their American commitments from selling their uranium either cheaper or free from restrictions.

Whatever the reasons for the loss of sales to France in 1957, they did nothing to thwart France's race to join the nuclear arms club, much to the dismay of the members of that club, and many others. In any event, seven years later, France was back again, seeking to purchase a larger supply of uranium. This time the protests from Washington were clear.

In February, 1960, France set off its first nuclear explosion at Reggane, in the desert sands of the Sahara, and General de Gaulle's *force de frappe* became a reality, without the help of Canadian uranium. Four years later, Denison Mines concluded a contract to sell $700 millions worth of uranium to France. Getting the deal approved turned out to be another matter.

By this time, Lester Pearson and John Diefenbaker had switched roles: Pearson was now Prime Minister, and Diefenbaker led the Opposition in the House. Pearson seemed clearly trapped between both a desire to sell uranium and a determination to improve relations with France, and the pressure to curb the military applications of uranium. Newspaper items provided accounts about what did – or did not – happen.

Financial Post, Toronto, January 18, 1964:

This week President de Gaulle was expected to make a formal request to his visitor, Prime Minister Pearson, that Canada sell uranium to France on a no strings attached basis, as we do to the U.S. and Britain. At the same time, Washington is putting behind the scenes pressure on Canada to do nothing to help advance France's independent military nuclear ambitions . . . If there is one thing that sets French tempers boiling it is being treated as a second class power while Britain retains some apparent higher position on the power ladder . . . Washington's anxiety is certainly based largely on its desire to limit the nuclear club. Ottawa officials suspect that there are other, less noble, considerations at work as well. Technical success of the heavy water reactor designed by Atomic Energy of Canada Limited, coupled with the decision to set up a heavy water production plant, have revealed once and for all Canada's nuclear ambition to take the lead in exports of commercial nuclear power stations, fuels and know-how.

New York Times, Paris, January 16:

The Canadian government is interested in selling uranium to France, where it would contribute to building France's independent nuclear force, Prime Minister Lester B. Pearson said tonight. While Canada opposes the spread of nuclear weapons, he said, she will take orders for uranium from France and from the United States . . . Mr. Pearson made his views known at a press conference tonight after two days of talks with President de Gaulle, Premier Georges Pompidou and foreign minister Couve de Murville.

New York Times, Ottawa, January 19:

Prime Minister Lester B. Pearson denied tonight upon his return from Paris that he had discussed the sale of uranium with President de Gaulle. He said he had no idea where such speculation arose.

Financial Post, January 25:

Prime Minister Pearson this week flatly denied that the subject had been discussed with General de Gaulle at all. Should France want to buy uranium, he said, it would have to be subject to the normal non-military terms, . . . Observers in Ottawa were confused because Pearson seemed to go out of his way to create the impression that he was willing to sell uranium with no strings attached. At a luncheon given by the diplomatic press association, Pearson turned to French Foreign Minister Couve de Murville and said he hoped he could 'persuade the minister to by Canadian uranium.' At a press conference, he expressed the view that there was no more contradiction in selling uranium to France for their nuclear strike force than selling to the U.S. . . . one of the Prime Minister's aides put forward the argument that if the U.S. was supplying KC-135 air-tankers for the *force de frappe*, there was no reason why Canada shouldn't supply the raw materials.

When Parliament resumed sitting in February, Opposition Leader John Diefenbaker was waiting, with his questions loaded. "I should like the Prime Minister to tell us something about his trip to Paris and Washington, because we want to get an authentic report," Diefenbaker declared. "I must say the reports we received indicate that there was a different stand taken by the Prime Minister in Canada from the one which he took in Paris . . . what took place? What is the position of affairs with regard to uranium?"

Diefenbaker never did get an answer, and negotiations with France continued for more than another year. There were sharp divisions of opinion within the cabinet. One view was that France still did not seem politically stable, and the possibility that the Communist Party might one day assume office was considered a continuing risk.

Pearson finally resolved the matter in a statement in the House on June 3, 1965, concerning "conditions applicable to granting of export permits" for uranium.

On the face of it, the brief statement appeared to say nothing new, merely re-confirming the past policy on safeguards restricting the use of uranium exported from Canada.

First there was the obligatory statement about the always anticipated growth in world uranium requirements for industrial use. Pearson said:

Canada holds a substantial portion of the known uranium reserves of the world and in the future may well be the largest single supplier for the rest of the world. It is vital that the Canadian industry be in the best possible position to take advantage of expanding markets for the peaceful uses of this commodity.

As one part of its policy to promote the use of Canadian uranium for peaceful purposes the government has decided that export permits will be granted . . . with respect to sales of uranium covered by contracts entered into from now on, only if the uranium is to be used for peaceful purposes. Before such sales to any destination are authorized, the government will require an agreement with the government of the importing country to ensure with appropriate verification and control, that the uranium is to be used for peaceful purposes only.

Pearson promised that within the terms of this policy, "the Canadian government will actively encourage and assist the Canadian uranium industry in seeking export markets."

The most important part of Pearson's statement was what was left unsaid. The statement meant that Canada would no longer sell uranium for military purposes to anyone, including the United States and Great Britain. Thus Canada would no longer discriminate against France. Giving up military sales to the United States and Great Britain involved no sacrifice. The policy was to apply only to new sales, which meant that the small amount left on the existing contracts would still be delivered to the United States and Great Britain. As for future military sales to these two countries, there were no prospects in any event, because they already had more than an adequate supply. But the new policy did mean that Canada was knowingly sacrificing nearly a billion-dollar sale to France, which had made it plain that it was not prepared to buy Canada's uranium under these restrictions.

If this loss was not sustained as a result of pressures by the United States and Great Britain, it was at least in accord with the policies of those two countries. That was made clear the following day when, under questioning in the House, Pearson said that there had been "consultations, before this policy was adopted, with the United Kingdom and the United States governments because of our previous association with them in regard to uranium policy matters." Despite the fact that it entailed a considerable commercial loss for Canada, the new policy was warmly applauded in the House by all the Opposition parties.

To soften the loss of the sales to France, Pearson at the same time also announced a government uranium stockpiling program. The program was intended to sustain production and employment at minimum levels over a five-year period.

"These purchases will be made at a price of $4.90 per pound of uranium oxide," Pearson said. They were to be made "only from companies which have previously produced uranium and will be limited . . . to the amount necessary to maintain an appropriate level of employment and production."

It was, in fact, the government's second stockpiling program. The first, in 1963 and 1964, involved expenditures of $24.5 million. The second involved an additional $77 million by the time it was completed in 1970. Biggest beneficiary of the two stockpiling programs was Denison Mines, which sold $80 millions worth of uranium to the government.

In Denison's 1965 annual report to shareholders, Roman greeted Pearson's action with a good news, bad news type of comment. Roman took credit for the stockpiling program, claiming it had resulted from Denison's initiative in completing a long-term supply contract with France's CEA. The stockpiling program, he told the company shareholders, gave Denison a five-year contract to sell 15 million pounds of uranium to the government, "a real turning point."

The loss of the sale to France was another matter. "[A] more realistic appraisal of uranium marketing is needed," Roman wrote. Such control on uranium exports, in Roman's view, was a "negative approach," insulting to the "national sovereignty and national pride" of the customer countries, and in any event would be impossible to administer. A more "positive approach" would be to recognize the "responsibility of the purchasing nation for the peaceful use of nuclear fuels which it buys from Canada or from any other nation," according to Roman.

> Trust is the essential factor in peaceful agreements, no less than in those defense agreements which Canada has also entered into with many of the European nations . . . Thus Canadian policy should evolve towards the responsibility of the purchasing nation for the peaceful use of uranium.

With such statements that seemed so self-serving, it was little wonder that Roman lost all his political battles. It was, however, about the most polite thing that Roman has ever said about how the government lost his big sale to France.

CONGRESS APPLIES AN EMBARGO

Miners in the United States had warmly applauded the action taken in November, 1959, by the Atomic Energy Commission to discontinue buying foreign uranium.

"We commend your committee and the Atomic Energy Commission for the decision made relative to the purchase of U_3O_8 from foreign producers," the Wyoming Mining Association wrote to Senator Clinton Anderson, chairman of the joint committee, two months after the AEC announcement. "With the growth of our domestic uranium industry, it is imperative that a major share of the domestic market shall be reserved for domestic producers."

Gordon Weller of the Uranium Institute of America almost radiated an atomic glow when he arrived before the Joint Committee the following month to remind the members of the wonderful accomplishments of the industry. Weller stated:

Without a doubt, the United States has outdone every nation in the world in its procurement of uranium, . . . our growing uranium supplies and our rapidly advancing nuclear-power technology will remove all doubts as to our long-range capabilities as a leading industrialized nation of the world . . . our supply of uranium assures us of our ability in the years immediately ahead to extend a helping hand to the under-developed countries of the world, to help improve their standards of living, which is so closely tied to power production, and to thereby broaden the commercial possibilities for all industrialized nations of the world.

Of course, should any under-developed countries have any uranium that they might wish to sell to the United States, well, that would be just too bad.

How much the AEC's decision to stop buying foreign uranium had affected the industry in Canada was hinted at by the AEC's director of procurement, Jesse Johnson, in a speech to the National Western Mining Conference at Denver, early in 1963. "Canadian reserves, once reported at nearly 400,000 tons of U_3O_8, are now estimated on a recoverable basis to be less than 300,000 tons," Johnson said. "With only one company scheduled to be producing by 1970, revival of Canadian production will be a major undertaking."

While the miners welcomed the protection of the AEC, there was a cloud on their horizon: how long would the protection last? As long as the Atomic Energy Commission was the sole U.S. purchaser of uranium, there seemed little reason to worry. The Atomic Energy Act of 1946 gave the AEC an exclusive monopoly on the ownership of all nuclear materials in the United States. This was modified somewhat in the 1954 amendment to the act, which allowed power utilities to own and operate nuclear power reactors. The enriched uranium they required to fuel their plants, however, had to be leased from the AEC, and the AEC was still the only one allowed to buy uranium from the producers. The AEC's Jesse Johnson, however, had already warned the miners that at some point they would have to look to the commercial market for their sales. In that event, the power utilities would presumably be free to buy uranium from anyone, including foreign producers.

Legislation introduced in Congress in 1963 did, in fact, propose that the power utilities would buy their uranium supplies directly from the miners, and that the uranium would be enriched at the big AEC plants on a toll basis. More than 90 per cent of the world's nuclear power reactors, including all of the U.S. reactors, cannot use natural uranium as fuel. It must first be enriched, increasing the portion of fissile uranium 235 from 0.7 per cent in natural uranium to about 3 per cent in the material used for reactor fuel. The enriching process is very costly, and in the 1960's the United States had the only plants outside of the Soviet Union that were capable of providing this service. Even foreign power utilities – unless they had one of the few reactors that could use natural uranium, such as the Candu reactors built in Canada – would have to have their uranium enriched in the United States. (Some west European utilities later obtained uranium enrichment from the Soviet Union, while eventually the U.S. monopoly of this service is likely to be overtaken by new and planned enrichment plants in western Europe and elsewhere.) This enrichment service to be provided by the AEC, the *New York Times* noted, "is expected to have an important effect for encouraging foreign countries to use enriched uranium reactors developed in the United States."

In hearings before the Joint Congressional Committee on "private ownership of special nuclear materials," held in July and August, 1963, AEC member Dr. Robert W. Wilson noted that "special nuclear material is the only article of commerce for which private ownership is forbidden." The proposed legislation would cure that.

If the uranium miners saw a threat from imported uranium resulting from such private ownership, the AEC stood ready to meet their concerns.

"If it is desired to avoid competition of foreign ore with the domestic uranium mining and milling industry, the commission would be willing to restrict toll enrichment of imported source material up to July 1, 1973, to situations in which the resulting source material would be re-exported," Dr. Wilson stated. "Moreover, such action may become necessary in view of possibly substantial effects on the balance of payments problem."

What Wilson was saying was that the AEC would, for example, permit Canadian or South African uranium to be imported into the United States, enriched by the AEC so that it could be used for fuel by nuclear power plants, and then re-exported to, say, West Germany. But it would be prepared to exclude the use of foreign uranium in U.S. nuclear power plants "if it is desired to avoid competition of foreign ore."

It was not difficult to guess how the miners would respond to that suggestion. The day after Wilson's statement, Richard Bokum, president of United Nuclear Corporation, appeared before the committee to claim that if foreign uranium imports were allowed,

It would destroy much of what are now considered economic ore reserves [in the United States] and it would completely destroy the incentive for exploration for additional uranium reserves in the United States . . . unless this tolling provision and private ownership create the incentive within the uranium industry, there probably will be no exploration until the middle of the 1970's.

In the same breath that he sought protection from foreign imports, Bokum accused European nations of being "nationalistic" in not wanting to buy from the United States. Bokum told Representative Chet Holifield that he did not think the United States would manage to sell many nuclear power reactors in Europe. "These countries are nationalistic," Bokum said. "They don't want to buy from America. They will get the technical know-how and you will be able to sell the first generation [of power reactors], but you will never sell the second."

Only foreign countries, it seems, suffer from nationalism. At home, it is called patriotism.

Engelhard Industries, Inc., the U.S. sales representative for the South African uranium producers, was the only voice raised before the Joint Committee in 1963 to protest the proposed import embargo. Lawrence C. Burman of Engelhard wrote to the Joint Committee:

> What appears to be proposed, is a firm embargo for ten years on all foreign uranium which might be used in fuelling domestic reactors. I doubt whether there is any other mineral product imported into the United States in competition with domestic sources to which such rigid restrictions are applied.

Burman predicted that such an embargo would result in a two-price system. "One price in the United States for domestic power reactors: a second and lower price where the U.S. producers will come out from behind the wall to compete for foreign business."

The Joint Committee hearings on "private ownership of nuclear material" were resumed in June, 1964, when again a parade of witnesses sought the protection first proposed by Dr. Wilson.

Richard Newlin of the Anaconda Company endorsed the proposal to enrich foreign uranium that would be re-exported, since this would "tend to keep the cost of enrichment down and to enhance the prospects of foreign purchases of U.S. reactors." But enrichment of foreign uranium for use in the United States "is an entirely different matter. It is well known that certain foreign uranium is produced under government support or as a low-cost by-product, and any incremental uranium from such a source would be very low cost indeed." There was no acknowledgment that U.S. uranium "was produced under government support" – just a suggestion that there was something wrong when other governments did the same thing.

Dean A. McGee, president of Kerr-McGee Oil Industries and a business partner of Senator Robert Kerr of Oklahoma, a powerful Senate spokesman for the oil industry, told the committee that Canadian production would soon "be concentrated in one mill operating at near capacity from substantial reserves. Its costs are expected to be at least as low as the average of U.S. producers, which means substantially below a number of U.S. producers." Uranium from South Africa would be even lower cost, according to McGee. "If this incremental and by-product foreign uranium is permitted into the very limited domestic market, the domestic mining and milling industry will have great difficulty in surviving. If any domestic producer survives in the face of such competition, it is likely to be only the larger and more efficient producer." McGee predicted that if foreign imports were permitted "the discovery and development of adequate domestic reserves of uranium will not occur, leaving electric utility and other private users of uranium, as well as the U.S. government, again dependent upon foreign supplies."

In 1963, the AEC had suggested that the ban on the use of foreign uranium might apply until 1973, but in the hearings the following year the date had been extended until 1975. Bokum suggested to the Joint Committee that "The year 1975 should be a flexible target date, and subject to the determination of the AEC and the Joint Committee that there is sufficient market to support the domestic industry."

Five years earlier, the miners had told the Joint Committee that imports of high-cost foreign uranium would be a disguised form of foreign aid. Now they were arguing that the danger lay in the lower cost of foreign uranium.

The only U.S. miner who seemed prepared to meet foreign competition head on was Robert W. Adams, president of Western Nuclear Inc.

"We are not concerned about 'low cost' foreign uranium destroying our domestic market," Adams told the Joint Committee. "I believe that we can do better in a competitive market than some operators think we can . . . if we wish to compete all over the world for the sale of reactors and reactor systems, we had better be willing to compete all the way down the line, including fuel." Adams derided the suggestion that South African gold producers would dump their by-product uranium on the U.S. market at fire-sale prices. "It does not make sense to me," Adams said. "For the very reason that their supply is a by-product, sales are not a requirement to stay alive. I think it is reasonable, therefore to assume that they will hold off for a higher price on their limited production."

In opening the 1964 hearings, Chet Holifield, chairman of the Joint Committee's sub-committee on legislation, said that among the "principal issues" to be dealt with was the question: "Should some restrictions be imposed on the importation of foreign uranium concentrates for enrichment and sale on the domestic market?"

AEC chairman Glenn Seaborg already had the answer. "To provide additional assurance of maintaining a viable domestic uranium-producing industry, it is the Commission's intent not to toll enrich uranium of foreign origin, except where the enriched product is to be re-exported," Seaborg had said at the opening of the hearings.

As the hearings drew to a close, there was one final question: was the proposal to exclude the use of foreign uranium in U.S. nuclear power plants in keeping with U.S. commitments to its international trading partners? Representative Craig Hosmer of California put the question to Joseph A. Greenwald, director of international trade with the State Department.

"We are talking about bringing foreign ores in for toll enrichment here and permitting it to be sold on the domestic market," Hosmer told Greenwald. "There are some people who want to tell the AEC, 'You are not going to be able to do this for quite awhile.' We want to know if that way of keeping foreign ore out – which is not by tariffs and not by quotas, but in effect operates to keep the foreign ore off the domestic market – we want to know if that violates, not the spirit, but the words of GATT" (General Agreement on Tariffs and Trade).

Greenwald responded that such "discriminatory limitations

on the domestic use of enriched foreign ores would be in direct conflict with our international commitments under GATT."

Greenwald quoted the relevant GATT article, which provides that:

> . . . the products of the territory of any contracting party imported into the territory of any other contracting party shall be accorded treatment no less favorable than that accorded to like products of national origin in respect of all laws, regulations and requirements affecting their internal sale, offering for sale, purchase, transportation, distribution or use.

The Department of State, however, was willing to go along with the proposed embargo, as a temporary measure.

"While we consider that this is contrary to our GATT commitments, our feeling is, if it is done on a transitional basis when moving to a new kind of arrangement, that it could probably be worked out," Greenwald told the committee.

AEC chairman Seaborg interposed: "That is what I understood."

"[A]s long as we made clear we intended to move to a complete observance of our international obligations," Greenwald elaborated, "I think other countries would recognize this as a special situation, and we should not have too much difficulty internationally."

On August 26, 1964, President Lyndon Johnson signed the legislation amending the Atomic Energy Act and ending the government's eighteen-year monopoly on the ownership and supply of fuel for nuclear reactors.

"This is another step toward achieving full use of the force of the atom for peaceable purposes for the benefit of all mankind," the president declared at the signing ceremony in the White House cabinet room. "That is our objective and that is our prayer, and all of our efforts will be directed along that line."

The legislation allowed utility companies to buy uranium directly from the miners; provided for the enrichment of the uranium by the AEC, starting in 1966, at rates designed to give "reasonable compensation to the government"; and directed the AEC to withhold the enriching of foreign uranium for U.S.

reactors whenever it was considered that such imports would undermine "the maintenance of a viable domestic uranium industry."

The AEC did not officially invoke this measure until two years later, but, in order to reduce the existing government stockpile, the AEC did not start enriching privately owned uranium until 1966. Thus, the effect was that the embargo on the use of foreign uranium by U.S. power plants came into effect on the day the president signed the legislation. The temporary measure that was in "direct conflict" with American trade commitments was to last fourteen years before a gradual phase-out was to start, and twenty years before it was due to be completely removed. In 1977, U.S. power utilities were permitted to import a maximum 10 per cent of their uranium requirements, the restrictions reducing each year thereafter until 1984 when all import restrictions were scheduled to be eliminated. Well before the restrictions were lifted, there were renewed demands that the embargo again be imposed.

ANOTHER LOSS FOR ROMAN

If Stephen Roman was just a bit upset when the government of Canada blocked Denison Mines' $700 million sale of uranium to France in 1965, he was even more upset by the unexpected action that Ottawa took five years later. This time the government stepped in to stop a negotiated sale to the subsidiary of an American oil company, of the 36 per cent interest in Denison Mines controlled by Stephen Roman and the Roman Corporation.

In early 1970, Denison was still scratching hard to find enough sales to keep the world's largest uranium mine from being shut down. Market value of Denison shares had plunged from a high of $80 to less than $20. Sales to potential U.S. buyers were blocked by the embargo that Congress and the AEC implemented in 1965. Denison's sales to the Canadian government stockpile, which had kept the mine in operation for the past five years, had just about run out. Denison was producing a small amount of uranium for the Tokyo Electric Power Company, and in January had announced a second, larger contract with the Japanese buyer for $300 million worth of uranium to be delivered over a 10-year period, starting in 1974. The new Japanese contract would keep Denison's mine and mill operating at only half capacity, and meanwhile a large inventory of unsold uranium was accumulating. Tough sales competition also appeared to be in store from new uranium discoveries in Saskatchewan and Australia, where high-grade ore lying near the surface could be produced and sold at prices lower than the deep mine at Elliot Lake could match.

These were the conditions that existed when the Toronto *Globe and Mail* on Saturday, February 28, 1970, carried a brief item reporting that Roman and the Roman Corporation were negotiating with an unidentified buyer for the sale of their interest in Denison. The prospective buyer was later identified as Hudson's Bay Oil and Gas Company of Calgary.

The report that control of Denison Mines was about to change hands came at a time of mounting concern over the extent of foreign ownership of Canadian companies. Foreign investors, primarily American, owned some 80 per cent of the country's oil and gas industry, and more than half of the mining and manufacturing industries. The Liberal government of Prime Minister Pierre Elliott Trudeau was under increasing pressure to take effective action.

When Parliament met Monday, March 2, 1970, Trudeau was ready to take the first step to limit foreign ownership of firms in the natural resources sector, by blocking the sale of Denison. After the stock markets had closed, Trudeau interrupted an emergency debate on foreign wheat policy to read a terse, two-paragraph statement, in the House of Commons:

> Last week the government of Canada learned that a substantial ownership interest in Canada's largest uranium mining company might be passing into non-Canadian hands. The government cannot delay making its position clear because it is understood the transaction may be close to completion.
>
> Our reservations about the change of control of Canadian uranium resources are such that if necessary the government will introduce an amendment to the Atomic Energy Control Act, to take effect as of today, to prevent such a transaction.

Roman and Hudson's Bay Oil still hoped to proceed with the sale, despite Trudeau's announcement in the House. They had already signed a letter of intent, prior to Trudeau's statement, outlining the general principles of agreement, although extensive negotiations were still required before a final contract could be signed. A news conference was set for March 20 at Denison's offices in Toronto at which Roman and Hudson's Bay Oil president Lindy Richards planned to announce that a formal deal had been signed.

Under the proposed deal, Roman and the Roman Corporation were to receive $104 million ($94 million in cash and notes and $10 million in Hudson's Bay Oil shares) in return for their shares that represented 36 per cent ownership of Denison. An offering to other Denison shareholders would be made on the same basis.

(Hudson's Bay Oil was owned 65 per cent by the Continental Oil Company of the United States, and 15 per cent by the Hudson's Bay Company, with its headquarters then in London. It was organized in 1926 to explore mineral rights, which the Hudson's Bay Company had retained from its former ownership of nearly half of North America, granted by England's King Charles II in 1670.)

The evening before the press conference planned to announce the sale of Roman's interest in Denison, Energy Minister Joe Greene made another statement in the House on the government's still evolving policy to limit foreign ownership of uranium mining firms. Greene announced that the government would limit foreign ownership in new uranium mines to 33 per cent. Foreign owners of uranium companies, with either existing mines or mineable ore bodies, would be allowed to retain their holdings, but any future sales of such holdings were to be made to Canadian residents until the foreign ownership was reduced to 33 per cent.

Faced with this announcement, Roman and Hudson's Bay backed off from the planned signing of their agreement in Toronto the next day. Roman told reporters that it would be up to the courts to determine whether the regulations could be applied retroactively to block the sale. "The deal has been completed," Roman said. "It was signed before March 2. Formal and definitive agreement was to have been signed today."

Hudson's Bay Oil president Lindy Richards, however, was not prepared to press the issue, telling reporters that there was no question of his company testing the agreement in the courts because no contract existed. "The general principles were scratched out on a piece of fool's-cap signed by the two negotiators," Richards said. "But it was only general principles. We realized a lot of details would have to be clarified before a formal contract was signed. We had hoped this might have been possible today."

Roman was bitter about the government's new policy, calling it "arbitrary and discriminatory," and claiming that it was "obviously directed at one company and one situation – at Denison and Roman. I think it's a pretty sad thing to establish a national policy on the basis of that kind of approach. It is something that, in my opinion, should not happen in a democratic country . . . I think it's asinine, a completely asinine policy."

Roman claimed that with the deal, the larger financial resources of Hudson's Bay Oil could be used to keep the mine in operation for the next three or four years, until increased sales made it a financially viable operation. Without those financial resources, he said he would have to consider shutting down the mine, and laying off nearly 1,000 employees. It would have been a drastic step, not only because of the lay-offs but because the cost of putting back into production a mine that has been shut down and flooded for several years can be as costly as putting a brand new mine in operation.

Government officials in Ottawa were never entirely certain whether Roman's threat to shut down the mine was simply a bluff to get more government help, but if that was the purpose, it worked. Late that year, Denison and the government reached an agreement for a new, four-year stockpiling program to buy production from the mine, to be financed 25 per cent by Denison and 75 per cent by the government. This time, however, before the "joint venture" stockpiling program had run its four-year course, Denison had managed to sell the entire stockpile, at a profit to both itself and the government.

The government, meanwhile, was still trying to figure out exactly how it would apply its policies to limit foreign ownership in uranium mining. In May, Energy Minister Greene told the House that the policy would not be implemented by regulations issued by the government, as previously announced, but by legislation, which would shortly be submitted to Parliament. In September, he told the House that "the government is preparing legislation to be introduced to Parliament during the forthcoming session, but it will take some additional time for this legislation to be made ready."

It did, indeed, take some additional time. Ten years later, the legislation had not been introduced in Parliament. Nor had regulations been issued. Thus there never was anything in law to prevent Roman's sale to Hudson's Bay Oil, merely an announcement by the government that it intended to pass such a law, an intent that it never acted upon.

Reflecting upon the loss of his big uranium sale to France, the loss of his sale of shares to Hudson's Bay Oil, and the loss of his $100 million law suit against the Prime Minister and the Energy Minister, Stephen Roman later had every reason for wry satisfaction. Each loss had made him enormously richer. They forced Denison to hang on to more of its reserves of uranium; they forced Roman to hang on to his shares of Denison. Later, the price of uranium and the price of Denison shares both rose dramatically. The 100 million pounds of uranium that Denison wanted to sell to France in 1970 for $700 million were sold a decade later for about $4 billion. The shares that Roman had agreed to sell in 1970 for $104 million were, by 1980, worth more than $360 million. (Roman and the Roman Corporation also increased their holdings in Denison, and by late 1980, Roman's share of the interest was worth about $150 million.)

GULF'S LUCKY RABBIT

The search for new uranium reserves had been at a standstill for nearly a decade until the mid-1960's. Then, for a brief period, there seemed to be brighter prospects ahead for uranium demand, and once again the prospectors headed for the hills. This time it was not weekend prospectors who loaded Geiger counters in the back of pick-up trucks, but more seasoned veterans – mining syndicates and oil companies – that took up the search.

One of the first in the field was a group of seven Calgary-based penny oil companies, led by New Continental Oil Company, which pooled their resources in 1967 to conduct an airborne radiomagnetic survey of the Athabasca sandstone basin in northern Saskatchewan. The basin covers an egg-shaped area of some 40,000 square miles, stretching across the northern end of Saskatchewan, southeast of Lake Athabasca. Geolo-. gists reckoned that the Athabasca sandstone may have acted like a giant sponge, soaking up uranium from waters that swept across the basin more than a billion years ago. Uranium had already been found along the northwestern rim of this basin, at Beaverlodge Lake, and it seemed a good bet that there might be other ore deposits to find.

For its aerial survey, New Continental equipped a twin-engine Beechcraft Baron with a gamma ray spectrometer to measure and record radioactivity; an altimeter that provided a printed record of the flight elevations; and cameras that provided a continuous photographic record of the survey areas. Manned with a pilot, a navigator, and an equipment operator, the small aircraft flew 15,000 miles of flight surveys across the Athabasca basin that summer. At a field office in Uranium City, the results were plotted on maps by a geologist and a draftsman.

Based on the survey results, New Continental and its partners filed on claims covering nearly 2,000 square miles along the rim of the basin. Others were also entering the play – some were even there before New Continental – including Gulf Mineral Resources Corporation of Denver, a subsidiary of Gulf Oil Company of Pittsburgh; Denison Mines; the French-owned Mokta (later AMOK Ltd.), and others.

The following summer, New Continental made a deal with Gulf to explore its properties. The 900 square miles of permits held by Gulf Minerals were pooled with the much larger spread held by New Continental. Gulf would pay all the costs of exploration and placing a mine into production, when and if an ore body was found. The New Continental group would get a share of any net earnings that might result. Gulf put a twenty-man exploration crew into the field, using two helicopters, a small plane on floats, and three core drilling rigs, to follow up on the broad leads provided by the aerial survey.

On December 3, 1968, Saskatchewan Premier Ross Thatcher

and Gulf Minerals' exploration vice-president Dr. James Early held a press conference in Regina to announce one of the most exciting mineral discoveries in the province's history. A Gulf core hole near Rabbit Lake, drilled at an angle to a depth of 500 feet, had intersected nearly 200 feet of ore grade mineralization in the Athabasca sandstone, averaging approximately 0.6 per cent uranium, three times as rich as the ore at Elliot Lake. Further drilling would be required to determine the extent of the deposit and whether or not it would be large enough to warrant the cost of a mine and mill. Investors, however, figured that they already had a pretty good idea of what the answer would be. On the week of the announcement, the stock market added one billion dollars to the price of Gulf's outstanding shares.

Gulf's Rabbit Lake find led to one of the world's largest uranium plays, promising to eclipse even the ore reserves along the big Z at Ontario's Elliot Lake. By 1980, seven uranium deposits had been found in the Athabasca sandstone basin, estimated by the Saskatchewan Mining Development Corporation to contain some 250,000 tons of uranium, about 5 per cent of the free world total. The figure seems likely to increase, with Canadian, American, French, British, German, and Italian firms spending, in 1980, close to $100 million in the search for more uranium in the Athabasca sandstone basin. Individually, the uranium deposits in the Athabasca basin are much smaller than at Elliot Lake, but the costs are significantly less, with each ton of ore containing three or four times as much uranium, and the deposits lying close to the surface.

After further drilling had confirmed that Rabbit Lake, the first of the discoveries in the basin, contained some 45 million pounds of uranium, the problem confronting Gulf was whether or not it could find a buyer. As Denison was finding, there was more uranium in 1970 than there were buyers. A mine and mill would cost an estimated $50 million, and the Saskatchewan government had promised to help out by spending $15 million to construct a road into the remote mine site.

To find a buyer for the uranium, Gulf Minerals turned Uranerzbergbau G.m.b.H., a uranium producer affiliated with one of West Germany's largest power utilities, and known more simply as Uranerz. By early 1970, Gulf and Uranerz had negotiated a letter of intent for joint development of a $50 million mine and mill at Rabbit Lake, capable of producing 2,250 tons of uranium per year. As it was finally worked out, interest in the project was to be held 49 per cent by Uranerz Canada Limited, a newly formed subsidiary of the Bonn firm; 46 per cent by Gulf Minerals Canada Limited, another new subsidiary of Gulf Oil of Pittsburgh; and 5 per cent by Gulf Canada Limited, about two-thirds owned by the Pittsburgh firm. The key to the arrangement was the commitment by Uranerz to take not only its share of the Rabbit Lake production, but also, if called upon, to purchase Gulf's share at minimum stipulated prices. Gulf would be free to sell its share of the production elsewhere at higher prices if it could, but if not, it knew it could get at least a minimum price from Uranerz. Without such an arrangement Gulf could not see a market developing for several years which would have justified proceeding with the Rabbit Lake development, Gulf Mineral Resources lawyer Roger Allen later testified.

After the letter of intent had been signed, it still took a year of perilous negotiations – held in Toronto, Denver, San Diego, and Bonn – before a final agreement was reached and signed. One of the problems was the announcements by Prime Minister Trudeau and Energy Minister Greene of the government's intentions to limit foreign participation in new uranium mining ventures. The precise terms by which existing arrangements would be excluded from the proposed legislation, or "grandfathered," were announced by Joe Greene in September. Under this grandfather clause, the Gulf-Uranerz arrangement would be permitted, since a letter of intent had been signed prior to Trudeau's March 2 announcement in the House, provided that the deal was completed and signed before December 31.

Gulf and Uranerz continued to hammer out the terms of a final agreement, working against the December 31 deadline. A final meeting was called for Toronto on December 30 at which the agreements were to be signed. At the Toronto meeting, however, the Uranerz representatives became "very concerned" about the possibility that Ottawa might not permit the Rabbit Lake uranium to be exported, according to Roger Allen's later testimony in the suit in Chicago against the uranium producers. If Ottawa ever blocked the exports, Uranerz could wind up having to pay for all of the production from the mine, unable to either sell it or use it. Such a situation, Allen said, "could end up breaking the company." Finally, "after dinner on December 30 an arrangement was agreed upon" which provided for re-negotiation by Gulf and Uranerz in the event that exports were prohibited by Ottawa, and with provision for arbitration if the two parties failed to agree on terms. With this settled, the Gulf and Uranerz representatives signed the documents at 11:40 p.m. on December 30 – 20 minutes before the government deadline.

With the signing of the agreement in Toronto, Rabbit Lake was scheduled to come into production in 1975, the first new uranium mine in Canada in nearly two decades. Within a little more than a year, plans to develop Rabbit Lake were once more to be placed in jeopardy.

CHAPTER SIX

The Stage is Set

Signs of surplus uranium supplies at distress prices, with fears of worse to come, were to be found everywhere in 1971.

The U.S. Atomic Industrial Forum noted that the American industry "was plagued with over-capacity," while abroad "most mills were operating at less than capacity or are simply adding to inventory . . . new mills are being built in Canada, Niger and South Africa, despite the pedestrian progress of nuclear power plant sales." The Forum noted that the governments of Australia, Canada, France, South Africa, Great Britain, and the United States held 80,000 tons of uranium stockpiles, four times as much as the annual free world production.

Nuclear Industry magazine reported that some mines, in order to keep costs below selling prices, were high-grading – digging out only the best grades of ore and leaving the rest in the ground. "The majority of the reserves left behind will not be recovered at any price once the mines have been abandoned," *Nuclear Industry* stated.

In August, the Nuclear Exchange Corporation of Menlo Park, California (Nuexco) advised its customers that, "The uranium market in Europe is giving additional evidence of distress. There are some organizations in need of cash which are offering their stocks of material at deeply discounted prices." It reported that several hundred thousand tons of uranium oxide had been offered "for immediate delivery as low as $3.55 a pound."

An internal Westinghouse memo estimated that discovered reserves in Australia had increased in one year from 20,000 to

200,000 tons, and that the cost to produce this could be as low as $2 a pound.

"The world price of yellowcake is being held, rather weakly, at about $U.S.6 a pound," the Australian *Financial Review* reported in July. "Australia is in a position to knock the bottom out of this market by entering into contracts at considerably lower prices for big, long-term supplies," the newspaper stated. It claimed that the large Nabarlek deposit of Queensland Mines "could be quarried profitably at $3 a pound and could probably make money as low as $1 a pound." Such prices, it said, "would be ruinous to any mine known anywhere else in the non-Communist world." It added that this could "trigger the government stockpiles of Canada, France and South Africa on to the market." With a stockpile of up to 8,000 tons, "the French have already panicked," according to the report, offering uranium at $5 and reportedly considering prices as low as $3 a pound.

There were other assessments that the low prices could lead to later shortages, and a resulting price explosion.

Eldorado president William Gilchrist, in the Crown corporation's 1971 annual report, warned that "any utility or nation which bases an appreciable and expanding portion of its electrical power generation capacity on nuclear energy should make sure that it has firm sources of supply." Gilchrist claimed that "the prices prevalent today cannot possibly" result in the investments in new mines that he said would be needed to meet future demand.

Nuexco warned that "exploration, development and mine and mill planning is being sharply curtailed as a consequence of the present low uranium prices." It predicted that "demand by 1975 will exceed presently existing USA production capacity," adding that "the uranium industry in the middle of this decade will bear watching."

THE EMBARGO EXTENDED

The root of the problem facing the Canadian mines was the U.S. embargo that prohibited the use of foreign uranium in American nuclear power reactors. Ottawa maintained a steady drum-fire of diplomatic notes, discussions, and public statements, seeking removal of the embargo.

"The Canadian government has made repeated representations to the U.S. government with respect to the United States 'viability embargo' against imported uranium," Ottawa declared in an Aide Memoire delivered to the U.S. Department of State in 1970. "Despite numerous assurances since it was introduced that the embargo was temporary, no progress has been made toward its removal." The note pointed out that Canada's uranium industry "developed in response to U.S. requirements," was operating at one-third of current capacity, "by contrast with the United States uranium producing industry which is operating at close to full capacity . . . The Canadian government views this situation with growing concern and draws the attention of the U.S. government to the fact that this embargo conflicts with U.S. obligations and Canadian rights under the General Agreement on Tariffs and Trade . . . The Canadian government therefore requests as a matter of urgent concern that the U.S. government undertake to remove the embargo by a specified early date."

The American response to the Canadian demand was spelled out by the Atomic Energy Commission on October 13, 1971. Far from announcing an early date to remove the embargo, the AEC proposed to defer consideration of this matter until "the latter part of the present decade." In addition, the AEC outlined plans to dispose of its 50,000-ton stockpile, with safeguards intended to avoid disruptions to the uranium market within the United States but without any provisions to avoid disruptions to foreign markets.

"The Australian government is most concerned" about the latest AEC announcement, Canberra declared in a cable fired to Washington. It protested that the plan to dispose of the stockpile "contains no explicit provisions designed to avoid disruptions in markets outside of the United States" and that there had been no consultations with other governments whose interests would be affected. "The Australian government would welcome the early announcement of a definite date for the relaxation of the import embargo on foreign uranium to assist the normalization of world trade in this commodity."

Washington, however, paid no more attention to Canberra than it had to Ottawa.

The plan to dispose of the AEC's 50,000-ton stockpile was soon modified into a scheme which would force both U.S. and foreign nuclear power plants to buy from the government stockpile at prices which were estimated at double the existing market price.

The method was later described by U.S. Congressman Craig Hosmer, a member of the Joint Committee on Atomic Energy, as "jimmying the tails assay."

"The option to even consider this gimmick arises from the historical accident of AEC's considerable stockpile of uranium built up from policies in the 1950's to encourage uranium exploration," Hosmer explained at hearings before the Joint Committee. "Some very clever persons suggested," according to Hosmer, that the stockpile could be reduced by adjusting the amount of fissile uranium left in the tailings of the AEC's three huge diffusion plants at which natural uranium was enriched to fuel grade material for most of the free world's nuclear power plants.

The scheme was as complex as it was cute. It related to the composition of natural uranium, which comprises two isotopes. Uranium 238, which is non-fissile and useless for bombs or power plants in its natural state, constitutes 99.3 per cent of natural uranium.* Fissile uranium 235 comprises the remaining 0.7 per cent of natural uranium. Only a very few nuclear power plants, such as the Candu, are able to use natural uranium containing just 0.7 per cent U 235 as plant fuel. The others require a fuel in which the U 235 has been enriched to about 3 per cent. The less U 235 is left in the tailings of depleted natural uranium from the enrichment plant, the less natural uranium is required to produce a given amount of plant fuel. However, minimizing the amount of U 235 left in the tailings also increases the amount of electricity used in the enrichment process. Conversely, reducing the amount of extracted U 235 increases the amount of natural uranium required and reduces the amount of electricity used in the enrichment plants.

In essence, the AEC's plan was to extract from the uranium oxide processed for power utilities less of the U 235 than the customer paid for. This would require additional natural

*The fertile uranium, however, can be converted into fissile plutonium, the basis of breeder reactors, which create more fuel than they use. In 1982, the first commercial breeder reactor was nearing completion in France.

uranium to provide the stipulated volume of enriched fuel. The extra volume would come from the AEC's stockpile. In a paper delivered in 1977, a uranium specialist in Canada's department of energy, estimated that the AEC was, in effect, charging $10 to $12 a pound for this make-up uranium provided from its stockpile, at a time when uranium was selling in U.S. and foreign markets at $5 to $6 a pound. The AEC was able to do this because, outside of the Soviet Union, it had the only uranium enrichment plants then in operation.

AROUND THE WORLD WITH JOE GREENE

The fire-sale prices of non-American uranium, and the looming competition from low-cost Australian supplies, were very much on the mind of Canada's Energy Minister Joe Greene when he flew to Canberra, April 28, 1971, for a week of discussions with Australian, Japanese, and French government officials.

John James Greene – to everyone, the plain, amiable, Joe Greene – seemed, in fact, more concerned about the condition of the uranium market than the condition of his heart. Greene, a lanky fifty-one-year-old Toronto lawyer with a thatch of white hair, had suffered two previous heart attacks that threatened to end his political career. A former RCAF pilot who had earned a Distinguished Flying Cross during the Second World War, Greene had been a Member of Parliament for eight years, a cabinet member for six years, and Minister of Energy for three years. In 1968, he had run for leadership of the Liberal party, losing out to Pierre Trudeau. The scrappy lawyer had bounced back from the two heart attacks shortly after the Liberal leadership contest, and now seemed undaunted by the rigours of his mission to Australia.

Among those accompanying Greene on the Canadian government mission to Australia were Atomic Energy of Canada Limited president J. Lorne Gray, hungry for sales of the Crown corporation's Candu nuclear power reactor; Deputy Energy Minister Jack Austin, who was later to emerge as the key Canadian figure in the uranium cartel; Gordon MacNabb, Assistant Deputy Minister of Energy; and John Runnalls, who had recently joined the energy department from Atomic Energy

Canada as a special adviser on uranium matters. Runnalls later acted as secretary for the Canadian section of the cartel. His detailed notes and meeting minutes, brought to light in the subsequent U.S. investigations, provided perhaps the most detailed account of the cartel's operations.

Joe Greene's mission had more than just uranium marketing on its agenda. Australia was considering the construction of a nuclear power plant, and Canada wanted to get the contract to build it. There was also a contemplated billion-dollar plant to enrich natural uranium into fuel-grade material for use in nuclear power plants (although the Candu plants are one of the few that use natural uranium). Competing sites for the enrichment plant were Australia and Canada, and possible backers included Australia, Canada, Japan, and France. France not only wanted to participate in such a project, but wanted it built with French, rather than American, technology.

Reporting later in the House of Commons on the Australian talks, Joe Greene said that they "were the most comprehensive of their kind concerning natural resources ever conducted between the two countries." Greene's report to Parliament, however, was long on generalities and short on specifics. He noted that Canada and Australia had a common interest in uranium marketing during a period when "the market may be soft," and that it was in the interest of both countries "to get optimum prices for our raw resources." He also noted that a Candu reactor "could be made available to meet Australian needs." No mention was made of the fact that Japanese and French government officials were also involved in the talks.

New Democratic Party Leader David Lewis responded that Greene could "save himself the trouble if he would refrain from bringing this kind of meaningless nonsense before the House . . . if he has nothing to say it is much better not to say it."

David Lewis would have been more enlightened had he been able to read the confidential cable that the U.S. Embassy in Canberra forwarded to the State Department in Washington, summarizing the discussions on the basis of "informed sources." "Canadians reportedly desired establish consultative mechanism re sale of minerals (particularly uranium and nickel) to prevent excessive competition developing with respect sales, particularly to Japan," the cable reported. "Australian side allegedly refused co-operate but agreed continue discussions." As well, Canada appeared to be losing out on its hoped for sale of a nuclear power reactor for Australia's proposed Jervis Bay plant, and Atomic Energy Canada president Lorne Gray "reportedly had serious dispute" with Australian Atomic Energy Commission chairman Baxter, "charging AAEC had reneged on promise accept Candu." (In any event, the plant was never built.) As for the billion dollar enrichment plant, the Australian and Japanese were "not enthusiastic re joining with French and/or Canadians in establishing plant in Canada," preferring a site in Australia. Bertrand Goldschmidt apparently won agreement for "secret formal talks in Paris" concerning French participation in the contemplated enrichment plant.

There were continuing hints in the trade publications that Canada was not making much progress in its efforts to get some kind of pricing agreement for uranium sales.

Nucleonics Week quoted Greene as having invited Australian National Development Minister Reginald W. C. Swartz to make a reciprocal visit to Ottawa for more talks "as a warning to uranium buyers in the world that they can no longer pit Canada against Australia." Greene also reportedly made it clear that the private sector would be included in any mechanism to firm up uranium prices. "If we reach some specified accord regarding the price of uranium, certainly we will bring the private sector in, including corporations like Rio Tinto-Zinc which are so big globally in uranium," Greene is quoted as stating. "Otherwise, a few well co-ordinated buyers could bring prices down."

A month later, on June 10, *Nucleonics Week* reported that "Australian officials are skeptical that a uranium collaboration would serve their interests and point out that Canada has a 26.5 million-pound stockpile to get rid of." The uranium industry in Canada, however, was said to be "more interested in binational collaboration than its Australian counterparts . . . industry in both countries doubts that a joint uranium policy could be effective without the co-operation of other nations such as France, Britain, West Germany, the U.S., and even Czechoslovakia." On July 15, *Nucleonics Week* reported that "The Canadian-Australian talks on a joint uranium price and processing policy now are at a standstill, reportedly in recognition of the practical need to bring other uranium producing, as well as consuming nations, into such an agreement to be effective."

Within five months, Joe Greene was heading another travel group from Ottawa, this time on an around-the-world tour. First stop was Tokyo, to be followed by Singapore (where Greene was to confer with National Development Minister Swartz and other Australian officials), Iran (to talk about oil matters with the Shah), London, Paris, and Bonn. Greene and his officials were anxious to talk with the Japanese about the continuing problem of trying to sell a Candu reactor, about the fading hopes to build a uranium enrichment plant in Canada, but mostly about the price of uranium. Canada was very worried that the Japanese would want to re-negotiate the price of $9 a pound that they were paying under the contract to buy uranium from Denison Mines. The price was well above prices then being offered. The risk was that Canada might either lose the sales that were keeping the Denison mine in operation, or get caught in a disastrous price war.

Joe Greene did not make it around the world on this trip. In Tokyo, he suffered a third heart attack, and this time the fighting lawyer was unable to fight back to a full recovery.

Greene and his officials had spent Monday, September 27, 1971, in negotiations with Japanese and industrial and government officials; had signed an agreement covering an exchange of research information on the production of heavy water (which allows the Candu reactor to use natural uranium); and had managed to persuade the Japanese not to renegotiate their uranium purchase contracts with Denison. On Tuesday, Greene had visited a Japanese nuclear power plant, and on Wednesday was scheduled to visit a large steel mill. That morning, his wife found him unconscious in the bathroom, where he had just showered. He was rushed by ambulance to a hospital, his left side partially paralyzed by the stroke. Greene resigned from the energy portfolio in January, and was later appointed to the Senate, not long before he died.

JACOB AUSTIN AT THE HELM

After Greene's heart stroke, the balance of the Canadian around-the-world mission was led by the next ranking official in the party, Deputy Minister Jack Austin.

Jacob Austin, Q.C., Calgary born, Harvard and Berkeley educated, was thirty-nine when he had joined the Energy Department as Deputy Minister in 1970, at the invitation of Prime Minister Trudeau. Equipped with a brilliant mind and an engaging personality, Austin brought a wide range of experience to his new job; former law professor at the University of British Columbia; an active law practice in Vancouver; a one-time candidate for Parliament; and a business executive involved in a number of mining and forestry companies. He also carried some handicaps: he had lost his only bid for election to Parliament; the mining ventures he had promoted turned into spectacular failures; and he was to face a $70,000 tax fight with the Department of National Revenue. For nearly four years, Jack Austin was the central Canadian figure in the uranium cartel, but in 1975 he was the centre of a controversy in the House of Commons over his tax problems.

Although details of the Austin tour have not been made public, it seems certain that plans for the formation of the cartel took shape during these discussions. After meeting with Australia's Development Minister Swartz in Singapore, Austin's party flew next to Tehran, and then to London. Included in the discussions at London with the British government were representatives of Rio Tinto-Zinc. In Paris, Austin met with Pierre Taranger, head of the French atomic energy commission, the CEA; Bertrand Goldschmidt, and Michel Houdaille, head of France's uranium marketing organization, Uranex. Taranger, according to informed sources, told Austin that the uranium industry was hemorrhaging. Prices had been driven down in the previous six months by 20 per cent, and Taranger predicted that they would fall another 20 per cent in the next six months. With a large government stockpile, and low-cost supplies coming into production from Gabon and Niger, he warned that France was prepared to meet any price competition. "Parts of the industry will bleed to death for sure," Taranger declared. There was, he suggested, only one solution: an agreement among uranium consuming and producing nations that would set a floor price to keep the industry alive.

From Paris, Austin and party travelled to Bonn, where the proposal for a floor price was put to officials of the West German government. The German government was sympathetic, but it was not prepared to do anything. It preferred to leave negotiations for uranium purchases entirely in the hands of the power utilities, without any government intervention. West Germany represented the largest European market for uranium. It was, reportedly, the lack of any support from Bonn that convinced Austin that the uranium producing countries would have to act without the support of the consuming countries to avert the threat of what Austin perceived could be "an unmitigated disaster."

While Austin sought to prop up uranium prices, he was unaware of another force that was helping to drive prices down. That force was the Westinghouse Electric Corporation, the world's largest commercial buyer and seller of uranium. The problem was that Westinghouse was contracting to sell uranium that it had not contracted to buy. In effect, it was dumping on the market billions of dollars worth of phantom supplies.

In considering measures that might help prop up the price of uranium, Austin could not help but be concerned about the Gulf-Uranerz mine at Rabbit Lake, scheduled to come on production in 1975. Any effective measures would almost certainly involve some allocation of the limited available market among the Canadian mines. Rabbit Lake had apparently already carved out a significant portion of that market. If the planned output at Rabbit Lake were to be cut back in any arrangement to allocate the market, the whole $50 million project could wind up being shelved. That would certainly incur the wrath of the government of Saskatchewan. But one way or another, Gulf would have to be involved in any plan that emerged.

Nicholas M. Ediger, a forty-two-year-old geologist from Manitoba who had worked for Gulf for twenty years in western Canada, was vice-president and general manager of Gulf Minerals Canada Limited, based in Toronto. On December 8, 1971, Nick Ediger travelled to Ottawa to keep an appointment for an invited meeting at the monolithic offices of the federal Department of Energy, Mines and Resources on Booth Street, with Jack Austin and Assistant Deputy Minister Gordon Mac-Nabb. Ediger summarized the meeting in a file memo, later produced in the uranium litigation in the United States. He wrote:

> Canada is holding discussions with both the producer and consumer nations with respect to agreeing on a world floor price for U_3O_8. Canada and Australia agree that the floor price should cover operating costs plus capital recovery at a reasonable rate of interest, together with an additional amount which would provide an incentive for high-risk exploration. It is Canada's view that $6 per pound U_3O_8 is the least amount that will accomplish this. Additional talks between the producer nations will be held in 1972.

There was no mention of additional talks with the consumer nations.

On January 27, Austin called a meeting with representatives of Canadian uranium producers to discuss the upcoming talks. Gulf declined the invitation to attend.

On the morning of Monday, January 31, 1972, Henry Armstrong at the Canadian Embassy in Washington placed a phone call to A. S. Friedman, acting director, division of international programs, in the U.S. Department of State. On the phone, Armstrong read the text of a telegram he had just received from Ottawa. The telegram read:

> Please advise appropriate authorities of Canada's initiative in calling a meeting in Paris on February 2 of government officials from Australia, France, South Africa and Canada to explore all facets of present uranium market problems.
>
> Stress that the meeting was called because of our concern with the continuing chaotic price situation which could reduce exploration to a point endangering the adequacy of supplies in latter part of this decade. Also advise that the meeting was called to complement one of major producers only, called unilaterally by Uranex of France for

February 3 and 4. Further details will be provided on return of Canadian representatives.

Ottawa had called the meeting of government officials; Uranex had called the meeting of corporate representatives. In some cases, the corporate representatives were government officials.

The cartel was about to be launched.

CHAPTER SEVEN

Members
of The Club

When members of the uranium cartel spoke of themselves as "the club," they may have been subconsciously reflecting the real precursor of the cartel.

The "club" may have existed long before the cartel was organized in Paris, February, 1972. The members of the club were from Paris, London, and Johannesburg. They had interests in nearly all of the non-American uranium mines then operating throughout the free world. They were connected by a complex web of interlocking corporate shareholdings and directorships. They maintained close commercial liaisons with their governments.

In Paris, the club was represented by the corporate interests of the government of France, and the Rothschild family, headed by Baron Guy de Rothschild, with the latter's interest focused in a holding company called Société Imetal. In London, there was the Rio Tinto-Zinc Corporation Limited, inevitably referred to as "the giant British mining house that controls enterprises around the world." In Johannesburg there was Harry Oppenheimer, who in fact does control the largest mining enterprise in the world, the Anglo-American Corporation of South Africa.

If members of the club had common concerns involving the marketing of uranium, they would have had little difficulty in discussing such problems among themselves. Nor would they have experienced much problem in discussing these matters with their governments.

There were unconfirmed reports that the cartel was organized at the instigation of this club. Certainly, the new uranium deposits being developed in Saskatchewan and Australia would diminish the alleged domination of the non-American market by the club, unless an expanded structure were organized. One published report speculated that the cartel had been organized as the result of a suggestion by Rio Tinto-Zinc to the government of France. Another published report claimed that it was organized as a result of a suggestion by Rio Tinto-Zinc to the government of Canada. (Joe Greene did nothing to allay this suspicion with his comment, quoted in *Nucleonics Week*, that RTZ would be included in any plan to help prop up prices.)

Even after the cartel was a going concern, there were hints that it was dominated by the club. In a letter to Jack Austin in 1973, Nick Ediger of Gulf Minerals Canada complained of "the continued domination of the 'Inner Club' . . . and the 'Star Chamber' atmosphere" at a meeting of the cartel's operating committee. He identified the "inner club" as Uranex, RTZ, and the Nuclear Fuels Corporation (Nufcor), sales agent for the South African producers, principally Anglo-American.

There was a mystique about the club that made it seem larger than life. It sprang from the very mention of legendary names like Rothschild and Oppenheimer, and from the tangle of interwoven shareholdings and directorships. Interlocking directorships among firms that are supposed to compete in the same field have been forbidden in the United States, ever since the trust busters broke up John D. Rockefeller's Standard Oil Trust in 1911. Such interlocking holdings conjure up an image of men conspiring to become – in Samuel Johnson's phrase – "rich beyond the dreams of avarice."

All of the strings of power held by the club, by RTZ, by Anglo-American, and by Imetal, were said to lead ultimately into the hands of Baron Guy de Rothschild in Paris.

"[T]he Rothschilds of France and England have an interest in nearly every major uranium mine in the world," *Forbes* magazine reported in January, 1975. "[B]ut for a few independent uranium companies in Canada and possible increased Australian production, the function of the Uranium Producers' Forum [another name applied to the cartel] could be performed at a board meeting of Imetal."

Canadian Business magazine, in 1977, asserted that RTZ is "controlled by the Rothschild clan" and described the Rothschilds of France as "the uncontested first family, the crown princes of the uranium industry. There is not a uranium producing nation in the free world which is not home to at least one of the local branches of RTZ, Imetal and Anglo-American." According to the *Canadian Business* article "no one has yet been able to calculate how many billions" of dollars Baron Guy de Rothschild made as a result of the uranium cartel.

Sadly, for the sake of drama, the reality of the club was less sensational than the myth, particularly the myth of the Rothschild control.

If the club was so powerful, why was the price of uranium so low?

Through the interlocking directorships, the club members may well have discussed uranium marketing matters in a manner that, in the United States, is illegal and considered anti-competitive. Beyond doubt they had good access to their governments. But American uranium miners hardly suffered from any lack of protection from the U.S. government, a form of protection later described by a U.S. Justice Department official as "massively anti-competitive."

Finally, the assertion that Baron Guy de Rothschild of Paris was the principal beneficiary of the 1974-77 rise in world uranium prices, missed the mark by hundreds of millions of pounds of uranium. The man who benefited most from the price rise was not a baron at all, but a former Slovakian peasant in Toronto. In terms of any individual stakes in uranium, that of Stephen Roman's in Toronto was far greater than that of the Rothschild clan in Paris.

A study by Getty Oil Company, produced in 1977 at the Congressional committee hearings headed by Representative John Moss, suggests that the amount of uranium controlled by RTZ, Imetal, and Anglo-American at the time of the formation of the cartel in 1972, amounted to about one-quarter of the free world total, excluding the United States. The RTZ group of companies, with uranium ore bodies in Africa, Australia, and Canada, held about 17 per cent of the non-American free world total; French-controlled companies, with ore bodies in France, Gabon, Niger, and Canada, about 15 per cent, of which Imetal's share was certainly no more than 3 per cent; and Anglo-American, with possibly 5 per cent. By contrast,

Roman's Denison Mines held 13 per cent of the then-known uranium reserves outside of the United States and the Soviet bloc – four or five times the amount controlled by the Rothschilds' Imetal.

THE HOUSE OF ROTHSCHILD

It has been said by *Forbes* magazine of the Rothschilds that, in the twentieth century, "they made a great fortune into a small one."

Founded in the late 1700's in the teeming Jewish ghetto of Frankfurt, Germany, by Mayer Amschel Rothschild, the House of Rothschild spread to Paris, Geneva, Naples, and London where it became the wealthiest and most financially powerful dynasty that Europe has ever seen. The Rothschilds built railways, controlled factories and mines, loaned the British government the money to buy the Suez canal, and financed kings and empires.

Rothschilds still grace the boards of many great corporations, but they control few of them. Wars, depressions, and a host of other troubles have shrunk the House of Rothschilds to a pale shadow of its former power and prestige.

The commercial interests of the family cousins in France were, until he handed over the reins to his son David in 1979, headed by Baron Guy, and centred in their principal holding company, Compagnie Du Nord (later folded into Banque Rothschild). At a time when Baron Guy de Rothschild was said to be making untold billions of dollars from uranium, the price of Compagnie Du Nord shares on the Paris bourse was sliding steadily downhill, from 68 francs in 1969 to 23 francs in 1976, when uranium prices were at their peak. In 1976, Compagnie du Nord, described as the "flagship of the French branch of the house of Rothschild," turned in a meagre profit of $5 million; in 1977 it posted a stunning loss of $6.3 million.

One of the large enterprises that the French Rothschilds purchased control of nearly a century ago was the Rio Tinto Company, later to become the Rio Tinto-Zinc Corporation. By the mid-1970's, Compagnie du Nord's interest in RTZ had shrunk to one-half of one per cent.

Still, the Rothschilds of France are not without assets and influence. Until he was succeeded by son David, Baron Guy sat as chairman of Banque Rothschild, chairman of Compagnie du Nord, and chairman of Compagnie du Nord's largest asset, a 20 per cent interest in Société Imetal. Other large shareholders of Imetal include Harry Oppenheimer's Anglo-American Corporation, with 5 per cent; American Metal Climax with 11 per cent, and Compagnie Financière du Suez, with 6 per cent. Imetal, with a large group of mining and metal interests, ranked 176th in *Fortune* magazine's 1980 list of the largest corporations outside of the United States, and its 1979 earnings of $56 million were almost identical to those of Stephen Roman's Denison Mines. (Roman's stake in Denison, however, is much greater than the Rothschild interest in Imetal.)

The directorships that linked the Paris, London, and Johannesburg mining houses at the time of the cartel were complex. Imetal's board of directors included Harry Oppenheimer, head of Anglo-American Corporation of South Africa, and the late Sir Val Duncan, chairman of RTZ until his death in 1976. Baron Guy, in turn sat on RTZ's board, as did S. Spiro, chairman of Anglo-American's British affiliate, Charter Consolidated. RTZ director J. L. Dherse sits on the board of Compagnie Financière du Suez, one of the largest shareholders of Imetal. In 1981, the influence of the French Rothschilds diminished further when the government of France took over ownership of Banque Rothschild, and most other French banks.

THE MINE AT RIO TINTO

Stretching eighty miles across Andalusia in the southwest corner of Spain lies the Iberian pyrite field, one of the great mineralized belts of the world. Richest of all the mines along the Iberian field is the Rio Tinto. Its output of copper, gold, and silver has helped finance empires for thousands of years, from the time of the early Phoenicians, to the Roman empire, and finally the present-day commercial empire of the Rio Tinto-Zinc Corporation of London.

No one knows when men first started to dig the ores of Rio Tinto, but there is a legend that the first tunnels into the hill called Cerro Salomon were the lost mines of King Solomon. Certainly they were the lost mines of the Roman empire that had laid abandoned for a thousand years before they were re-discovered in the late 1500's by search parties sent out by King Philip II of Spain. It had been hoped that the Rio Tinto might help rescue the monarchy from financial collapse, but sporadic efforts to make them productive mines during the following 300 years proved more often a burden than an asset to the royal treasury.

The year 1873 found Spain in the chaos of civil war, the army away fighting a rebellion in Cuba, the monarchy toppled, armed mobs controlling much of the country, and the president of the new republic in charge of a bankrupt government. A number of metal-bound wooden chests, shipped from London, were smuggled through France and across the Pyrenees by rail and cart to Madrid. They contained more than $422,000 in gold pieces, the downpayment for the sale of the money-losing royal mines at Rio Tinto, arranged by the new republican government to a syndicate of London bankers for a total price of $3.5 million.

Most of the big mining companies of the time thought that Rio Tinto would never make a profit. However, Hugh Matheson, a London-based Scottish banker, persuaded a group of financiers otherwise. Matheson's plans were to strip out the ore at Rio Tinto at an unprecedented rate by means of open pit mining, and build a railway to the coast to slash transportation costs. To carry out the plan, Matheson and his partners organized the Rio Tinto Company in 1873, which acquired the property from the syndicate and issued public shares that soon became the darling of European investors. Rio Tinto, soon mining ore at the rate of 700,000 tons a year, had become the largest single employer in Spain. (Rio Tinto staff from England introduced soccer in Spain.)

The English company had been operating for little more than a decade before the Rothschild family of France became involved, through a breathtaking but ultimately disastrous plan, which sought to gain a monopoly on the world supply of copper.

The price of copper, like the price of so many other commodities, was subject to wild fluctuations. In the first 13 years after the Rio Tinto company was formed, the price bounced around in a range between $38 and $108 per ton. Hyacinthe

Secretan, whose French company was one of the largest copper buyers and manufacturers of brass and copper products, set out to stabilize the market by cornering the world supply of copper, with financial backing from the Paris Rothschilds and other French banks.

The plan was simple. Secretan would contract to buy copper from the big mining companies at fairly high and guaranteed prices, and the mines in turn would agree to limit production. To put the plan into effect, Secretan entered into secret contracts, first with Rio Tinto, then with other copper producers in 36 separate countries, giving him control of 80 per cent of the world production. Any excess copper on the market was bought by Secretan, and held in a stockpile. At first the plan worked, and copper prices soared. With the profits, the French syndicate, led by the Paris Rothschilds, was able to purchase control of a number of mining companies, including Rio Tinto.

But the cartel soon faced the problem that threatens every monopoly: high prices attract and bring on new supplies and competition. By 1888, world copper production exceeded sales by one-third, and Secretan was nearly $7 million in debt in a futile effort to buy the copper that was flooding the market. Unable to keep the copper prices up, and unable to meet his purchase contracts with the mines, Secretan went broke; one of the directors of his company committed suicide.

Secretan had not learned the lesson that the Oppenheimers later applied so successfully with diamonds. A cartel can only continue to function if it succeeds not just in keeping prices from falling too low, but also from rising too high. Presumably Secretan had never heard about what members of the uranium cartel called "orderly marketing."

In the authorized history of RTZ, *Not On Queen Victoria's Birthday*, author David Avery writes that it was during this time that the French Rothschild family, "acting as always in great secret, was able to become the dominant shareholder" of Rio Tinto. Avery adds that the Rothschild's "dislike of putting too much down on paper makes it difficult to gauge the extent to which the Rothschilds influenced Rio Tinto policy."

Through years of profits and lean years of losses, through depression and boom times, through war and peace, the great mine at Rio Tinto kept yielding its copper, providing the

London-based house with funds to invest in other enterprises, in South Africa, Rhodesia, and the United States (where its first investments were not successful).

It was not a dynamic Rio Tinto Company that emerged from the Second World War. Its head office in London had been run by a war-time staff of six people. The big mine in Spain had barely been kept going through a civil war and a world war with antiquated machinery and was losing money. A large modernization program to make the mine viable would have meant unemployment for many of the 11,000 miners, which the Spanish government was not prepared to allow. (Later, under Spanish ownership, the mine force was reduced to 5,000, while production was substantially increased.) There was a bitter division among the board of directors about whether Rio Tinto should continue as an active mining enterprise, or simply an investment holding company which would collect dividends from dwindling assets.

A new board of directors, including such bluebloods as former Secretary of Foreign Affairs Anthony Eden, opted for an aggressive role for the company. A power-house team was assembled to breathe new life in the venerable institution. Mark Turner, a London banker then serving in the postwar administration of the British sector of Berlin, agreed to serve as managing director for a brief but vital three years. Val Duncan, a war-time colonel who had served on the planning staffs of Generals Eisenhower, Montgomery, and Alexander, was hired, succeeding Turner as managing director. Later, he became chairman. Mining engineer Roy Wright was hired as overseas manager, and RTZ geologists were soon scouring the world for minerals and investment opportunities. (According to author David Avery, when Wright was offered the job, he responded that "as far as he knew, Rio Tinto had no overseas business to manage. 'That's quite true,' came the reply. 'But we soon will have.' ") Turner and Duncan were both later knighted.

Rio Tinto's first big postwar venture was arranged with Rothschild help. Newfoundland was still a British colony when Prime Minister Joey Smallwood came to London after the war in search of investment capital. He found it through N. M. Rothschild & Sons, the English bank in the family, and the result was the British Newfoundland Corporation. Organized in 1953 by a group led by Rio Tinto – and including Anglo-American – Brinco was given exclusive mineral, water power, and forestry concessions in Newfoundland and Labrador. The group completed the billion-dollar Churchill Falls hydroelectric project in Labrador in 1973, which was purchased the following year by the Newfoundland government.

In 1954, Rio Tinto sold the bulk of its interest in the big Spanish mine for nearly $8 million, providing a fresh injection of capital. (In 1978, RTZ increased its interest in Rio Tinto Minera, still operating the ancient mine, from 5 to 25 per cent). The same year that the Spanish mine was sold, Roy Wright arranged the purchase of Joe Hirshhorn's uranium and other mining properties in Canada. In 1962, the Rio Tinto Company was merged with the Consolidated Zinc Corporation to form the present-day RTZ.

There is no plaque or sign on the outside of the plain, rather drab six-storey bulding on quiet St. James Square in southwest London that identifies it as the headquarters of the Rio Tinto-Zinc Corporation, possibly the second-largest mining concern in the world. There is a dignified and unrushed calm inside the building, matching the prim little park that it faces. Like Anglo-American, RTZ is not an operating mining company, but a "mining house," providing varying degrees of financial, managerial, technical, exploration, and marketing services to the scores of firms around the world which comprise the RTZ "group," and in which the parent firm holds varying ownership interests. The group includes such giants as Conzinc Riotinto of Australia, that country's largest mining concern, with interests in copper, coal, iron ore, aluminium, uranium; Rio Algom Limited and Brinco Limited in Canada; U.S. Borax & Chemical Corporation, makers of the familar twenty-mule team borax products, in the United States; Palabora Mining Company, with a huge copper mine in South Africa; Rossing Uranium Limited, with a large, low-grade uranium mine in Namibia; and scores of others. Ownership of RTZ is broadly held, mostly by English investors. The company has said that "no shareholder or group of affiliated shareholders holds a controlling interest" in it. With assets of more than $7 billion, the RTZ group reported earnings of two-thirds of a billion dollars in 1979, of which the parent company's share was nearly half.

When Val Duncan died in 1976, Mark Turner returned to the company, again serving as chairman until his death in 1980. It is very much a cosmopolitan twenty-two member board that runs the affairs of Rio Tinto-Zinc, with directors from Canada, Australia, South Africa, and the United States, as well as Great Britain. It is also very establishment, with half a dozen lords and knights on the board. It has had close ties with Britain's Conservative Party. While Anthony Eden in 1946 left his position as Britain's Secretary of Foreign Affairs to become a member of the board, in 1979 Lord Peter Carrington left his position as RTZ's executive in charge of governmental relations to join Margaret Thatcher's cabinet as Foreign Secretary. It is not the sort of group that would have much enjoyed the experience of having been hauled in front of an American judge at the U.S. Embassy in London and forced to plead the fifth amendment under U.S. law. Not really cricket.

HARRY O AND THE DIAMOND CARTEL

While the Rothschild dynasty has declined, Harry Oppenheimer's Anglo-American empire has continued to thrive, based on gold, diamonds, and the longest running cartel in history.

The stable of some 260 companies controlled by Harry O – as he is sometimes called – provides 30 per cent of the entire world production of gold; markets 80 per cent of all the diamonds produced, including gems from the Soviet Union; is the largest producer of platinum; a leading producer of copper, coal, uranium, vanadium, and mining explosives; includes one of the world's largest commodity trading firms; industrial subsidiaries that produce steel, machinery, food, chemicals, and assemble automobiles; and an investment portfolio in some 90 companies ranging from banks to breweries. Assets of the major companies controlled by Oppenheimer were estimated at more than $15 billion in 1980, with earnings in excess of $1 billion. So large is the group, that it accounts for one-third of all of South Africa's exports, and 10 per cent of the nation's gross national product.

The base for this commercial empire was built at the turn of the century by Ernest Oppenheimer, the fourth of ten children of a middle class Jewish cigar merchant in Friedberg, Germany. Sir Ernest began his career in London, 1899, as a clerk for a diamond merchant, and by the time he was twenty-two he was in Kimberley in charge of the firm's buying office. He got into gold mining in 1917, when he formed Anglo-American with the help of a U.S. mining engineer, Herbert Hoover, later President of the United States. Ernest Oppenheimer moved into the big time in the 1920's when he won the mining rights to the confiscated Germany colony of Southwest Africa, now Namibia, where diamonds are still sifted out of beach sands. In 1929 he purchased De Beers Consolidated Mines from empire-builder Cecil Rhodes, just in time to see the stock market crash and the Depression of the 1930's drop the price out from under the bottom of diamonds.

When the price fell, Oppenheimer invested all the capital he could find in buying more diamonds, keeping them in inventory until prices began to rise, then slowly releasing them onto the market. This classic approach – buy low, sell high – has been religiously followed by De Beers ever since.

The secret of Oppenheimer's successful diamond monopoly lies not only in propping up prices in times of slack demand, but equally important, keeping prices down in times of surging demand. Large price rises could bring on new supplies, bust the trust, and ultimately lead to a price collapse. By restraining both rises and falls in the prices for diamonds, De Beers has attained the ultimate in "orderly marketing."

Harry O assumed command of this empire after his father's death in 1957, when he was forty-six. Despite a few notable mining and investment failures, his empire has continued to expand steadily, greatly helped by the rapid surge in gold prices in 1979.

At the pinnacle is the private family holding company, E. Oppenheimer and Son, which manages to control this empire with an 8.2 per cent interest in Anglo-American. Anglo-American does not directly own or operate a single mine. It provides financing and management services for other companies, which it effectively controls, and receives its revenues in the form of managerial, financial, and technical fees, dividends, and commissions on sales.

From Anglo-American, the chain of control that stretches

through some 260 companies in South Africa, Europe, and North America, becomes incredibly tangled. Anglo-American owns 30 per cent of De Beers, and De Beers owns 41 per cent of Anglo-American. The principal interest in England is a 36 per cent holding in Charter Consolidated, which in turn holds interests in a wide range of other companies, including a 4 per cent interest in Rio Tinto-Zinc. In 1980, Anglo-American extended its domination of the gold mining industry by purchasing controlling interest in London's Consolidated Gold Fields for $340 million. Consolidated's South African mining interests provide 12 per cent of the world's gold production, and the acquisition boosted Oppenheimer's direct or indirect control to more than 31 per cent of the world total.

In North America, the Oppenheimer interests are centred in the Bermuda-based Minerals and Resources Corporation, which includes on its board of directors such notable bankers as Walter B. Wriston, chairman of Citicorp, and Cedric E. Ritchie, chairman of the Bank of Nova Scotia. Minorco, as it is called, is owned 32 per cent by Anglo-American, 16 per cent by De Beers, and 15 per cent by Charter Consolidated, with the other 37 per cent of the shares publicly held. Among Minorco's subsidiaries are Hudson's Bay Mining and Smelting in Canada, and Engelhard Minerals and Chemicals in the United States.

Engelhard, through its Phillips Brothers division, emerged in the late 1970's as one of the world's largest commodity brokers, marketing more than 150 different types of basic industrial commodities; steel, oil, copper, grain, gold, fertilizers, cement, sugar, and others. Oil has been the premier item, largely responsible for boosting Engelhard's sales from an annual rate of $1.4 billion in 1968 to $18 billion by 1979.

While Oppenheimer's business thrives, the biggest threat is from a deadly cross-fire of political and racial tensions and the ever-present risk of revolution by South Africa's 17 million blacks to overthrow the hated policies of apartheid imposed by the country's 4 million white Afrikaaners. Anglo-American's empire was built with the help of cheap wages paid for black labour. Yet Harry Oppenheimer has consistently been among the staunchest opponents in South Africa to that country's apartheid policies.

CHAPTER EIGHT

The Cartel is Born

If the Rothschild, Oppenheimer, and Rio Tinto-Zinc interests did, in fact, operate in the fashion of a club, in an effort to exert control over world uranium supplies and prices, it must have been a stormy club.

At least it was stormy enough when they got together with other producers to officially organize a cartel, with more than a little help from their governments.

"None of us really wanted to be at those meetings," according to an insider who later confided to the author. "But no one could risk not being there. If you weren't there when the pie was being sliced, you would worry about whether it was your pie that they were carving. And if you were there, you worried about the trouble you might be getting into."

The minutes and reports of the semi-secret cartel meetings in Paris, London, Johannesburg, Nice, Toronto, Sydney, Geneva, and Las Palmas, suggest that trust at these meetings was in far shorter supply than uranium. They were there to pursue arrangements felt to be in their common interest. Common interest may be a noble concept, but self-interest is the driving force of business competition, and the competitive instinct dies hard.

Nevertheless, it was the idea of curbing competition that brought corporate and government officials to Paris for a series of meetings on February 1 to 4, 1972.

There were two sets of meetings at Paris, at which plans for the formation of the cartel were discussed. There was one set of meetings held by government officials, and another set of meetings held by company officials. In some cases, the companies were government-owned. That allowed some people to attend both sets of meetings.

Not all of those who later became members of the cartel were represented at these initial meetings in Paris.

Canada, France, and Australia were represented at the meetings of government officials, but South Africa was not. The industry meetings included companies from Canada, France, and South Africa, but not Australia. Rio Tinto-Zinc did not participate directly at this first gathering, but was represented by its Canadian subsidiary, Rio Algom.

The Canadian delegation at the government meetings was headed by Assistant Deputy Energy Minister Gordon Mac-Nabb, and Eldorado president Bill Gilchrist, with further representation from the Canadian Embassy in Paris and the Department of Industry, Trade and Commerce. The French delegation was led by Pierre Taranger and Bertrand Goldschmidt. From Australia, there were M. C. Timbs of the Australian Atomic Energy Commission, D. J. Gates of the Department of National Development, and a representative from the Australian Embassy in Paris.

Six companies were represented at the series of separate meetings called by France's Uranex, four of them from Canada. The Canadian firms included Uranium Canada Limited, the Crown firm that handled the Canadian government's $100 million uranium stockpile; Eldorado Nuclear Ltd., the government-owned uranium producer; Denison Mines; and Rio Algom. The other two companies at the Paris meetings were Uranex, and South Africa's Nufcor. Gordon MacNabb and Bill Gilchrist sat in on the meetings of government officials, as well as the meetings of company officials. (Gulf Minerals people were later to complain that it was sometimes difficult to tell whether the people from Ottawa were speaking for the government of Canada, or for the commercial interest of the two government-owned companies.) There is no record to indicate that Jack Austin was present at these initial meetings in Paris, although he was an active participant at subsequent meetings.

Disagreement apparently started even before the first meeting was held. It involved the question of who should be included in the discussions. Pierre Taranger of the French CEA wanted the conclave limited to existing uranium producers. He had wanted the new producers – the Australians and the Gulf-Uranerz partnership in Canada – brought in at a later stage, after the cartel had been established. Jack Austin had argued that the Australians should be brought in at the start. It is not clear why South Africa was not represented at the first meeting of government officials, unless it was because of the harsh criticism that Taranger planned to level at the uranium sales policies of that country.

A confidential eight-page report on the discussions held by the government representatives, indicated that the delegates had little difficulty in outlining the nature of the problems that confronted them.

The first problem was the price for non-U.S. uranium. Four dollars and fifty cents a pound was not enough to keep a lot of the existing mines in business. "The French believe that Nufcor is primarily responsible for the current situation as it has been desperately in need of a cash flow and therefore had consistently under-cut other producers," the report states. "The French believe that the South Africans now realize that past policies had been seriously in error and to the detriment of South Africa."

The French also suggested that within the next three years, the price of uranium should be increased to $6.25 per pound. To achieve this, "utilities and other consumers must be made to realise that assurance of supply of uranium after 1980 is heavily dependent on securing now, prices which will encourage exploration for uranium and development of deposits."

Another problem was the extension of the U.S. import embargo, announced by the U.S. Atomic Energy Commission ten weeks before the Paris meetings. "When the United States needs to import supplies to cover the short fall in the domestic market, it could be expected that the U.S.A. would allocate import quotas to cover the short fall only," according to the report. "At present it is realistic to regard the United States market as being closed to non-U.S. producers for many years, whilst other world markets would be open to U.S. producers and possibly exploited if the world price for uranium rose to more remunerative levels." The American policies thus faced the world producers with two problems: exclusion from the U.S. market, and possible competition from U.S. supplies.

The biggest problem, however, was that in the short term there was lots of uranium, and little demand. In addition to production already covered by sales contracts, it was estimated that there would be a further 100,000 tons of non-U.S. uranium available for sale during the six-year period to 1977, and a demand for perhaps only 26,000 tons of this.

If that were not bad enough, the new Australian producers were eager to come on with a supply that could capture all of this uncommitted market, at prices that no other uranium producers could match.

The answer to this problem was devised by the meeting of the company convened by Uranex. "This first meeting was to be used to prepare the climate for future meetings which might lead to the orderly regulation of the uranium market . . . It was envisioned that the Club would agree upon a price for uranium from time to time . . . the Club could meet as frequently as proposals for contracts came forward and it would examine all aspects of the uranium market and seek to ensure that each producer obtained a fair share of the market." The classic formula for a cartel: restrict production in return for higher prices.

The French suggested that a "fair share" of the anticipated 26,000-ton demand for the aspiring new producers in Australia would be in the order of 1,200 tons. "The broad objective is for the producers themselves to try and obtain an agreement," the document concluded. "However, it was recognized that producers cannot come to an acceptable agreement without collaboration of the respective governments."

Results of the Paris meeting were reviewed with the Australian companies by government officials at meetings held in Canberra on February 28, and at Sydney on March 2. L. F. Bott, Secretary of the Department of National Development, told the miners that the Australian government "would like to see a logical and profitable development of Australian resources," according to notes summarizing these meetings. "The government would do what it could to assist in this objective but believed that the industry itself must supply the initiative and take a major role. He suggested that the various uranium companies should join together and set up a representative committee with a spokesman to liaise with the Commonwealth Government [the government of Australia] and with world producers at future meetings proposed in Paris."

If that sounded as though the government were trying to push the companies into assuming the responsibilities of participating in a cartel, it did not seem to bother the Australian companies. They would go to the next meeting in Paris in March, with John Proud, chairman of Peko-Wallsend Ltd., as their spokesman.

The Australians, however, were not about to be pushed around by the big boys in the club. "The general view was that Australia should be prepared to co-operate with other world groups, but only if Australia was fairly treated," the notes reported. Several Australian companies were said to be "sufficiently advanced in their planning and marketing that they intended to proceed in any case. It was considered that the overseas group . . . really did not appreciate the very strong position of Australia. In fact, if Australia chose to stay outside of a world producers' club, it was likely that the idea would collapse.

"Mr. Proud stressed the need for extreme secrecy."

Gulf and Uranerz Canada, the two Canadian companies that did not go to the first Paris meeting, were meanwhile kept informed by Ottawa. On Monday, February 14, 1972, Gordon MacNabb phoned Nick Ediger to invite Gulf to a meeting that Wednesday to review what had happened in Paris. MacNabb stated that "it is very essential that Gulf Minerals attend the meeting on Wednesday from Canada's point of view, and in Gulf's best long-term interest," according to a file memo that Ediger wrote. "Mr. MacNabb was particularly concerned because he felt that the production from Rabbit Lake during the period in question could be regarded as totally uncommitted and, therefore, subject to any machinery that might be agreed upon to allocate demand and establish floor prices."

The implication of this was clear enough. Gulf had, by selling a 49 per cent interest in its Rabbit Lake mine, secured a market through its German partner. MacNabb was suggesting that if the arrangement were not recognized, sales of Rabbit Lake uranium might be cut back, possibly to the point where construction of the mine, then underway, might have to be halted. MacNabb was hinting that if Ediger wanted to protect Gulf's interest, he had better come to the meeting on Wednesday.

On Tuesday, Ediger got another 'phone call, this time from Austin, who "also issued a very strong invitation for Gulf Minerals to attend the meeting." In his file memo, Ediger says that he "explained that we had some serious concern about being represented at a meeting which would discuss what was, in effect, prorationing." Austin responded that Gulf "would be acting irresponsibly if it chose to ignore the discussions."

Austin had a particular, and compelling, reason for wanting to ensure that Gulf and Uranerz participated in the emerging plans for a uranium cartel. Canada – like almost every other nation – has a double standard about certain anti-competitive measures. They may be legal if they affect only the commerce and interests of other nations. Under Canada's Combines Investigation Act, a cartel of Canadian producers concerned with export sales may, under certain conditions, be legal. The effect, in this case, seemed to be that the contemplated uranium export arrangements would be legal only if all Canadian uranium producers participated in the scheme. Otherwise, the producers that did participate, including the government's two Crown corporations, could be guilty of breaking Canadian criminal law. It was imperative that Gulf be roped in.

Gulf, however, had strong reasons for not wanting to join. It already had a market for its uranium, and there seemed to be a risk that it might lose part of that market. It was also concerned about the risk of violating antitrust laws; not only the Canadian laws that Gulf Minerals Canada was subject to, but the American laws that its parent in Pittsburgh was subject to. Ottawa felt strongly that Gulf Minerals Canada was a Canadian corporation, doing business in Canada, incorporated in Canada, and subject to the laws of Canada. That would be cold comfort for the Pittsburgh parent if it ever found itself in a U.S. court as a result of actions by its Canadian subsidiary, even if that subsidiary were acting in accord with Canadian law.

Nick Ediger, as manager of Gulf Minerals Canada, was not about to try to resolve this problem on his own. It was discussed in a telephone conference call to Denver involving four people: Ediger; Willard Z. (Bud) Estey, then outside counsel for

Gulf Minerals Canada, and later a Justice of the Supreme Court of Canada; Sinesio Zagnoli, vice-president of parent Gulf Mineral Resources in Denver; and Roger Allen, staff lawyer with Gulf Mineral Resources.

Following the 'phone call, Zagnoli sent a Telex to E. B. Walker at Gulf Oil's headquarters in Pittsburgh, indicating the degree of concern. "Until the meeting tomorrow we have little to go on, but it seems clear that if they would reach an agreement along the lines indicated, the German deal [with Uranerz] may be effectively nullified and we would have the risk of operating the plant at part rates and high unit costs," Zagnoli wrote. "The Canadians suggested that prorationing would include all Rabbit Lake uranium . . . Under these circumstances, the economics of the project as prepared are not valid. One alternative that must seriously be considered immediately is stopping the project."

Rabbit Lake was then the only uranium mine in the world under construction.

The decision reached during the telephone conference was that Ediger and Estey would attend the Ottawa meeting.

Rio Algom and Denison were also represented at the Ottawa meeting, as were the two Crown companies. One of the first questions was whether the Rabbit Lake production would be considered committed, and thus exempt from any sales allocation plan. According to Ediger's file memorandum, "Denison and Rio Algom agreed that Rabbit Lake production could properly be left out of any discussion of allocation formula." That would have removed one of Gulf's main concerns about joining the cartel, if it had been the final word on the subject.

At the meeting, Jack Austin informed the producers that "the cabinet has sanctioned participation" by the Department of Energy and the two Crown companies "in any exploratory discussions concerned with a working mechanism to allocate demand and establish a floor price, in the period 1972-77," and that the government "took no exception to discussions among Canadian producers with respect to export markets," Ediger wrote in a file memo.

Ediger also noted that under the Combines Investigation Act, "any agreement to control exports which has the effect of reducing the volumes of export, is illegal . . . Any agreement which has an effect on the domestic price as a result of fixing an export price is also illegal." Those were perilously narrow confines within which to structure a legal cartel, and the government would soon be forced to find a way to circumvent the problem.

For the record, Gulf made it clear that it was not prepared to participate in a cartel. "Mr. Estey advised all present of Gulf's concern about the implications of these discussions with respect to both Canadian and United States antitrust legislation," Mr. Ediger reported. "He went on to emphasize that Gulf's attendance at the meeting was in response to a strong invitation from the Department of Energy, Mines and Resources to provide information with respect to Rabbit Lake, and we had no intention of entering into discussions intended to allocate export markets or set prices."

That touched on an issue that would later become one of the key questions in the uranium litigation in the United States: whether or not Gulf was compelled by the Canadian government to join the cartel. Estey's statement seemed to make Gulf's position unequivocal, except for the next paragraph in Ediger's memorandum, dealing with the second meeting of the uranium producers to be held in Paris on February 21 and 22.

"Subsequent to the meeting, Mr. Estey spoke to both Mr. Austin and Mr. MacNabb privately with respect to Gulf's attendance at the forthcoming meetings in Paris," Ediger wrote. "They specifically recommended against Gulf's seeking an invitation and it was agreed that Gulf would not participate. However, Mr. MacNabb did agree to keep us informed."

Six days after the second meeting in Paris, MacNabb phoned Ediger to tell him what had happened, and to invite Gulf to the third Paris meeting, in March. At the February meeting, there had been a squabble about how much of the market Canada should get, and MacNabb assured Ediger that he had fought hard for Gulf's interest.

Another problem that had arisen in Paris involved a sale of uranium to Spain from the joint-venture stockpile held by Denison Mines and the Canadian government. It had been suggested that Canada be allocated about a third of sales anticipated during the 1972-77 period, some 9,100 tons. Uranex and

Nufcor had argued that from this 9,100 tons allocated to Canada should be deducted the sale of 4,500 tons to Spain and 3,700 tons of production from Rabbit Lake. This would provide the Canadian mines with 900 tons of new uranium sales during the period, instead of 9,100 tons – a difference of about $100 million.

As Ediger summarized the 'phone call from MacNabb in another file memo: "Mr. MacNabb stated that he was not very popular in Paris because he took a very hard line with respect to the status of the Canadian commitment to the Spanish utilities and the Rabbit Lake production through to the end of 1977 . . .

"Mr. MacNabb further stated that the government of Canada [i.e., the cabinet] intends to do everything possible to encourage the Rabbit Lake project. They fully recognize that they must treat it as if it were in existence today . . . They also recognize that the project is only viable if full production capacity is maintained, and because the project is important to the national economy, and the province of Saskatchewan, they will not take any action which will cause us to postpone our construction program or subsequently jeopardize our productive capacity."

Apparently at the Paris meeting, Nufcor had argued that the Rabbit Lake project should be delayed, because otherwise "it would drive Uranerz into bankruptcy. Mr. MacNabb did not attach much credence to this point of view. He also informed the meeting that it was not in Canada's economic interest to impede the project in any way.

"Mr. MacNabb then changed the subject to matters involving the Combines Investigation Act . . . Apparently, there is a provision in the Act whereby any agreement with respect to export markets is illegal if it has the effect of harming the export possibilities of other Canadian producers. Thus, Gulf and UCL as Canadian producers must be parties to any agreement, even if it is acknowledged that they would not be affected by the agreement.

"Mr. MacNabb stated that . . . it was necessary for us to be represented at the Paris meeting . . . In view of the delicate nature of this matter with respect to antitrust legislation and the relationship between Gulf and its partner, I asked Mr. Mac-

Nabb to write me a letter formally setting out his concerns and requesting our response. He agreed to write such a letter tomorrow."

The letter was never received. Apparently there was a change of thinking in Ottawa, and Ediger later received a 'phone call advising him that Gulf could forget about having to attend the third cartel meeting in Paris, after all.

In fact, the March 12 and 13 meetings in Paris raised some doubt about whether there would be a cartel.

"[T]he discussions amongst the uranium producers are not as yet successful," Rio Tinto-Zinc's chief world uranium salesman Louis Mazel advised Conzinc Riotinto of Australia chairman Rod Carnegie in a letter following the meeting. "In order to maintain, and hopefully improve, the uranium prices it will be necessary to come to a quota arrangement," Mazel wrote. The principal problems were the Rabbit Lake production with its sales contract with Uranerz, and the determination of the Australian producers to have an adequate share of the market.

The Australian producers had been represented for the first time at the talks by their newly appointed spokesman, John Proud. "I think that most producers were very much impressed by John Proud," Mazel assured Carnegie, but "equally amazed about the large quantities he felt should be produced by the Australians."

Although Gulf had not yet been invited to join the discussions, it was already being told that it was expected to participate in the contemplated producers' arrangement. The message came from Donald Stovel Macdonald, the strapping, six-foot-five, forty-year-old Toronto lawyer who less than three months before had succeeded Joe Greene as Minister of Energy, Mines and Resources. After a brilliant scholastic record (University of Toronto, Cambridge, and Harvard), and a short stint practising law, Macdonald had been elected to the House at a youthful age thirty. With his ready grin, blunt candour, and flashing temper, Macdonald had been dubbed "the Thumper" in his university days, a tag that the press gleefully picked up.

At a brief meeting in the minister's office on March 23, Macdonald had informed Nick Ediger, Bud Estey, and Roger Allen that a marketing arrangement by the uranium producers would be in Canada's interest, and he "urgently hoped" Gulf would participate. According to a Gulf memo, Macdonald "strongly implied that if the Canadian producers could not unanimously arrive at a position regarded as acceptable by the government, the government was prepared to enforce agreement by creating a uranium marketing board or in some other formal compulsory fashion."

(Another Gulf memo commented: "Bud Estey says Macdonald is key man; unfortunately, much of his authority is delegated to Austin, who seems to be less reliable.")

The Canadian producers met in Ottawa on April 10 at the request of Jack Austin to establish a position for the fourth Paris meetings, now set for April 20 and 21. Austin reported that the March meeting in Paris had "terminated with the direction that the Canadian producers determine if they could get their house in order to present a unified position; otherwise, further meetings in Paris would serve no useful purpose," according to a file note prepared by Gulf Mineral Resources lawyer Roger Allen. Rio Algom, Denison, and Eldorado claimed that their suggested sales allocations were "unacceptable and they will not join unless it is increased." Denison president John Kostuik argued that the Rabbit Lake mine should be deferred, or its production rate cut back. Rio Algom vice-president George Albino claimed that if the Rabbit Lake producers did not give up a part of their market share, "there was nothing further to discuss as Rio Algom would not completely remove itself from the market for this five-year period in order that the desires of the Rabbit Lake producers could be attained."

Failing to come to terms on how to share the market, the meeting turned to the other problem: whether what they were proposing was legal. Austin reported that "an opinion had been obtained from the Director of the Combines Investigation Branch that the arrangement is legal as it is presently understood by the Director but that it could later become illegal if orders have to be declined by Canadian producers as a result of the arrangement." Stripped of the jargon, this meant that if the cartel was to have any effect, it would almost certainly become illegal.

Gulf and UCL at this point, according to Allen's file memo, protested that even if it were legal under Canadian law, "their participation would be dependent upon a determination that it

129

would not result in violation of United States or German antitrust law."

That brought out a hint of the way in which Ottawa (or perhaps Jack Austin) would eventually arrange Canadian participation in the cartel. Gulf and Uranerz would have to obey Canadian law, not foreign law. The government would make the arrangement legal. Gulf and Uranerz would participate whether they wanted to or not. Roger Allen's file note spelled it out.

In blunt terms, Austin stated that "both Gulf and UCL are Canadian corporations operating in Canada and are accordingly subject to the laws of Canada," Allen wrote. "He again stressed the cabinet's desire for the producers to implement the agreement without the necessity of direct government implementation such as creating a uranium marketing board. However, if government implementation proved necessary he would advise that he felt sure it would be considered by the cabinet." Austin then told the producers that "a formal declaration would be sought from the cabinet (with the minister of justice present) that the arrangement is in the national interest of Canada." Once this was obtained "Gulf and UCL would be directed to participate in the arrangement if the other Canadian producers acquiesced in being so directed . . . Neither Gulf nor UCL were given an opportunity to agree or object to the Canadian government's direction to participate in the arrangement."

The meeting ended after "Mr. Austin polled the Canadian producers with the exception of Gulf and UCL" as to Canada's advice on whether another meeting in Paris seemed worthwhile. Eldorado president Bill Gilchrist said that "we must have the next meeting, but he frankly saw little hope of success." Austin then prepared a Telex to the cartel's pro-tem chairman, Pierre Taranger, of France's CEA, urging that "issues are so vital to all that a further effort should be made to bridge the gap." Whether the planned meeting in Paris would proceed would depend on what response Taranger got from the other countries.

From the executive offices in the granite-block, neo-Gothic Gulf Oil Building in downtown Pittsburgh, it appeared to the lawyers that Gulf was rapidly being manoeuvred into a position where it would either have to join the cartel, or get out of the uranium business in Canada.

Gulf's chief antitrust lawyer, Irwin W. Coleman, outlined the situation in a memo to the company's general counsel, Merle Minks, two days after Austin had strongly hinted that Gulf's participation would be directed.

"I have been informed that the producers, other than those in Canada, are not only ready, but anxious to proceed," Coleman wrote. "Apparently, the producers in Canada are ready to proceed except that our Rabbit Lake joint venture with the Germans has not at this time agreed to do anything. We are being pressured by the Canada government representatives to get in line and join the agreement."

"There is serious question as to whether Gulf can be a party to such an agreement, both under the Canada Combines law and the United States antitrust laws," Coleman wrote. "There is also a serious question whether our participation will render the Rabbit Lake project uneconomical. Based on present discussions, production at Rabbit Lake would be cut from the projected 6,190 tons during this period [1972-77] to 4,650 tons . . . Mr. Zagnoli is now studying the economics of the Rabbit Lake project under the proposed quota to determine if the project would be viable under such circumstances. If found affirmatively we then must assess the antitrust risk."

Coleman outlined what then seemed to be Ottawa's plan to put the arrangement into effect; agreement in principle at the Paris meeting planned for April 20 and 21. A declaration by the cabinet that the agreement "is in the interest of Canada and represents the policy of the Canada government." An opinion from the minister of justice "which will prevent any action being taken under Canada law against participants in the agreement, at least as long as the present government is in power." Direction by Ottawa to the producers "to enter into and participate in the agreement."

According to Coleman, Gulf's outside counsel in Canada, Bud Estey, had advised that the risk under Canadian law would be "minimal if the program as now contemplated is carried out." Coleman added:

On the whole, if the economics of the project are found to be satisfactory under the proposed agreement, I am of the opinion that we have little choice in the matter . . . Gulf Minerals Canada, Limited is a Canada company operating in Canada and subject to the jurisdiction of the Canada government. It must obey the laws, policy and directives of that government, or get out . . . Messrs. Allen, Estey and Ediger impressed upon me that a decision as to our course of action must be made in time to advise the Canada government and others participating whether we will attend the Paris meeting.

The meeting was eight days away.

The next scene in the saga was played out at either end of a Telex line, from offices in Ottawa and in Pittsburgh. It involved some posturing. The government of Canada was about to urge Gulf to participate at the next cartel meeting. Clearly, Ottawa must have Gulf in if it were to achieve the uranium marketing arrangements, which it had aggressively promoted. Yet Ottawa wanted the arrangements to be seen, for whatever reasons, as voluntary. Gulf wanted them to be seen as involuntary. If it were to be forced to join a cartel, it wanted the record to show that it had been forced.

In Ottawa, Deputy Minister Jack Austin drafted a Telex message addressed to Nick Ediger at Gulf Minerals Canada offices in Toronto, where it was relayed to Pittsburgh. At the law department in the Gulf Building in Pittsburgh, six men gathered to prepare Gulf's response to the anticipated request to attend the Paris meeting. The Gulf team consisted of Ediger; Sinesio Zagnoli, president of Gulf Mineral Resources in Denver; Roger Allen, Gulf Mineral Resources lawyer; Irwin Coleman, who was due to retire later that year as Gulf Oil's top antitrust lawyer; Roy Jackson, another Gulf lawyer who was due to succeed Coleman; and Wendell Ramsey, an economist.

The message arrived from Austin:

Telex from Taranger of Uranex has confirmed that April 20-21 meeting will be held in Paris . . . As you know, the Canadian government endorses the principle of such an arrangement as in the national interest and will look to Gulf Minerals Canada as a Canadian producer to take every reasonable step to ensure compliance. Please confirm that your company will be represented and let me know the names of your two delegates by Telex.

The Gulf people drafted a carefully worded response:

As you have advised that it is in the national interest of Canada that Gulf Minerals Canada Limited be represented at the Paris meeting of producers, please be advised that pursuant to your direction, Gulf will be represented by N. M. Ediger and W. Z. Estey. It must be stressed that such representatives' ability to acquiesce on behalf of Gulf to any arrangement which may be acceptable to other producers determined to be in the best interest of Canada, will be contingent upon a subsequent determination that the same does not result in Gulf violating any applicable antitrust laws, and further, its acceptability to Uranerz Canada Limited as co-owner of Rabbit Lake.

Before the response was transmitted, a telephone call was placed to Bud Estey in Toronto to get his advice on the wording. The future Justice of the Supreme Court of Canada did have a suggestion. The reference to possible violation of "antitrust laws," Estey suggested, sounds too American. Even if the response is coming from Pittsburgh, it would be better if it sounded more Canadian. The wording was changed to read ". . . does not result in Gulf violating any applicable law on restraint of competition."

A second Telex message addressed to Ediger was received the same day, this one from Energy Minister Donald Macdonald. Gulf was asked by Macdonald not only to join the discussions at Paris but also, along with the other Canadian producers, was strongly urged to comply with whatever marketing arrangements were agreed upon. Macdonald's Telex reads:

I have been authorized by cabinet to advise you that the Canadian government is concerned with the unstable situation in world uranium marketing; has followed carefully discussions amongst world producers; is prepared to allow Uranium Canada Ltd. and Eldorado Nuclear Ltd. to enter into an informal world producers' arrangement; that in order to be workable, all Canadian producers should participate; to advise you, as all existing Canadian producers have proposed to participate in such an arrangement, and the Canadian government is of the opinion that such an arrangement would be in the national interest, your company is requested to make every effort to adhere to the common terms.

Austin was later to cite this Telex as having "clearly expressed" the government policy that "it would not force Canadian producers into an arrangement." Perhaps not forced. Just voluntarily conscripted.

Canadian Embassy, 35 Rue Montaigne, Paris, April 19, 1972. Canada's uranium producers had gathered to review once more the posture they will adopt at the meeting of the international uranium producers, scheduled to start the following morning in the headquarters of the French Commissariat à l'Energie Atomique. Gulf Minerals Canada and Uranerz Canada will be represented for the first time. The meeting of the Canadians, called for 8:00 p.m., does not get underway until an hour later, and no one is in a good mood.

Ediger informs the group that Gulf will not agree to adhere to any terms set by the cartel without "first obtaining from the U.S. Department of Justice an expression that such adherence would not result in a violation of U.S. antitrust laws." (Later, after Ottawa passes a law forcing compliance with the cartel marketing arrangement, Gulf drops its plans to seek clearance from the Department of Justice.) Austin again responds that Gulf Minerals is a Canadian producer, subject to Canadian law. Uranerz lawyer Dr. Justin says his firm, too, has antitrust problems. The German government could seize the proceeds from any sale that violated German antitrust laws. Austin suggests that the sale could take place outside of Germany so that funds could not be seized. In that case, Justin responds, instead of seizing the money, the German government could seize the uranium.

Denison president John Kostuik was still upset about the Rabbit Lake project, and at remarks made at an earlier meeting by Uranerz Canada vice-president Karl Kegel. Kostuik threatened to try to block the grandfather clause which would exempt Gulf and Uranerz from having to be Canadian owned under the still-proposed uranium ownership legislation.

According to Roger Allen's file note,

Mr. Kostuik delivered quite a tirade against the 'so-called' Canadian producers constituting Rabbit Lake and, in particular, Gulf. He referred to the great sacrifices being made by the other producers to serve the best interest of Canada, while Gulf and UCL were taking an inflexible position which served only their own self interest . . . He referred to his resentment of being lectured to by Mr. Kegel in Ottawa as a so-called Canadian producer. He ended his 'flag-waving' tirade with a threat that if Gulf did not cooperate, he would exert all of his influence to the end that Gulf would not receive favorable treatment in the foreign ownership legislation now being drafted.

Despite the acrimony, the meeting did agree on one thing. They would ask at the meeting the next day for a minimum of 9,050 tons as Canada's share of new sales through to the end of 1972.

The discussions on the following two days by the twenty-three people who were attempting to carve up the non-American, free world uranium market were meticulously reported in thirty-four pages of minutes compiled by Dr. John Runnalls of Canada's Department of Energy, Mines and Resources.

Austin told the meeting that "only a spread of 5 per cent stood between an agreement or no agreement so far as the Canadians were concerned," according to Runnalls's minutes. "In other words, if the Canadian allocation could be increased by some 5 per cent of the available market between 1972 and 1977 he said the Canadians were willing to support an arrangement." The previous meeting in March had allocated sales of 8,100 tons to Canada, and now the Canadian producers wanted an additional 950 tons.

Pierre Taranger of Uranex dryly noted that the total of everyone's minimum demands was 20 per cent more than the anticipated sales, and under these circumstances, an arrangement seemed impossible. The problem, he said, lay with "the desires of the new producers" who "had not suffered enough as yet to realize the serious nature of the uranium marketing problems."

Jack Austin said he felt "somewhat crushed by the turn of events," and that the meeting would never have been called if it were known how much the Australians were going to demand. J. W. Shilling of Nufcor said that if the new Australians wanted to break into the market, there was no way to stop them, and the result would be a price war. Bill Gilchrist said no nation should sell its uranium resources under $5 a pound, and if the price were to drop below that, his advice to Eldorado's board would be to close operations. Rio Tinto-Zinc managing director Roy Wright remarked that the meeting "would gladden the hearts of all utility executives."

Taranger warned that the new Australian producers were about to repeat the same mistake that France had made earlier

> in creating new production which exceeded the market capacity. Today there was proof of this mistake in the size of their stockpiles and over-production . . . and France was paying. He was convinced that any new producer entering the market would be making the same wrong decisions as France had done earlier, and in his experience he had never seen that a wrong decision led to the making of money.

The Australians were not about to back down under this pressure. Six Australian companies had production plans which, before the end of the decade, would provide enough output for more than half of the total non-American market. Western Mining asserted that cartel or no cartel, it was going ahead with its plans and was prepared to sell uranium at $4 a pound. Taranger said that France could sell from its stockpile at $3 a pound, which, he claimed, would be more profitable than waiting 10 years to sell it at $6 a pound.

While the would-be cartel members fought among themselves, they paid little heed to the interests of two other uranium producers, the former French colonies of Gabon and Niger. The governments of these new republics had been seeking greater development of their uranium resources, Taranger reported. Niger alone had enough uranium to boost production by 5,000 tons a year. France had managed to delay these plans to expand production. Niger and Gabon had also been purposely kept out of the cartel. "So far the French had succeeded in excluding representatives from Gabon and Niger but it was not certain that this position could be preserved," according to Runnalls's minutes. When the cartel was organized, there were never any further hints that France might permit its former colonies to participate. The impression was that France treated her former colonies as though they still were colonies.

The duration of the planned cartel emerges as a subtle but crucial element of the Paris discussions. Ottawa had said that it was opposed to any extension of arrangements beyond 1977, as well it might. The longer such an arrangement was in place, the greater would be the difficulty of forecasting its effects, and the greater the risk of violating Canada's Combines law. Gulf, too, had said that it would not participate in any arrangement extending beyond the six-year period. It foresaw the possibilities of the U.S. embargo being lifted in the late 1970's, which would increase its exposure under U.S. antitrust laws.

The Australians, however, pressed strongly for an arrangement extending through 1980. Their new mines were not slated to come into production until 1975 or 1976, and a market allocation plan that lasted only through to the end of 1977 would be of little value to them.

Despite the thorny issues involved, Jack Austin hinted at a separate meeting of the Canadian caucus that he had in mind a separate arrangement extending well beyond 1980. He saw a need to stabilize prices not only in times of surplus supply, but in times of shortages as well. By the end of the 1970's, Austin said, "demand pressures then would be very high, and there would be just as much need to regulate the situation then, as now, when there was such an over-abundance of supply." Failure to curb rising prices at a time of shortages, Austin suggested, would lead to yet another boom-and-bust cycle.

Austin was finessing the Canadian producers with a very subtle ploy. Unknown to the producers, Ottawa had by this time decided that the legal risks in the arrangement as contemplated were unacceptable, even if the arrangement terminated at the end of 1977. Austin hardly wanted to confess this aspect to the producers, at this late stage. There was a way around the problem, but it would require some adroit manoeuvring. Ottawa could pass a law, by means of a regulation issued by the cabinet under the authority of the Atomic Energy Control Act, which would seem to make participation in the cartel legal, in spite of the Combines law. The cabinet, however, did not want to issue such a regulation unless it was requested by the producers to do so. An extension of the cartel's terms would make the risks more visible, and the producers would clearly see the merit in requesting the government to pass the necessary regulation. Austin's strategy would be played out during the next several weeks. It was not for nothing that he had a reputation as a master poker player.

Intense debate at the Paris meeting continued for two days. A commitment that the marketing arrangement would be extended until 1980 finally won acceptance of a plan of sales allocations and a tentative price schedule. The arrangement covered the period 1972-77, but it was agreed that it would later be revised and extended for a further three years. The price, in line with discussions at the earlier meetings, was set at $5.30 a pound, for deliveries made in 1972, rising to $7.10 a pound for deliveries in 1978. Sales to Japan, Korea, and Taiwan were to be 30 cents a pound higher, reportedly to cover the cost of commissions to agents involved in sales to these countries.

The estimated market of 26,000 tons for the 6-year period was allocated 33.5 per cent to Canada; 23.75 per cent to South Africa; 21.75 per cent to France (including Niger and Gabon); 4 per cent to the RTZ affiliates in Australia and Namibia; and 17 per cent to the new Australian producers. Each group came out with substantially less than its initial minimum demand. In Canada, for example, the Rabbit Lake producers lost sales of 1,000 tons, or about $12 million, under the allocation plan.

The tentative agreement was subject to confirmation by each group after they had all returned home to study the plan further. They were to advise Paris of their final decisions. "If one negative response was received, then there should be no more meetings," Taranger had warned. "If there was unanimity on the other hand, then the present working group should meet again." Barring a negative response, the next meeting was set for Johannesburg, May 29 to June 1.

Gulf was feeling the increasing pressure to get in line. An internal memo at Gulf's Pittsburgh head office on April 28 concluded that "failure on Gulf's part to submit to coercive pressure being applied by the Canadian government respecting Gulf's participation would almost certainly result in severe adverse economic consequences for Gulf, including a material deterioration of Gulf's relations with the Canadian government."

What Energy Minister Donald Macdonald was saying in

private about the need for an international arrangement to improve uranium prices, he was also saying in public, although in somewhat more guarded terms. In March he had told a House of Commons standing committee that "the government of Canada has taken steps for the holding of discussions at an international level regarding the state of the uranium industry . . . In the absence of international market stability, the development of the resources required for the nuclear power industry in the 1980's will not be ensured." In another statement, he declared that "it is critical that a resource exporter like Canada derives the capital from minerals and energy commodities to achieve much broader industrial goals and to make sure the national interest is protected in the international market place." He did not mention, however, that the discussions were being held not just with other governments, but with corporations.

While pushing for a producers' agreement, it was becoming increasingly clear in Ottawa that steering such an arrangement through the legal shoals would be a formidable task. Both the Combines' director of investigations and the Justice Department had advised the cabinet in March that such an arrangement held considerable risk of violating criminal law. The cabinet ordered a study of alternatives, including legislation to amend the Combines Investigation Act so as to exempt uranium marketing for a six-year period, or the establishment of a federal marketing agency. Either of these measures, however, would take a long time to put in place. Another way would be to pass a regulation under the Atomic Energy Control Act. The act already gave the federal government broad authority over virtually every aspect of uranium production and marketing. It would be a simple matter for the cabinet to issue a regulation under this act, authorizing the Atomic Energy Control Board to set uranium export prices and to allocate the export sales among Canadian producers, according to directions issued by the minister of energy. The regulation would be law. And the directions from the minister to the board would implement the export volumes and prices determined by the cartel. There would no longer be any question about the producers agreeing to the terms set by the cartel: they would be compelled by Canadian law to do so.

The next meeting of the Canadian uranium producers was

held on May 9 to discuss the upcoming meeting in Johannesburg – assuming there was enough agreement to hold another
meeting.

There was the by now routine argument about whose law
Gulf Minerals Canada would obey. Nick Ediger's file memo
records:

> I told the group the Gulf was diligently pursuing a legal
> opinion with respect to its position in the U.S., and be-
> cause of the potential gravity of the matter, it would take
> some time. Mr. MacNabb expressed his irritation at the
> extra-territorial effect of U.S. law. Albino, an American
> citizen, executive vice-president of Rio Algom, with a
> wholly-owned subsidiary producing in the U.S., sug-
> gested that Gulf was overly concerned.

There was some question about whether Gulf would attend
the planned Johannesburg meeting, and two different accounts
of Gulf's response. John Runnalls's minutes reported: "Mr.
Austin asked if Gulf was prepared . . . to go ahead in Johannesburg and take the associated risk. Mr. Ediger replied in the affir-
mative." But Nick Ediger's file memo contains a different account: "All Canadian producers confirmed that they would attend . . . No one asked me so I kept my mouth shut."

There was also discussion about an "aide memoire" that all
the Canadian producers were expected to sign at the Johannesburg meeting, stating that "All the undersigned Canadian uranium producers agree that it would be desirable to establish a
marketing arrangement in the period to the end of 1977." The
document, however, was ambivalent about a possible extension to 1980. It noted that "the major threat to the establishment of a suitable arrangement stems from the new Australian
producers" and that this threat "would be reduced considerably if an approximate allocation for all uranium producers
could be specified during the period 1978-80." It concluded,
however, that "there is no proposal at this time acceptable to
all Canadian uranium producers to enter into any arrangement
for the 1978-80 period." The holdout was Gulf Minerals.
Ediger had told the meeting, according to Runnalls's minutes,
that Gulf "could not contemplate an arrangement that would
extend beyond 1977."

The matter of the cartel's terms had still not been resolved when fourteen representatives of Canada's uranium producers met at the Presidential Hotel in Johannesburg on the evening of May 28 "to discuss the strategy to be adopted for the meeting of international uranium producers commencing the next day." It was time for Austin to play his hand, finessing the producers into requesting the regulation that would make adherence to the cartel arrangements a matter of Canadian law.

"Mr. Austin opened the meeting by indicating that the international discussions . . . would be difficult because the Australians would be going into these meetings feeling they had the whip hand," John Runnalls reported in his minutes. "The major problem would be the Australian allocation from 1978 onward . . . All the parties with the exception of Canada would insist on an agreement to the end of 1980."

There were pointed suggestions that the Australians, having learned of the proposed price schedule of the proposed cartel that they proposed to join, had been contracting to sell all the uranium they could, at prices below the cartel's tentative prices. If the Australians could not be trusted at this stage, Austin asked, "how would it be possible to look forward to a stable arrangement later?"

Most of the Canadian producers appeared willing, if somewhat reluctant, to extend the term. Eldorado president Bill Gilchrist said it would be "unwise" to go beyond 1980. Rio Algom vice-president George Albino said that the "Australian position was not an illogical one." Denison president John Kostuik said that he would accept an extension to 1980 rather than "be the one to prevent any possibility for an arrangement." Ediger said that there had to be "some firm termination date."

Now that the producers had agreed that the cartel period must be extended, Austin played his next card. He told the meeting that while there was a possibility that a marketing arrangement could run afoul of the Combines Investigation Act,

It seemed to be a reasonable business risk to accept an arrangement up to 1977. Beyond that, however, the risk of infraction of the act was substantial. Hence, the government of Canada, having listened to the advice of three separate departments on the issue, had decided that 1977 should be the limit of any arrangement. Mr. Phillips, [counsel for Uranerz Canada] remarked that if the Canadian government thought the risk was grave beyond 1977, the producers were certainly not going to be interested in extending the period.

Austin then reminded the producers of how the policy of the government "that it would not force Canadian producers into an arrangement . . . had been clearly expressed" in the Telex message sent to each of them by Energy Minister Macdonald on April 14. (Former Gulf Oil lawyer Roy Jackson was to later testify before the Moss committee hearings: "That is Mr. Austin's statement made in a position of posturing, as far as I am concerned.")

While he said that the government "had decided that 1977 should be the limit of any arrangement," Austin added that "the government was sympathetic to a longer term that would be applied not only during the demand scarcity but later on when there was a shortage of supply." There was, however, a catch. Because of its policy that it would not force anyone into an arrangement, "The government would not regulate . . . unless such a request was made."

The position thus seemed to be: no extension, no cartel. Extend the cartel and there was a grave risk of breaking criminal law. The government could resolve this by passing a regulation. But the producers would have to ask for the regulation. And they would have to make up their minds right away. "It would be necessary to reach a consensus at the present meeting," Runnalls's minutes reported, "because on the following day the Canadians would have to disclose whether or not they were prepared to enter into an arrangement extending into 1980."

Austin was asked how long it would take to pass such a regulation: no more than four to six weeks, he responded. Austin did not mention that he had already been ordered to draft the regulation. The Energy Department had already decided that this was the route it wanted to follow, and Austin went to the meeting to get the necessary request from the producers.

George Albino "asked if a request from Rio Algom and Denison would be sufficient. Mr. Austin replied that the action could be initiated with requests from the existing Canadian producers. Neither Gulf nor UCL would be asked to agree [they were not "existing producers" because the Rabbit Lake mine was not yet in production]. Nevertheless he wondered what their position might be. Mr. Allen replied that from Gulf's standpoint, compliance with the laws of the host government would be an overriding consideration.

"Mr. Austin then asked if Denison, Rio Algom and Eldorado agreed that they would request the government to proclaim a regulation under Section 9(c) of the Atomic Energy Control Act to specify price levels and volumes of [export] sales. Messrs. Kostuik, Albino and Gilchrist all agreed that they would make such a request."

Jack Austin had played his hand. Trump!

From this point on, the cartel was a matter of mechanics. The Johannesburg meeting agreed to a plan of allocating future sales until 1980 between the four producing countries and RTZ, with the new Australian producers getting a further increase, and the rest once more slightly cut back. For the final 3 years of the agreement, the new Australian producers would get the largest share of sales, 24.4 per cent, followed by Canada at 23.2 per cent. Procedures for allocating sales and rigging bids were established. It was decided that a secretariat would be established to handle administrative functions, and that the cartel would operate with two committees, a senior policy committee to handle the major issues, and an "operating committee" to handle more routine matters. Each of the five participants (Canada, Nufcor, Uranex, Australia, and RTZ) would appoint two representatives to the operating committee. Canada's representatives on the operating committee for the first year were Alan Lowell of Rio Algom and Mario de Bastiani of Denison.

The Johannesburg arrangement, Gulf lawyer Roy Jackson wrote shortly after, "constitutes an actual, but informal, intergovernmental agreement. The Canadian government, for policy reasons of its own, has avoided any treaty or other formal arrangement, and, according to Mr. Estey, will probably continue to do so."

On June 14, Austin wrote to Macdonald:

Attached for your consideration and signature is a memorandum to cabinet reporting on the recent meeting of uranium producers in Johannesburg and on the details of the marketing arrangements which they have concluded. The memorandum recommends approval of the terms of the arrangement and the drafting and promulgation of a regulation and/or direction under the Atomic Energy Control Act which would ensure Canadian producer compliance with the Johannesburg agreement and would effectively protect them from any litigation which might otherwise be possible under anti-cartel legislation.

All producers support the proposal . . . which would require compliance with the agreed terms of the marketing arrangements and thereby exempt the arrangement from the operation of the Combines Investigation Act.

Austin did not mention that this excluded support from Gulf and Uranerz.

The first meeting of the cartel's new operating committee was held at Cannes, France, in early July, at which André Petit was appointed to head the cartel's secretariat as a full-time job. Described as a man in his forties with an educational background in political science, economics, and law, Petit was on loan from the French CEA, where he had been a personal assistant to Bertrand Goldschmidt. In his new function for the cartel, Petit "would move to a completely independent office" of a wholly owned subisidiary of CEA called Société d'Etudes et de Recherches d'Uranium (SERU), according to a memo from Alan Lowell. "From the security aspect it was thought convenient that Petit would be 'buried' in the large CEA HQ building," Lowell wrote. (L. T. Gregg, appointed sales manager for Gulf Minerals Canada in July, 1972, and later a Canadian representative on the operating committee, testified in a deposition statement that the use of SERU "was felt to provide good security. It isn't the type of thing that some inquiring investigative reporter could wander into and start going through files and interviewing secretaries and things of that nature.")

After the cabinet had issued the regulation, Macdonald, in turn, on August 23, issued the first directive to the Atomic

Energy Control Board, setting the volume and prices of uranium export sales, other than to the United States, and allocating sales among the Canadian producers. It was the first of four such directives to be issued by Macdonald during a period of nearly two years, all of them reflecting the prices and allocations determined by the cartel. The only respect in which they differed from the cartel arrangements was that the government directions did not set higher prices to be charged to sales to "middlemen," and the Canadian prices were slightly lower than the others.

On the same day, Macdonald also issued a public statement:

> In order to stabilize the current uranium marketing situation and to promote the development of the Canadian uranium industry, I have today issued a Direction to the Atomic Energy Control Board covering such aspects as minimum selling prices and volumes of sales to export markets. Because of the nature of uranium export contracts it would not be in the public interest to diclose further contract details at this time.

The cartel was in business.

CHAPTER NINE

The Cartel Overtaken

The great uranium cartel was effective for a period of less than two years.

Its first impact on the market sprang from the Johannesburg meeting of May 29 to June 1, 1972, at which the uranium producers finally agreed to their first price schedule, an allocation of sales, and a method of implementing the plan through a secretariat whose job it was to see that sales were portioned out according to the quota system to each producing area. The quotas assigned to each of the major producing countries – Canada, Australia, France, South Africa, as well as Rio Tinto-Zinc – were then further portioned out among the individual producing companies in these areas.

For a year and a half or so, the fierce competition for sales in the limited market available to non-American producers, was curbed. The world uranium price was increased, almost to the point where it matched the prices paid to American producers.

There were plans hatched within the cartel for other bold measures. It was agreed that the Westinghouse Electric Corporation, the middleman buyer and seller of uranium whose low prices threatened the marketing structure established by the cartel, should be boycotted and eliminated as a source of competition. It was suggested that cartel members should refuse to sell uranium to Westinghouse, and there was a report of efforts made to block participation by Westinghouse in a mining development and exploration venture in Australia. Finally, there were suggestions of a secret agreement to extend cartel pricing arrangements into the United States, to boost not only world uranium prices but American prices as well, through conspiracy with U.S. producers.

The wonder, though, is that the cartel was cohesive enough to have any effect on world prices, let alone affect U.S. prices or actually implement a boycott. "The exciting part of cartel operations such as the uranium producers seem to have formed via Paris is to see how they all agree on prices and allocations and then each one scurries to find ways to cheat the others," John F. Lee, a vice-president of the marketing division of Engelhard Minerals and Chemicals Corporation, noted in a letter in early 1972.

Despite the problems, the cartel, aided by other factors operating in the market, had managed to boost the non-American price for uranium some $2 a pound by late 1973. Then the cartel was swiftly overwhelmed by events completely unrelated to its machinations.

DISSENSION IN THE RANKS

The competitive rivalry between firms, which not even the cartel could completely manage to suppress, is reflected in the rancorous debates that run like a continuous string through the minutes and reports of the cartel meetings, even after the major agreement achieved at Johannesburg at the end of May, 1972.

Alan Lowell, Rio Algom's vice-president in charge of marketing, reported to the other Canadian producers on the results of the first meeting of the cartel's new operating committee, held at Cannes, France, in July. He described "the rather acrimonious debate that had taken place with Louis Mazel who had accepted 200 tons of business" in Japan without approval of the cartel.

Mazel was RTZ's chief world uranium salesman. He was in constant motion all over the world, travelling in high style: London, Paris, Chicago, Washington, Bonn, Tokyo, Canberra, Geneva. The Cannes meeting was not Mazel's last run-in with the cartel. Mazel was adroit at slathering a thick layer of euphemism to cover the cartel's activities. Mazel wrote to Harald Melouney, general manager of Mary Kathleen Uranium in Melbourne, on May 2, 1972:

In your letter you mention a word which we would not even like to mention as some members of the club are rather worried about informal price agreements. I would like to stress very strongly that under all circumstances there can only be an unofficial agreement and whatever agreement is struck it should be on a *strictly confidential basis*. [Emphasis in the original]. For the outside world, all Paris and subsequent meetings will be in connection with the exchange of marketing information.

In an even more incredible statement, contained in another letter to Melouney, Mazel proclaimed: "It should be said that there is no 'producers' agreement' or anything like it. Some of the uranium producers discovered, during the exchange of information on supply and demand, that there are some similarities of ideas and each producer is applying these in his own way." Among cartel members, jet-setters all, Mazel was known as "the flying Dutchman." Others, less charitably, referred to him as "Louis the Lip." Eventually, Mazel's relations with other cartel members became so strained that he was briefly banished by RTZ to Brazil.

The meeting at which Lowell reported discussions of the operating committee at Cannes was typical of the sessions of the Canadian producers. It was held in a government office, a conference room of the Department of Energy, Mines and Resources at 588 Booth Street, Ottawa. There were thirteen people at the meeting to represent Canada's uranium producing companies. Seven of them were government employees.

The Canadian producers may have been titillated by Lowell's account of the acrimonious debate involving Louis Mazel, but there was not much greater harmony when they turned to discussing their own problems. During this discussion of the division of the sales allocated to Canada, the minutes recorded:

> [I]t was clear that Mr. de Bastiani thought the allotments for Denison and Rio Algom were too low and the Gulf-UCL amount too high, whereas Mr. Ediger felt strongly that the Gulf-UCL amount could not be reduced further without introducing serious economic difficulties for the Rabbit Lake venture. Mr. Austin suggested . . . the question should be tabled for another meeting.

By mid-April, 1973, at a meeting in Paris, cartel members were pressing for a more formal arrangement, closer to that of the Organization of Petroleum Exporting Countries. This would bring the cartel out in the open, end the façade of rigged bids, and – it was argued – provide the electric power utilities with greater assurance of uranium supplies, at stable prices. It would also involve more government intervention and regulation of the industry, with a further reduction of competition.

"With one exception, GMCL, the Canadian delegation agreed with this concept," Nick Ediger later wrote. "I do not regard it as being in the Canadian interest and certainly not in Gulf's long-term interest."

Ediger voiced his objections to this concept, as well as other aspects of the cartel, in a letter to Deputy Minister Jack Austin on May 10:

> [W]e are strongly opposed to any involuntary sharing of contracts with other Canadian producers, and are unalterably opposed to any involuntary sharing of contracts with non-Canadian producers. We would vociferously reject any attempt to create a Canadian uranium marketing board. At the present time, it is impossible for me to visualize any benefits for Canada from a more formal, publicly-recognized association of world uranium producers . . . The continued domination of this 'Inner Club' (Uranex, Nufcor and RTZ) and the 'Star Chamber' atmosphere at the recent operating committee can only work to the detriment of Canada. All of these factors force me to question the present or future benefits of Canada's continued participation in the arrangements.

Ediger complained that the Rabbit Lake project, involving not only the capital investment by Gulf and Uranerz but also a large investment by the Saskatchewan government for the construction of 330 miles of new roads to provide access, was being hampered by the cartel arrangements, slippages in the construction of new nuclear power plants, "and the success of some fuel manufacturers and brokers i.e., Westinghouse, using materials from 'undisclosed sources.' " The cartel arrangements, he asserted, "seriously frustrate" efforts by Gulf and Uranerz to aggressively market Rabbit Lake uranium in world markets. "I would like to stress that at no time did GMCL voluntarily seek to become a part of the producers' arrangement. However, we have tried to abide with both the spirit and the specific rules agreed to by Canada."

A more formal and publicly recognized cartel arrangement never got past the talking stage, however, and in October, at a meeting in London, the cartel was more concerned about a further price increase. The second schedule adopted by the cartel at the London meeting, sixteen months after the first price schedule adopted in Johannesburg, added about another dollar a pound to the price. But whether, in this instance, the cartel was really increasing the price was debatable. There were indications that the market was already starting to firm up, that the cartel may have been following, rather than leading.

Later the same month, Energy Minister Donald Macdonald sent another directive to the Atomic Energy Board, revising the export prices for Canadian uranium in line with the schedule set by the cartel at the London meeting.

The London meeting also raised another issue for Gulf, in the form of a request that it appoint L. T. Gregg to serve on the cartel's operating committee. Gregg, in charge of international uranium sales for Gulf Minerals Canada and its parent Gulf Mineral Resources since mid-1972, had already participated along with Ediger on the cartel's policy committee. Now, Assistant Deputy Energy Minister Gordon MacNabb was asking Gulf to get involved in the nitty-gritty of the cartel work with a representative on the operating committee. Alan Lowell of Rio Algom and Mario de Bastiani of Denison had represented Canada on the operating committee for more than a year, and Ottawa had decided that it was time for its own John Runnalls and Gulf's L. T. Gregg to take a turn.

MacNabb's request was followed by a more formal, written request from Jack Austin to Nick Ediger. "[T]he practice which the Canadian government favours is a rotation amongst nominees from the Canadian uranium industry," Austin wrote. "Under this rotation it is now the turn of Gulf Minerals Canada Limited as a member of the Canadian uranium corporate group to provide one of its members to serve."

Commenting on the request in a memo to Zagnoli in Denver, Ediger wrote:

For the past several months we have steadfastly resisted the blandishments of the Canadian government in respect to this matter. Our position has been that we do not want to increase our legal exposure, particularly since we do not believe that our representation on the operating committee serves our best business interests.

Ediger said that when the matter had been raised in London by MacNabb, "I once more told him that 'in addition to our potential exposure under U.S. antitrust legislation, I did not want to participate in the cutting of my own throat.' " Ediger continued in his memo:

We have continuously objected to the existence of the 'uranium club' and Canada's participation in it. However, in fairness it appears to have resulted in a new degree of market stability and higher prices, which should ensure the more orderly development of reserves and long-term surety of supply for the nuclear electric power plants of the world. The Canadian government appears determined to continue participating in the international arrangements, and with the current climate of economic nationalism I believe we should accede to their request . . . I feel it is going to be increasingly more difficult to maintain the co-operation and understanding we have received from the Canadian government in the past if we do not comply with Mr. Austin's request.

Gregg and Runnalls did join the operating committee, and one of the first meetings they attended in that capacity was in Johannesburg at the end of January, 1974. The Johannesburg meeting set the cartel's third price schedule, with an increase this time of $1.34 per pound. Ottawa once again confirmed the cartel arrangement with another directive to the Atomic Energy Control Board to boost Canada's export prices, to a level 30 cents per pound less than that set by the cartel. But by this time it was becoming increasingly clear that the cartel's prices were being overtaken by increasing prices caused by other factors, and the effectiveness of the cartel was nearly at an end.

A contentious issue at the Johannesburg meeting involved a

sale of uranium by Denison to Japan under a long-term price agreement that violated rules agreed to by the cartel in London the previous October, and another sale by Rio Tinto-Zinc to Spain that should, under the club rules, have gone to the Canadian producers.

Gregg later testified about the ruckus at the Johannesburg meeting in a deposition in connection with a law suit related to the cartel. The action that the other cartel members wanted to take because of the infraction of the rules by Denison "caused a great deal of debate, a great deal of anger, consternation and so forth in the Canadian camp," Gregg testified. "[T]here was going to be a very severe penalty assessed to Canada. Now to Canada, not Denison, to Canada, as a result of that." Denison had broken the club rules, and all the Canadian producers would be made to pay for the infraction.

> So Dr. Runnalls and I, at the end of each day of the operating committee meeting, would carry all this debate back, and the Canadian producers would hold a small Canadian producers' meeting in someone's hotel room and we would go for hours and hours discussing everything that had been said that day . . . about what the penalty was going to be and what bad guys Denison were, and on and on. And finally, the Canadian position that evolved was that, well, we are not going to accept any penalty right now. We will wait until we get back home and can debate it in more quiet circumstances.

The second issue was "an under-the-table" purchase of uranium by a Spanish company from RTZ, which Gregg said had been "engineered" by Mazel without the knowledge of the other members of the club.

Gregg testified in his deposition that Mazel

> tried to cover it up and he denied having done it, and then lied about it and covered up the facts of it. And he was examined at great length by all of us, and it got quite rancorous and almost physical at several points . . . it was considered by the members to be a very, very underhanded type of thing.

Gregg testified that the RTZ sale to Spain was "very, very

sizeable." It should have gone to the Canadian producers, "which would have put three or four of us in Canada – had we gotten all the contracts – in a very good position. We felt that Mazel's action had hurt us pretty badly."

"We, again, just as was the case with Denison, we discussed all manner of penalties that would be imposed against RTZ, and we even discussed kicking Mazel out of the whole affair." Mazel's response "ranged all the way from denial to lying to anger to striking back at Canada for having permitted the Denison deal." The result, according to Gregg, was that "several senior Canadian people" spoke to RTZ's managing director Roy Wright, and Mazel was transferred to Brazil.

In Gregg's view, the cartel "was certainly effective through the Johannesburg meeting of January of '74. I personally felt that it was losing its reason for being and was losing a certain amount of cohesiveness by the time of the April '74 meeting in France." One of the things that would have been essential to maintaining the cohesiveness of the cartel, according to Gregg, "would be getting RTZ and the South Africans to agree not to undercut everyone else."

The cartel held a few more meetings throughout 1974 and into 1975, but rapidly rising prices show how useless it was becoming. The cartel set its last price schedule in January, 1974. Five months later, prices being quoted for uranium sales were 25 per cent higher than the cartel's price schedule; in another four months, the market price was 60 per cent more than the cartel had set.

It was because of this that some observers viewed the cartel as little more than a joke. George White, president of the Nuclear Exchange Corporation, has said that he found the cartel amusing. Testifying as an expert witness called by a U.S. Congressional sub-committee, White described his assessment of the effectiveness of the cartel:

> I know they wouldn't appreciate this, but we felt they were pretty humorous. [White explained that] what would happen is that they would get together and they would decide on a new price. They would always be trying to catch up with our market. By the time they got started – you know, it takes a long time for an organization like this to do anything, because they were basically govern-

ment meetings . . . By the time they got around to making quotations . . . they were behind us again.

THE BOYCOTT OF WESTINGHOUSE

Possibly the clearest statement of planned, illegal antitrust activities of the cartel records relates to talk about boycotting Westinghouse and eliminating it as a source of competition in the uranium market.

From a memo reporting a meeting of Australian members of the uranium cartel:

> sales to middlemen, such as reactor manufacturers, eg., Westinghouse, General Electric, was to be discouraged and . . . any quotations given were to be 15 cents per pound higher than for equivalent sales to utilities.

From the minutes of a meeting of Canadian uranium producers in Ottawa, September 21, 1972:

> There followed a general discussion of the impact of Westinghouse bidding in Europe. It was believed that the maximum amount of uranium available in Westinghouse at the moment was 3,000 tons . . . considerably less than that required to fill the SSPB (Swedish State Power Board) order, for example. Some members thought that Westinghouse should be approached directly, whereas other views were that it would be a dangerous move. The consensus finally reached was that if the club was to survive as a viable entity, it would be necessary to delineate where the competition was and the nature of its strength, as a prelude to eliminating it once and for all.

From a memo, March 1, 1973, by Donald Hunter of General Atomic, a subsidiary of Gulf Oil Corporation:

> We have learned that Westinghouse has submitted a joint venture with Queensland Mines for approval of the Australian government. If this arrangement is approved, Westinghouse will be provided with up to two million pounds per year from 1975 to 1980, and 600,000 pounds per year post-1980 from Nabarlek plus additional quantities which may be found as a result of exploration at a

price approximately 40 cents per pound below the existing world market price. The proposed venture is approximately three months away from fruition and if it develops would provide Westinghouse with a potential source for U.S. reactor sales. [General Atomic was also then in the business of building and selling nuclear power reactors.] It would also provide a source for their substantial foreign shortage. We will work with GMCL to try to put pressure on the Australians to block the proposed arrangement.

The Australians hardly needed any urging from Gulf to try to block the Westinghouse venture, and there are suggestions that it had already been rejected by the Australian government long before Hunter wrote his memo.

Queensland Mines was a small Australian firm which owned the rich Nabarlek uranium deposit in northern Australia plus a 4,000-square mile exploration concession, but not much cash. It needed money to develop a mine and mill at its ore deposit, and to conduct further exploration on its concession in the limited time available before it would have to turn half of its concession back to the government. It had already received a loan of 3.5 million Australian dollars from the Australian government, but that was just a tiny fraction of what it needed. Queensland Mines proposed to farm out an interest in its Nabarlek holdings to Westinghouse in return for the required investment and exploration capital.

In July, 1972 – eight months before Hunter wrote his memo – the board of directors of Queensland met to review the proposed deal with Westinghouse. A representative of the government agency that had provided the loan to Queensland attended the meeting, and tipped off Westinghouse about what happened. A Westinghouse memo reported that the board "spent the whole day reviewing the Westinghouse offer. The board called Canberra many times. We don't know who was called. Our informant figures that the conclusion of the phone calls was that the Australian government would not allow Westinghouse (a middleman) to buy the Queensland output."

The following month, the Australian Producers Forum, representing six firms (Western Mining Corporation, Noranda Australia, Queensland Mines, Electrolytic Zinc, Pancontinental Mining, and Peko-Wallsend Ltd.) that each had large new uranium deposits in northern Australia, which they hoped to place into production, put more pressure on the Australian government to block out newcomers. These were the firms that had just elbowed their way into the cartel by threatening to dump low-cost uranium onto the market, and had forced the existing uranium producers reluctantly to move over and make room for them at the table. Now that they had got to the table, they were mouthing the same arguments that had earlier been applied against them, that the development of new mines (other than their own) should be delayed until the market improved.

"The Australian government has asked for the Australian producers to come to an arrangement which will increase orderly marketing of uranium and will maintain the price of uranium at a reasonable level during the market surplus," John Proud, chairman of the Australian Uranium Producers Forum, wrote to Reginald Swartz, Minister of National Development, on August 21, 1972. "The six companies which presently intend to produce uranium in Australia . . . are now parties to an arrangement which would meet the government's wishes . . . The greatest danger to maintaining the world marketing arrangement [i.e., the cartel] while there is a market surplus is that further substantial uranium deposits may be discovered and brought into production . . . by companies not a party to the arrangement." Proud specifically mentioned the possibility of Queensland Mines completing an arrangement with another firm to develop its exploration concession. He urged the government to "not grant export permits for uranium to other than previously named producers from already known deposits, until such time as the world market situation improves."

In asking for restrictions on the development of new Australian uranium mines, the six firms were to get far more than they bargained for. Within six months, Australia had a new government, which not only blocked Westinghouse but also, for some five years, blocked the six Australian firms from proceeding with the planned development of their mines.

As for the implication that the cartel would boycott Westinghouse by refusing to sell it uranium, the statements in the cartel records would have constituted a damning indictment, except for one thing. Few, if any, of the cartel members paid any heed to such suggestions. Evidence at the suit against Westinghouse by the electric power utilities indicates that members of the cartel in 1973 offered to sell to Westinghouse a total of 30 million pounds of uranium, for delivery between 1976 and 1980, at prices from $7 to $11 per pound.

The U.S. embargo did not legally prohibit American firms from buying and importing foreign uranium; it just prevented them from using it. A U.S. utility could contract for future purchase of foreign uranium if it were willing to take the risk that it would by then be allowed to use it. Or it could import foreign uranium and hold it in inventory in anticipation that the embargo would be later removed. Not surprisingly, few American utilities were willing to contract for the purchase of foreign uranium until it became clear that they would be allowed to use it. The Atomic Energy Commission announced its proposal in October, 1973 to phase out the embargo, and confirmed this a year later. Prior to 1974, foreign uranium accounted for only 4 per cent of the supplies contracted for purchase by U.S. utilities. In 1974, U.S. utilities contracted for the purchase of 33,000 tons of foreign uranium, and by mid-1977, 14 per cent of their purchase commitments was from non-American sources. Westinghouse, in 1973, was short of uranium supplies to meet its future contract commitments, not only to U.S. utilities but also to overseas utilities, and was thus in a better position than most American buyers to make use of non-U.S. uranium.

(Urangesellschaft offered Westinghouse 1 million pounds; Gulf's General Atomic offered 2 million pounds; Gulf Minerals Canada, 5 million pounds; Nufcor, 15 million pounds; Eldorado, 7 million pounds. The large offer from Nufcor was made in August, at a price of $8.13 a pound rising to $11.04 for deliveries during the period 1976-1985. Less than three months later, when the Tennessee Valley Authority sought long-term uranium purchase contracts, the best prices it could get were in a range of $12 to $16 a pound. In 1974, Eldorado offered Westinghouse another 5 million pounds, for delivery over a 10-year period at a starting price of $8.50 a pound.)

The attitude which seemed to prevail within the cartel was that whatever rules or suggestions were agreed upon should be strictly observed – by other members.

THE CONSPIRACY AT OAK BROOK

In a suit later filed against twenty-nine uranium producers, Westinghouse charged that members of the cartel conspired with American uranium producers to extend the cartel pricing into the United States and "undertook . . . to raise prices in the United States above prevailing competitive levels." The allegation by Westinghouse was that the American producers agreed not to oppose the removal of the U.S. embargo on the use of foreign uranium in American reactors, in exchange for an undertaking by the foreign producers that they would not sell into the U.S. market at low prices.

Westinghouse charged that the U.S. producers knew that the Atomic Energy Commission embargo "was unlikely to be lifted without the approval or at least the acquiescence of the major United States producers of uranium." Thus, according to Westinghouse, the foreign producers "commenced a series of meetings and communications with the major U.S. uranium producers" during which "the foreign defendants and their co-conspirators advised the U.S. producers of the agreements which the participants in the cartel reached from time to time and invited the co-operation, agreement and acquiescence of the U.S. producers in furtherance of the goals of the cartel and the combinations and conspiracies."

The key meeting at which this conspiracy is alleged to have been hatched involved members of a sub-committee of the U.S. Atomic Industrial Forum, an industrial association comprising uranium miners, manufacturers of reactors and other nuclear power equipment and electric power utilities, and representatives from the Rio Tinto-Zinc organization.

Early in 1973 there was increasing speculation within the nuclear power industry as to when the AEC uranium import embargo might be lifted, and conflicting views as to whether it should be lifted. The Atomic Industrial Forum appointed an ad hoc committee charged with the task of formulating a position which the AIF could then advance in anticipated hearings on the question by the Atomic Energy Commission. Chairman of the ad hoc committee was Robert Adams, president of Western Nuclear Corporation. Adams could be expected to be favourably disposed toward lifting the embargo. In the public hearings held by the Congressional Joint Committee before the embargo was imposed in 1964, Adams was the only American uranium producer to testify that the protection was not required, that if the United States was going to compete in foreign markets for sales of nuclear power reactors it ought also be prepared to compete with foreign uranium.

The crucial meeting was held at the annual conference of the Atomic Industrial Forum, at Oak Brook, Illinois. There were some 200 delegates at the conference, from mining companies, power utilities, manufacturers, the Atomic Energy Commission, and from the United States, Canada, Great Britain, France, Australia, and Japan. But it was at a much smaller meeting held by the ad hoc committee, at 10:00 a.m. on March 26, 1973, in room 601 at Stouffer's Oak Brook Inn where the plot was allegedly hatched. There were eight people present: five from U.S. uranium mining companies, including Ralph Stewart of Pioneer Nuclear; E. D. J. Stewart of Pioneer Mining; William Bush of United Nuclear; and Robert Adams; Emmanuel Gordon, a staff member of the AIF; Alan Lowell from Rio Algom; and two from RTZ, Miss Frances Millett and Peter Daniel.

The representatives of the non-American producers on the ad hoc committee felt that "they should have some part of the U.S. market at an early date so as they wouldn't have to close down all their operations," Adams later testified. "[T]he American producers were somewhat sympathetic to that view."

Shortly after the Oak Brook meeting, on April 12, Louis Mazel wrote to Adams to express his appreciation "that you were able to invite members of our staff as non-American producers to attend your ad hoc committee . . . [W]e fully agree with your suggestion that in 1980 about 30 per cent of U.S. requirements can be fulfilled under a quota system from non U.S. sources," adding, however, that imports be permitted to start sooner, with a suggested quota of 5 per cent for 1977, building up from there.

In his letter to Adams, Mazel provided an

> example of how we operate the world market concept . . .
> In this context I would like to emphasize that it is certainly not our idea nor the idea of any other non U.S. producer to sell into the U.S. market at low prices. All of us would really like to maximise our profits and are therefore very much more interested in U.S. prices than in non U.S. prices.

The "world market concept" referred to by Mazel is a method used to sell uranium under long-term contract, with the price to be determined prior to each year's deliveries by reference to the prevailing world market price. The catch, it has been alleged, is that the prevailing world market price was rigged by the cartel.

The Atomic Energy Commission did propose, in late-1973, that the embargo be lifted in stages, starting in 1977. Following public hearings, this proposal was confirmed in late 1974.

Whether the Atomic Industrial Forum and the ad hoc committee that met in room 601 of Stouffer's Oak Brook Inn had any influence on the removal of the embargo is open to question. The ad hoc committee felt the embargo should be phased out. But within the entire Atomic Industrial Forum, according to Adams's later testimony, "we did not have unanimity." As a result, the only recommendation that the AIF came up with, was that the Joint Congressional Committee on Atomic Energy should hold hearings on the question "for expression of views of all interested parties."

It is up to the courts to determine whether cartel members conspired with American producers to illegally raise American uranium prices. But on the face of it, there is something incongruous about a conspiracy to restrict competition by means of removing the restrictions on imports. And American producers hardly needed any help from the world cartel in restraining competition. They already had a monopoly on most of the world's market for uranium.

THE UNKEPT SECRET

One of the essential characteristics of a conspiracy is that it is secret. Members of the uranium cartel kept repeating how urgent it was to keep their arrangement a matter of great secrecy, and there was at least one suggestion that they ought to deny that any arrangement at all existed. But if that was truly the intent, the cartel members must have been blabbermouths, as unable to keep secrets as they were to refrain from undercutting one another from time to time.

There never was any secret that a cartel was formed by the uranium producers and the governments of Canada, Australia, France, and South Africa. Only the details of the arrangements agreed to by the cartel were missing. And even some of these leaked out, to the cartel's arch-rival, the Westinghouse Electric Corporation.

Part of the lack of secrecy seemed to be due to the government of Canada. Ottawa appeared to have a compulsion to keep Washington informed about what was happening. And what it did not state explicitly, it implied readily enough.

Prior to the formation – as previously reported – Ottawa informed Washington about the first meeting to organize the cartel at Paris in February, 1972, including who was going to be there and what was going to be discussed.

Following the initial meeting, Ottawa sent a 500-word summary to both the U.S. Department of State and the U.S. Atomic Energy Commission outlining the topics discussed at the meeting of the government representatives, including "a general discussion on possible price stabilization mechanism." The summary said that no details were available about the parallel meetings held by the producers "as a result of undertakings given by producers to each other." It added, however: "It was understood that at the producers' meetings such matters as floor prices and market allocation would be reviewed." Price agreements and market sharing are, of course, the essence of a cartel.

Government communiqués were not the only sources of news that a cartel was being formed. The initial meeting was widely, if briefly, reported in newspapers such as the *Wall Street Journal*, which said that the talks "suggested moves to co-ordinate uranium production and marketing policies."

The most detailed account was carried by *Nucleonics Week*, a U.S. trade publication that on February 17, 1972, carried a detailed story headlined "Paris uranium meeting fails to make any giant steps toward cartel." The item provided a fairly com-

161

prehensive account of the meeting, including the names of most of those who attended, the initial reluctance to admit the new Australian producers into the proposed club, and the threat by the Australians that they could sabotage the plan because they "would be able to outproduce and undersell everyone else."

Even the U.S. Central Intelligence Agency knew that a cartel was being formed. In a cable to Washington from Paris on March 8 (an excised copy of which was later released under the U.S. Freedom of Information Act), the CIA reported that "there was a brief announcement of a meeting in Paris attended by uranium representatives from South Africa, Canada, France and Australia. While the announcement said nothing about the objectives of the meeting, it is perfectly clear to those in the uranium business that its principal goal was the establishment of a cartel to set prices and market quotas." The CIA, however, had managed to uncover fewer details than those published in *Nucleonics Week*.

The follow-up meeting in Australia of producers and government officials was well reported in the *Financial Times* of London. "Organizing of uranium marketing on a national basis, rather than through individual companies, is understood to have been one of the objectives spelled out at the Paris meeting," the *Financial Times* reported from Canberra.

When the cartel members finally agreed to a price schedule and market allocation plan at their Johannesburg meeting at the end of May, 1972, the news was promptly reported by the Nuclear Exchange Corporation in its monthly report to subscribers. It was described as the "formation of a cartel-like uranium marketing agreement," which would "establish price floors starting at about the $6 level in 1972" (the actual starting price was only $5.40).

When Energy Minister Donald Macdonald issued the first directive to the Atomic Energy Control Board setting uranium export prices and allocations, on August 23, 1972, it did not take the news media long to figure out that Macdonald was, in fact, implementing a cartel. The day after Macdonald's announcement, the Toronto *Globe and Mail* reported that the issuance of the regulations "has increased speculation" that Canada, France, South Africa, and Australia "are moving to

162

carry out a cartel-like arrangement that was worked out in Johannesburg, South Africa, last May 29-30." Similar speculation was reported by the *New York Times*, the *Wall Street Journal*, and *The Guardian* of London, among others.

The U.S. government did not seem upset about the cartel plans, according to reports in both the *Wall Street Journal* and *The Guardian.*

The Guardian reported:

> [A] Nixon Administration source said price increases for uranium produced in Canada and other countries would improve the prospects that the U.S. could sell more of its uranium to buyers abroad, including the Japanese who are negotiating with the U.S. on purchases of enriched uranium to power Japan's nuclear electric generating plant.

The Guardian, in fact, had put its fingers on one of the major limitations in the ability of the cartel to raise uranium prices. The foreign producers could not raise their prices beyond U.S. levels – if, indeed, that high – without attracting competition from American uranium, while still remaining blocked out of the American market.

Right from the start, one of the best-informed sources of what the cartel was up to was Westinghouse. Starting in 1972, Westinghouse's Nuclear Fuels Division, which buys and sells uranium, maintained a file on the cartel. Information was provided from sources in Canada and Australia, and Europe. More than two dozen Westinghouse letters, memos, and Telex messages, introduced years later as evidence in the trial at Richmond, discuss the cartel's activities, where it met, when it met, and the prices that it set.

Westinghouse apparently even gave some thought to joining the cartel, through participation in joint venture uranium mining and exploration projects in Australia. "PKW [Peko-Wallsend Ltd.], activities are one means for Westinghouse to remain a member of the club of companies," one memo states. "Club rules are set by government, yet unless a member disqualifies himself, the government would not force a member from the club by unconstitutional means." In another memo, a Westinghouse representative in Australia advised headquarters in Pittsburgh: "I think it is too early to pull out of Australia and believe some sort of toe-hold should be maintained to legitimize our claim to being an explorer and member of the 'club.' "

WHY URANIUM PRICES SOARED

When the uranium cartel was formed in 1972, the price for non-American uranium was under $5 a pound, and the U.S. price was about $6. Three years later, the world price was about $25, and rising.

What happened?

One of the first things that happened was that plans to develop the big uranium ore deposits in northern Australia were frozen for more than five years.

On August 25, 1972, the Australian government announced it had approved 3,349 tons of uranium export contracts by Mary Kathleen Uranium and Queensland Mines. They were the last Australian uranium export contracts approved until after a further announcement, on August 25, 1977, by Prime Minister Malcolm Fraser that a ban on Australian uranium mining would be lifted. Originally scheduled to start producing in 1975, the first output from these rich deposits was delayed until 1981.

The freeze on Australia's uranium supply followed the election in December, 1972, of Prime Minister Gough Whitlam's Labor Party and the bitter nuclear debate that became one of the most divisive issues in Australia's history. The full impact was not immediately apparent, as the new Australian government initially announced that it would defer the approval of new uranium export contracts "for the time being." But as the delay stretched out and the availability of Australian supplies became highly uncertain by late 1973, it was a major factor in the outlook for the world uranium supply and demand balance, and prices.

It had been expected that before 1980, Australia would become the world's second largest, and lowest-cost uranium producer. Deferral of the Australian production was substantially offset by delays in construction of nuclear power plants, and a sharp drop in the growth rate of world electricity demand, but the effect on prices was still significant.

164

The rise in uranium prices that started in 1975 was actually led by U.S. government actions and policies. The most important of these was a decision by the Atomic Energy Commission requiring U.S. power utilities to enter into long-term, fixed commitments for the enrichment of their uranium at the AEC plants, and to ensure that they had the uranium supplies to meet these commitments. Previously, the utilities had generally contracted for purchase of about three to five years of uranium requirements; now they were pressed into covering their requirements under much longer term contracts with the miners.

In a 1975 analysis of the uranium price rise prepared for Westinghouse by a university economist, James H. Lorie, and a Washington consultant, Celia Star Gody, the authors pointed out that "Inquiries from utilities for long term supplies were reported to have covered only 15,000 tons of materials in 1972, but rose to 150,000 tons in 1973. Kerr-McGee, a larger supplier, reported requests for bids covering 255,000 tons of U_3O_8 in the last half of 1973 and the first half of 1974." This new AEC policy did not change the amount of uranium that would be required – but it did intensify competition for long-term purchase contracts. It was this AEC policy change, according to Lorie and Gody, that provided "an initial impetus toward higher prices."

Another factor was a still further change proposed by the AEC in its uranium enrichment process, reducing the amount of nuclear power plant fuel recovered from natural uranium, the net effect of which would have been to increase the demand for uranium by as much as 20 per cent. While this proposal was later dropped, it was one of the factors bearing on the outlook for uranium supply and demand in the fall of 1973, and thus on prices.

Growing uncertainty about when, or if, government policies would permit depleted uranium from nuclear power plants to be re-processed for the recovery of plutonium was another factor. Plutonium is a suitable fuel for nuclear power plants, and in the early 1970's, it had been anticipated that it would soon supply a substantial portion of these fuel requirements. But plutonium can also be used to make bombs, and there were strong arguments advanced in 1973 that plans for uranium recycling should be cancelled in order to help curb the proliferation of nuclear arms – a policy later adopted by the Carter administration.

"In terms of uranium supply, the incremental U_3O_8 required in the absence of plutonium recycle would, in the face of an already tightening supply situation, certainly lead to further upward movement in the long term price structure," Nuexco reported in its bulletin on October 22, 1973.

Behind all of these factors, according to some authorities, was an even more fundamental cause. The cost of producing uranium, at least in the United States, had risen, and sooner or later price would have to follow cost. During the fifteen-year period to 1970, the price for uranium had been cut nearly in half. At the same time, miners were having to dig more ore for every pound of uranium (an average of 4 pounds per ton in 1970 compared with 5.8 pounds in 1955) and dig it from greater depths. The costs of wages, supplies, and equipment had also risen greatly.

Increased costs, the freeze on Australian production, the move by U.S. utilities to cover more of their uranium requirements with long-term purchase contracts, the delay in plans to produce plutonium, the possibility of a change in operation of the AEC enrichment plants requiring more uranium – all these were factors tending to push up prices, allowing the cartel at its October 8 and 9, 1973, meeting in London to add a dollar a pound to its price schedule.

The price set by the cartel at its London meeting was $6.70 a pound for deliveries made that year, rising to $9.70 a pound for uranium delivered in 1978.

The first indication that prices might be rising faster than the cartel could keep up with, came within weeks of the London meeting. The U.S. goverment-owned Tennessee Valley Authority, the largest electricity producer in the United States, had invited 53 American and foreign uranium producers to submit bids on supplying up to 86 million pounds of uranium over the period 1979 to 1990. Only three bids were received. Urangesellschaft offered uranium at prices to be negotiated. Kerr-McGee Nuclear Corporation and Western Nuclear offered a total of 20 million pounds, at prices between $12 and $16 per pound plus further increases to reflect 100 per cent of the escalation of general prices – about double the prices set by the cartel.*

The fuse that was to set off the world-wide explosion of energy prices was lit two days before the cartel's meeting in London.

On October 6, 1973, Egyptian and Syrian armed forces launched an all-out attack on Israeli-held territory on the east bank of the Suez Canal and in the Golan Heights. The latest Arab-Israeli war was underway.

In support of the political objectives of the war, the Arab oil producing states embargoed oil supplies to selected countries (the United States, the Netherlands, Portugal, South Africa, and Rhodesia), cut back production rates, and boosted oil prices by nearly 400 per cent in four months. Never before in history had the price of a basic raw material risen by so much so fast.

In parts of Europe and Japan, rationing of gasoline and fuel oil was imposed, service stations were closed, Sunday driving was banned, and use of electricity was sharply curtailed. The winter and spring months of 1974 saw U.S. motorists waiting for hours in line-ups at the gasoline stations that weren't closed; highway speed limits cut to 55 m.p.h.; year-round daylight savings time; and coupons printed for a national program of gasoline rationing.

Economists and marketing experts have disagreed in their assessments of whether or not the oil embargo and rise in oil prices contributed to the parallel explosion in uranium prices that started in 1973 and continued into 1977.

---

*The lack of bidding was due in part to the fact that "bidders took exception to the terms and conditions of the bid invitation," Erik Kraven, in charge of TVA's uranium procurement, later testified at the Moss Committee hearings. TVA had experienced the same problem in 1970 when it had sought 27 million pounds of uranium but could get bids on only 11 million pounds, despite the fact that "the uranium market at that time was definitely depressed, with a strong buyer's market." One of the TVA bid conditions which caused Gulf Minerals Canada to decline to make an offer was a requirement that it stipulate that its bid had not been discussed with any other uranium producers. Gulf Minerals' L. T. Gregg told the Moss committee that Gulf Minerals had not discussed with other producers any bids that it made for U.S. sales, but had, of course discussed other bids as a participant in the cartel.

In their study for Westinghouse, James Lorie and Celia Gody concluded that the "most important" of the factors causing the uranium price rise "were the developments in the international petroleum market, which then spread throughout the energy field."* While that was a widely-held view, there were others who have argued that the rise in oil prices contributed very little, if any, to the increase in uranium prices.

Those who argue that the oil price had no effect on uranium prices point out that it takes at least a decade to plan and build a nuclear power plant, so that the rise in the price of other fuels could have no immediate effect in increasing the demand for uranium. Moreover, the increased cost and shortages of oil supplies had still not, by 1980, resulted in any increase in planned nuclear power plant construction in the United States. Thus, according to this thesis, any resulting effect on uranium prices was simply "psychological."

There were, in fact, profound effects on the price of uranium resulting from the actions of the Arab oil producing nations and the Organization of Petroleum Exporting Countries.

Even if the oil crisis did not increase the demand for uranium in the United States, it created a keen awareness by the power utilities about the importance of assuring future uranium supplies for their nuclear power plants, thus providing an additional impetus to enter into long-term purchase contracts.

There were far more compelling effects than this, however. The most important was the decision by France, early in 1974, to launch the world's most ambitious program of nuclear power plant construction, intended to provide 70 per cent of the nation's electric power generation by 1985. It was a program that would soon require investments approaching 10 billion dollars a year. To ensure an adequate supply of uranium for this expanded program, France abruptly stopped further ura-

*Although Westinghouse asserts that the cartel caused uranium prices to rise, this factor is barely mentioned among the many causes listed in the study Lorie and Gody did for Westinghouse. Their only mention of the cartel is contained in a single sentence: "Finally, there have been recurrent reports concerning a uranium 'cartel' or 'club' including Canadian, Australian, French and South African producers." It was not until a month after their study had been completed that the cartel documents were first publicly disclosed.

nium export sales. In 1972, France had a government stockpile of 10,000 tons of uranium, which it was threatening to dump on the market at prices as low as $3 a pound. Two years later, it had decided not to export uranium at any price.

Another effect of the OPEC actions was the withdrawal of South Africa from the uranium export market. The soaring oil prices had sent gold prices soaring. Higher gold prices resulted in South Africa mining lower grade ore. This in turn resulted in a reduction in the amount of uranium produced as a by-product. South Africa withdrew from the uranium export business.

By mid-1974, there was only one country in the free world offering to export uranium: Canada. And even here, there was a reduction in the amount being offered. In 1972, Donald Macdonald had said that Canada's only uranium market was the export market. But in the wake of OPEC's actions, Ottawa foresaw the possibility of an expanding domestic nuclear power industry, and a need to reserve adequate uranium supplies to meet its own needs.

"The world uranium market, which was in desperate straits only a year ago, is rebounding quickly as utilities rush to seek out long-term and secure sources of supply," Macdonald told Canada's provincial premiers at an energy conference in January, 1974. "In the light of this change we are moving to firm up the uranium export policies . . . proven reserves of uranium will be required to be held at all times to meet, at a minimum, the fuelling requirements of Canadian reactors, whether in existence or committed . . . As fuel prices rise, Canadian utilities will be turning more and more to nuclear generation which, especially with the Candu reactor, is better equipped against increases in fuel costs than oil or coal." The net effect of the policies implemented by Ottawa was to withdraw a further 80,000 tons of uranium reserves from the export market.

"[T]he change in the uranium situation from a buyer's to a seller's market has been completed, and the new situation is characterized by rising prices and the reluctance of many producers to make . . . firm offers," Nuexco reported on February 19, 1974.

When the uranium cartel met at Johannesburg nine days

later to set its third and final price schedule, it seemed to be still trying to catch up with the "new situation."

The cartel added from $1.80 to $2.80 per pound to its line of prices. The price was set at $8.50 per pound for uranium delivered in 1974, rising to $12.50 for deliveries in 1978. The new price schedule came into effect in March. Three months later, Nuexco reported that the U.S. spot market price had risen to $10.50 per pound; $14.00 by October; $16.00 by January, 1975; $26.00 by July, and still rising.

Once more the market had zoomed past the cartel, and its effectiveness now was over.

Contemplating the outlook as seen early in May from the offices of Mary Kathleen Uranium in Melbourne, Harald Melouney expressed his thoughts in a brief memo:

> Australia: Due to the present policy of the Labor Government, no company is permitted to enter into new contracts and all companies are keeping out of the market.
>
> South Africa: As a result of the current high prices for gold the mines are operating at a lower cut-off grade which results in a reduced production of U_3O_8. The South African companies have largely withdrawn from the uranium market.
>
> France: Also out of the market.
>
> Canada . . . two opposing forces. One strong force believes that Canada should withdraw from the Producers' Club and arrange uranium sales on a government-to-government basis. The other wishes to remain in the club . . . only one Canadian company, Denison Mines, is quoting for business at the present time.
>
> The supply situation is viewed with such concern by Mr. Roy Wright and others that a special, high-level meeting of the policy committee of the producer's club will be held in London at the end of May.

No report of the May meeting is available, but it can be speculated that the cartel was concerned with two pressing problems: how to meet the anticipated demand from reduced available supplies, and how to keep the price from getting out of line, which would inevitably result in yet another bust.

In September, Robert D. Niniger of the U.S. Atomic Energy

Commission assessed in a memo the same factors that Melouney had examined in May, came to the same conclusion, and added that the usefulness of the cartel had probably passed.

"We have talked to most of the members of the so-called foreign supplier 'cartel,' " Niniger wrote. "It is apparent that they agreed to stop undercutting each other and by 1973 had established some general minimum price level . . . It has obviously had some effect on price, but it is not wholly responsible for the extremely large increases of the past twelve months. The usefulness of the supplier's club has probably now passed."

There was every reason in 1974 for the AEC to conclude that the time had arrived when it would be safe to cautiously and slowly peel back the protection of the temporary uranium import embargo. Demand seemed strong, prices were high, foreign-sourced uranium was limited, and there seemed no risk that lifting the embargo would open the floodgates to a tide of low-cost imports that could damage the domestic producers.

Thus, as had been generally expected, the AEC on October 25, 1974, confirmed its proposal of a year earlier to lift the embargo in stages, permitting imports to provide as much as 10 per cent of U.S. requirements in 1977, the quota gradually increasing until by 1984 there would be no restrictions.

The AEC made it clear, however, that it would continue to have a tender regard for the welfare of the industry it had created, nurtured, and protected for so many years. In announcing the phased removal of the embargo, the AEC stressed that it "will monitor U.S. dependence on foreign uranium supply and will take appropriate measures if it determines that the extent of domestic use of foreign uranium threatens to impair the nation's common defence and security *or the viability of the domestic uranium producing industry.*"

CHAPTER TEN

He Who Sells
What Isn't His'n

He who sells what isn't his'n
Must buy it back, or go to prison.
Anonymous

From the office on the twenty-third floor of the Westinghouse building at Gateway Center, Pittsburgh, there is a spectacular view of the valley where the Monongahela and Allegheny Rivers merge to form the Ohio, at the apex of the business district known as Pittsburgh's "golden triangle." The office is decorated with abstract art, and the motorized glass doors open and close ever so smoothly and silently. It is late 1976, and the office is occupied by Robert F. Kirby, a tanned, lean six-footer who seems youthful for his fifty-seven years. He plays golf with his friend Arnold Palmer, and at home relaxes playing jazz on an enormous Hammond organ in the style of another friend, Lionel Hampton. Kirby has worked for the Westinghouse Electric Corporation since 1946, after serving in the U.S. Navy as an electronics engineer, and has been chairman of the board and chief executive officer since February, 1975.

Kirby had precious little time to sit back and enjoy the view. Since taking command at Westinghouse less than two years before, he had made a good start on resolving some deep-seated problems that had brought the fortunes of America's oldest and second largest maker of electrical equipment to its lowest point in decades. But now the giant, multi-national firm was locked in a legal battle, and fighting for its very survival.

Westinghouse's earnings had been falling dramatically for five years when Kirby took over as chairman: from $3.80 per share in 1969 to $2.06 per share in 1971, and 31 cents per share in 1974. Its misfortunes had been well chronicled in the financial press.

Founded in 1886, Westinghouse in 1976 manufactured some 8,000 products, from light bulbs to giant turbines for some of the largest electrical power plants. More than half of the nuclear electrical plants in operation throughout the world used reactors built by Westinghouse or its licensees.

It had also acquired what the *Wall Street Journal* called "a hodge-podge of unrelated businesses" – radio and television broadcasting; soft drink bottling; a record company that had some smash hits with the Beatles; a watch company; office furniture; land development; sewage treatment plants; mass-produced houses; publication of books and learning materials, and many more. Not all of these were smash hits in the earnings department.

To handle these diverse activities, Westinghouse had 125 separate division managers, each with responsibilities for a particular group of products or services, in both United States and foreign markets. Sometimes the result, according to *Fortune* magazine, was a lack of co-ordinated effort. When a Westinghouse salesman called on a businessman in Saudi Arabia, *Fortune* reported, "the Saudi reached into his desk drawer and drew out the business cards of twenty-four other Westinghouse salesmen. Spreading them on his desk, the Saudi exasperatedly inquired: 'Who speaks for Westinghouse?' "

With profits skidding, the 125 Westinghouse division managers were also under the gun to produce immediate results, often without much regard to the long-term effects. A Westinghouse vice-president, A. P. Zechella, is quoted as stating that a Westinghouse manager is "measured on his return on investment. The average life of a unit manager is three years. He's not concerned about how the product might do ten years from now."

Joseph C. Rengel, Westinghouse vice-president in charge of Nuclear Energy Systems, in later court testimony, suggested that the time frame was even shorter. "I don't look at anything longer than a year or a year and a half as being anything more than we could handle," Rengel stated. "I have enough short-term problems that take my time completely, and I don't spend much time on the long-term aspects of the business."

By late 1976, Westinghouse was well on its way to solving many of these problems. Under Kirby's direction, some of the money-losing divisions had been sold; changes were being made in the management structure to improve long-term planning and co-ordination of effort; and profits were climbing back from the low point of 1974.

Sometimes though, while an earlier problem might have been solved, its effects linger on much longer, creating new problems, as in the case of the uranium problem. To fuel the nuclear reactors it had sold (and to help sell them), Westinghouse had contracted to provide electric power utilities with large volumes of uranium at fixed prices, but had failed to make arrangements to obtain this material. To buy these supplies at prices prevailing in 1976 would result in Westinghouse suffering a loss of billions of dollars. Now it was being sued by the power companies for failure to deliver the uranium at contracted prices. Unless this problem could somehow be resolved, Westinghouse could be bankrupt.

One possible escape for Westinghouse would be to establish that its problems in fulfilling its uranium delivery contracts had resulted from an illegal price conspiracy by uranium producers. This was exactly the charge that Westinghouse brought that year in suits against twenty-nine uranium producers, at the time that it was being sued by the electric utilities. If it could make the charges against the uranium producers stick in court, Westinghouse might be able to recover any loss resulting from its supply shortfall and the suits brought by the utilities. It might, in fact, even wind up with a very large profit, under the triple damage award provisions of U.S. antitrust legislation.

From his office in the Gateway Center, Robert Kirby had no way of knowing, in late 1976, whether the legal battle would ultimately lead Westinghouse into liquidation, or a windfall profit of billions of dollars.

One thing he did know, though, was the seriousness of antitrust charges. Westinghouse itself had been found guilty of participating in a price fixing conspiracy in the mid-1950's, involving what was then the largest antitrust case brought before a U.S. court.

174

In 1961, Westinghouse, General Electric, and twenty-seven other firms were found guilty of having conspired to fix prices, rig bids, and divide markets over a period of at least eight years, involving some $15 billion in sales of electrical equipment. Seven corporate officials were sentenced to jail, and twenty-four others received suspended jail sentences. Fines totalled $1,924,500.00, including $372,500.00 against Westinghouse and $437,500.00 against General Electric.

"This is a shocking indictment of a vast section of our economy, for what is really at stake here is the survival of the kind of economy under which this country has grown great, the free-enterprise system," Judge J. Callen Ganey declared in handing down the sentences.

Despite the court's findings, Kirby continued to believe that Westinghouse and General Electric were not guilty, that the penalties Westinghouse had to pay resulted in its providing faulty equipment to power utilities, and that it was thus the consumers who had to pay in the end.

Kirby's views on the electric price-fixing conspiracy were later expressed in his testimony during the trial of the suits brought against Westinghouse by the power utilities:

> In the electrical price fixing case, settlements were made which cost the people that were involved huge sums of money . . . as a result of that, from the Westinghouse standpoint, we were seriously hurt as far as putting in the sort of plant and test equipment and so forth through a change in size of turbine generators, for example. Subsequently, most of the vendors had difficulty with that equipment. They were not as reliable as they should be. Consequently, it eventually cost the utilities a great deal of money.

Kirby said he had "read a great deal about" the case and had "talked to the people who were involved. I believe if you go through that process, you will find that the conclusion was that Westinghouse and GE were not guilty; yet we wound up paying gigantic sums of money."

Kirby had quite a different view about the alleged price conspiracy by the uranium producers, however.

Less than a dozen blocks across town from Gateway Center is the headquarters of Gulf Oil Corporation. If Westinghouse were to collect any enormous sums from its law suit against the uranium producers, it was here that the burden would fall the heaviest. Gulf was the most exposed, because, through its Canadian subsidiary, it was the largest firm that had participated in the cartel, the only U.S. firm that was an active member, and because Westinghouse would almost certainly find it more difficult to collect any judgements against foreign members of the cartel.

"This was one of the massive rip-offs of all time," Kirby has been quoted as saying about the alleged uranium price conspiracy. "And from what I have seen, it was directed from Pittsburgh."

WESTINGHOUSE DEFAULTS

On Friday, September 5, 1975, Westinghouse officials telephoned twenty-seven utilities with which it had contracted to supply uranium, arranging appointments for the following Monday. On Monday, the Westinghouse people showed up at the offices of the utility companies throughout the United States, as well as three in Sweden, with surprise notifications that Westinghouse would not fulfil its uranium supply contracts.

In its notifications, Westinghouse set out that it had contract commitments of nearly 80 million pounds, and a contracted supply of only 15 million pounds, or 65 million pounds short. A court was later to rule that under a disputed contract, Westinghouse owed an additional 7 million pounds, which brought the shortfall to a total of 71.8 million pounds, equal to 2 years of total U.S. uranium production.

Westinghouse had contracted to supply this uranium at an average price of about $10 a pound. The market price at the time the utilities were notified was about $25 a pound. The problem was to get worse. After the notifications had been received, the utilities scrambled to purchase from other sources the uranium they had expected to receive from Westinghouse. This helped drive the price up higher. Within three months, the price had increased to $35 a pound; $41 a pound by mid-1976, and a peak of about $44 a pound. At the peak price, the shortfall represented a potential loss of nearly $2.5 billion

176

for Westinghouse, more than the entire equity owned by the company's shareholders. (The price, however, was later to settle back, to a level of about $25 a pound in 1981.)

In its notifications to the utilities, Westinghouse claimed that it was legally excused from delivering the uranium at contracted prices because it would be "commercially impractical." Westinghouse proposed a settlement to the utilities, whereby it would, in effect, ration out among the utilities its 15 million pounds of uranium in inventory and would also provide some 50 million pounds, which Westinghouse proposed to produce from its own reserves, but at much higher prices than stipulated in the contracts.

The Westinghouse position was that it was excused from providing the uranium at contracted prices under the provisions of section 2-615 of the Uniform Commercial Code. A Westinghouse vice-president was later to refer in a memo to the company's action as "the 2-615 caper."

Section 2-615 of the Uniform Commercial Code "excuses a seller from delivery of goods contracted for, when his performance has become commercially impracticable because of unforeseen supervening circumstances not within the contemplation of the parties at the time of contracting."

An official comment attached to this section of the code declares:

> Increased cost alone does not excuse performance unless the rise in cost is due to some unforeseen contingency which alters the essential nature of the performance. Neither is a rise nor a collapse in the market itself a justification, for that is exactly the type of business risk which business contracts made at fixed prices are intended to cover. But a severe shortage of raw materials or of supplies due to a contingency such as war, embargo, local crop failure, unforeseen shutdown of major sources of supply or the like, which either causes a marked increase in the cost or altogether prevents the seller from securing supplies necessary to this performance is within the contemplation of this section.

Another official comment states:

There is no excuse under this section, however, unless the seller has employed all due measures to assure himself that his source will not fail.

The uranium Westinghouse proposed to provide in lieu of contracted deliveries was to be produced by means of new technology. Three sources were envisioned. Solution mining of a uranium deposit held by Westinghouse subsidiary Wyoming Mineral Corporation at Bruni, Texas, would be the main source. Instead of conventional mining, a water and chemical solution would be pumped down wells into the underground deposit, pumped back to the surface, and the uranium extracted. A second source involved producing uranium as a by-product of phosphate production. And a third potential source involved the acid leaching of uranium present in minute amounts in the tailings from copper mines.

Westinghouse offered to provide 50 million pounds of uranium to the utilities from these sources, for the cost of production. As part of the offer, it also proposed to sell to the utilities new uranium reserves, which Westinghouse might find and develop, these later volumes to be sold 50 per cent at cost and 50 per cent at market price.

If accepted by the utilities, the offer would have enabled Westinghouse to avoid any loss under its contract commitments, and possibly even earn a substantial profit from its future uranium production. The trouble with the proposal, as far as the utilities were concerned, was that the cost of uranium Westinghouse offered would be about double the price at which Westinghouse had contracted to deliver the 72 million pounds.

None of the utilities with fixed price contracts (although even the fixed price contracts had some provision for cost escalation), accepted either the Westinghouse argument that it was legally excused from meeting its obligations, or the Westinghouse offer of alternative higher cost supplies.

Seventeen suits were brought against Westinghouse for its failure to perform. Three of the suits by utilities with head offices in Pittsburgh – Duquesne Light Company, Ohio Edison Company, and the Pennsylvania Power Company – were tried before Pennsylvania State Court Judge I. Martin Wekselman. Three more suits were brought in Sweden by utilities to whom

Westinghouse had contracted to deliver nearly 12 million pounds of uranium. The eleven other suits were consolidated in the U.S. District Court in Richmond, Virginia, before U.S. District Judge Robert Merhige Jr.

The first trial to get underway involved the three suits brought before Judge Wekselman in Pittsburgh, starting in October, 1976, and finishing six months later. Much of the evidence presented at this trial was ruled by Judge Wekselman to be confidential, but was later made public by a U.S. Congressional committee.

The principal trial in the Westinghouse default case was the one in Richmond, Virginia, before Judge Merhige, a diminutive Yankee with a clipped New York twang, a man with a breezy informality who had once played football for Notre Dame.

By the time this trial started in September, 1977, nearly two years had been spent in the discovery process, with lawyers examining millions of pages of documents in search of relevant evidence. As a typical example, Virginia Electric Power Company alone provided an estimated 450,000 pages of documents for inspection by Westinghouse lawyers.

Westinghouse hired 40 lawyers for the case, rented 17,000 square feet of space on 4 floors of an office building in Richmond, installed 10 photo copying machines, and spent a reported $25 million a year in legal fees.

Merhige, at one point during trial, remarked that the lawyers appeared to be challenging the capacity of the paper industry. "They can't cut down trees fast enough for you guys," he said.

During the Richmond trial, Judge Merhige listened to evidence for eighty-six days. Fifty persons testified from the witness stand, and depositions from another one hundred and twenty six people were read into the record. More than 8,500 exhibits were introduced in evidence. The transcript ran to 21,000 pages.

HOW WESTINGHOUSE DUG ITS PIT

The evidence presented at the Richmond trial provides an insight into how Westinghouse got caught owing nearly $2.5 billions worth of uranium. It suggests that the affairs of Westinghouse were about as disorganized and unco-ordinated as those of the cartel.

Part of the problem may have stemmed from the rapid turn-over of Westinghouse people handling the company's uranium business. The Nuclear Fuel Division nominally had the responsibility for the design, manufacture, and marketing of nuclear fuel, including the purchase and resale of uranium. During the five year period from 1970 to 1975, a succession of five different people headed the Nuclear Fuel Division. The "uranium management" section of the Nuclear Fuel Division was specifically responsible for buying uranium and, hope-fully, developing the company's own uranium production. Within the same period, four different people headed the Uranium Management section.

While the Nuclear Fuel Division was responsible for buying and selling uranium, the marketing people in the Water Reac-tor Division were also involved. To help sell the reactors, the Water Reactor Division-Marketing, at times reduced the sales price for uranium – in at least one instance by as much as 70 cents per pound – without first informing those who had to buy the uranium. Uranium Management soon found it had a prob-lem. It was unable to buy uranium at prices as low as it had been sold. If they paid more than the sales price, it would become apparent that Westinghouse was operating its uranium business at a loss. The immediate problem was averted by a simple expedient. For a period of nearly five years, from January 13, 1970 to November 18, 1974, Westinghouse pur-chased no uranium. During the same period, it contracted to sell tens of millions of pounds of uranium.

Selling uranium it did not have represented a sharp change in Westinghouse's initial procedure in this new field. A commer-cial market for uranium did not exist in the United States until 1966, when the Atomic Energy Commission first allowed private firms to purchase, own, and sell uranium. Westing-house quickly emerged as the world's largest non-government purchaser of uranium. For four years, it meticulously main-tained a careful balance between the amount it had contracted to sell and the amount it had contracted to purchase.

In February, 1970, Westinghouse first offered to sell large volumes of uranium that it did not have. In separate proposals to a number of different utilities, Westinghouse offered a total of 15.5 million pounds of uranium. It took a calculated risk that the profit it would earn from fabricating this uranium into fuel bundles for nuclear power plants would exceed any loss that it might sustain as a result of higher than expected prices.

Donald J. Povejsil, then general manager of the Nuclear Fuel Division, spelled out in a memo the calculated business risk in one of these sale offers, involving six million pounds of uranium. Povejsil reckoned that the price Westinghouse might have to pay for the uranium would, at worst, be no more than $1 a pound in excess of the offered price, and that the loss would be more than offset from profits on the fabrication business.

> Assuming no relief from recycle uranium or plutonium, we are taking a risk on something in excess of six million pounds of U_3O_8. Thus we are risking approximately $6,000,000 of unexpected price rise in U_3O_8. The expected margin from . . . the fabrication involved is presently estimated to be about $18 million on an escalated basis. This margin is deemed sufficiently large to justify the risk of unanticipated price rises in U_3O_8 in that period.

None of the uranium which Westinghouse offered in February, 1970, was sold, as a result of which the company did not get into a short position until later. But by February, 1973, Westinghouse was short 34 million pounds of uranium.

Westinghouse seemed to be doing a thriving and profitable business as a commodity broker, buying and selling uranium – as long as it did not worry about the commitments it would face down the road. The 1973 "strategic plan" of the Nuclear Fuel Division notes:

> Our uranium activity to date has been profitable and has helped to sell Westinghouse plants and fuel fabrication . . . From 1968 to 1972 purchase-resale not only significantly assisted in the sale of plants and fabrication . . . but produced 20 million dollars in income before taxes on an average investment of 0.7 million.

While the shortfall mounted, Westinghouse continued to reject opportunities to buy uranium. On January 11, 1973, Stewart Early, one of the Westinghouse people who was to seek favourable purchases of uranium, wrote to his boss, Chris

DeSalvo, head of Uranium Management, reporting that Allied Chemical had offered to sell Westinghouse three to six million pounds of uranium at a per pound price which Early said was "about $1.00 below cartel prices." The offer was not accepted.

Senior management seemed unaware of the problem that was emerging. On March 19, 1973, John F. Simpson, president of Westinghouse's Power Systems Company, told financial analysts at a seminar in New York that Westinghouse had "firm commitments for uranium that match our requirements throughout the terms of all our contracts." In fact, the company was 34 million pounds short.

The short position took a giant leap the following month, when Westinghouse offered 21 million pounds of uranium to 5 utilities, in connection with sales of the company's "standardized nuclear unit power plant systems" – or SNUPPS.

Chris DeSalvo at Uranium Management, worrying about the growing shortfall, wanted the offer of 21 million pounds to the 5 utilities withdrawn. He wrote to Ted Stern (who had headed the Nuclear Fuel Division for sixteen months but was then vice-president of newly created Water Reactor Division), claiming that "our uranium situation requires a serious review of this case." DeSalvo said the offer had been "made prior to our revised policy of not aggressively pursuing uranium sales until our present inventory situation is rebalanced." He said he felt "compelled to make this request in view of my top management concern for our inventory situation."

Tom Ritner, who was in marketing at the Water Reactor Division, did not want to lose the sale of the SNUPPS. He wrote to Stern: "It is the unanimous opinion of WRDM [Water Reactor Division-Marketing] management that our present position could be seriously jeopardized if we made such a major change in our offer as raising uranium prices or withdrawing our uranium quotation." Stern decided to let the offer stand. The sale was made. Westinghouse's shortfall then approached 60 million pounds.

DeSalvo kept looking for opportunities to buy uranium, still hoping to cover the shortfall at less than Westinghouse's sales price. In August, 1973, he wrote to Reginald Worroll of the Nuclear Fuels Corporation in South Africa, inquiring about the possibility of buying 15 million pounds over a 10-year period at a price of around $6.50 a pound. Worroll wrote back saying that the suggested price is "significantly below . . . prevailing market price." DeSalvo responded with another letter to Worroll, saying, "I would concede that the offered price was somewhat low." He did not offer a higher price.

The same month, Stewart Early wrote a memo to another associate in the uranium management section: "W prides itself at being able to buy uranium below the market prices . . . therefore, the expected U price should not be used for the make-buy decision but something less than the expected price . . . most top management have been sold by CAD [Christy A. DeSalvo] on the idea that W can buy more cheaply than anyone else."

Not only was Westinghouse failing to contract for supplies to cover its long-term sales commitments, it also sold uranium from its inventories in order to improve the short-term profits generated by the Nuclear Fuel Division. The division found that its inventory of uranium was more than enough to meet its requirements for a period of three or four years, and by selling some of this "excess" inventory it would realize a profit. In 1972 and 1973, Westinghouse sold 16 million pounds of uranium from its inventories, sales that totalled more than $100 million. The deliberate gamble was that uranium prices would not increase by any significant amount for several years, so that replacement for the supplies sold from inventory could then be purchased at favourable prices.

Walt Dollard, who headed the Nuclear Fuel Division for two years, testified at Richmond on the strategy involved in these inventory sales.

Dollard said that when he took over as manager of the Nuclear Fuel Division in August, 1972, "there was a large inventory of uranium and it looked like there would continue to be a large inventory for some period of time . . . it seemed that the price in the long term would eventually have to go up, but that the present prices looked like what one would expect to have for a period of time until the inventories had worked off." He said that the question that had faced him was: "Would I sell this now with the expectation that five years later I could buy it back at an equivalent price plus interest?" His department "looked about whether or not they could reduce the inventory, and made a conscious decision that if they did they could procure replacement uranium at a price equivalent to what they sold it for, plus interest charges."

It was a disastrous gamble, and one that ignored the advice of Westinghouse's own uranium consultant. Consulting mining engineer, Dr. David A. Robertson of Toronto had been warning Westinghouse for more than four years that uranium prices would increase, and increase rapidly. In a report provided to Westinghouse in February, 1968, Robertson predicted that the United States would "have great difficulty" in supplying its uranium demand at prices equivalent to $25 a pound, in 1968 dollars. In a 1971 report he warned that "demand will exceed supply from presently known reserves in 1975." In yet another report to Westinghouse, in April, 1973, Robertson said: "It remains our conviction that substantial increases in price will occur in the medium term, and we believe that the recent price movements represent the beginning of this trend."

In April, 1974, a senior management committee at Westinghouse ruled that it "endorses a corporation and division policy not to speculate on uranium futures." It was too late – the damage was already done. In any event, the company continued for several more months to sell uranium that it did not have.

Westinghouse chairman Donald Burnham did not learn of the company's uranium shortfall until February 8, 1974, at a meeting of the company's "major projects review committee," comprising senior Westinghouse officials. Even then, it was slow to act. A hand-written note by DeSalvo nearly six months later stated: "NFD [Nuclear Fuels Division] is under instructions from Mr. Burnham not to quote uranium at firm prices to customers without a backup supply."

The Nuclear Fuel Division, at the February 8 meeting with senior management, recommended the best way to meet the company's shortfall in its uranium supplies: "The cornerstone of our preferred strategy is to enter into production through development of new-technology production methods."

Westinghouse was resting its hopes on a slender reed. Since 1969, Westinghouse, through its subsidiary Wyoming Mineral Corporation, had participated with Homestake Mining in a modest joint-venture program to find and develop uranium in the United States. Some uranium had been found, but none had been placed into production. The joint venture with Homestake was terminated in February, 1974. Homestake took the uranium reserves that could be mined by conventional means; Westinghouse took the reserves that would require unconventional mining.

The major deposit acquired by Westinghouse was the uranium in the sandstone deposit at Bruni, Texas, which Westinghouse figured to produce by solution mining. The trouble was that no one really knew whether or not this system would work, and Joe Bach, the mining engineer in charge of Wyoming Mineral, figured it would require two years just to find out.

When Westinghouse got around to trying to produce the Bruni uranium by solution mining, it ran into some problems it had not expected. In earlier work at the site, a number of holes had been drilled into the sandstone deposit. "We found they had forgotten to mark a lot of the holes," Kirby testified at the Richmond trial. "So when we began drilling our holes and started pumping liquid into it, we started finding it coming out of a lot of holes we didn't know existed. Things like this at the beginning really slowed us up a little bit."

Kirby, who had been president of Westinghouse's Industry and Defense Company, was not aware of Westinghouse's uranium shortfall until after he had been appointed vice-chairman of the company in the fall of 1974, an interim step before his appointment the following March as chairman and chief executive officer.

Kirby learned about the shortfall at a briefing for the Westinghouse board of directors in September, when approval was being sought for expenditures to develop some of the new production technology. It was mentioned at this meeting, Kirby testified, that "we had supplies that would carry us out into 1978. This was 1974; so that gave us a four-year period to get all these things together. That seemed like quite a long time." Kirby said that he "felt reasonably confident for a variety of reasons. Price had gone up, but that had been caused, in our opinion at that time by the oil embargo, the OPEC situation and so forth. I felt that prices would start to drop back to a more normal cost-price relationship."

"[W]e were attempting to pick up reserves," Kirby continued

185

in his testimony. "We picked up a few. We had a fairly strong program on it. I even got a few phone calls myself, I think from prospectors. At least they sounded like they were talking from somewhere way out west."

If Kirby was not too concerned about the problem in 1974, there were others in Westinghouse who appeared to be, including John Simpson, president of the Power Systems Company, who called for an examination of unorthodox measures. In a memo to the Nuclear Fuel Department and the newly created Nuclear Energy Systems in July, 1974, Simpson wrote:

> I would like the divisions to examine other alternative approaches to reducing exposure. These include gaining relief from terms of the sales contracts, cancelling the plant and uranium contracts, bringing antitrust suits against the uranium producers, and similar approaches which might be viewed as unorthodox but which may become necessary.

It was the first mention in Westinghouse of possible antitrust action, and – contrary to some other reports – suggests it was not the release of the Mary Kathleen documents in September, 1976, which first turned Westinghouse's thinking along this direction. Two years after Simpson's memo, more than three months before the release of the MKU documents, and five months before it instigated its suit against the producers, Westinghouse advised the U.S. Department of Justice that it had evidence of an international uranium cartel and an illegal price conspiracy involving U.S. producers.

While Simpson sought unorthodox means to escape the uranium shortfall problem, there were others within Westinghouse who appeared to believe that the company was the architect of its own troubles. John Mellor, in Uranium Management, wrote to DeSalvo on June 25, 1974:

> I am very disturbed at our continued offering to sell U_3O_8 in association with plant fabrication, even on a 'cost plus' basis . . .
>
> Our past sales policy where we interposed ourselves between the primary producer and the primary buyer prevented or delayed the rise in uranium prices by eliminating a market transaction at significantly higher

prices. While we have no risk on a cost-plus transaction in itself, the basic effect of our policy is to prevent the formation of a true market. I suggest that it is in our interest to allow a true market to form as soon as possible, albeit at $20 a pound or greater so that producers will be encouraged to explore and install capacity as far as possible, bringing supply into balance with demand for 1978 onwards, with concept of stabilization of prices at more realistic levels.

On November 18, Westinghouse purchased 2 million pounds of uranium from Duke Power Company. It was the first uranium that Westinghouse had contracted for purchase in four years and nine months, and it covered less than 3 per cent of the amount that it was short.

While Westinghouse was later to claim that illegal conspiracies resulted in artificially high prices for uranium, a Westinghouse employee was writing that Westinghouse had created artificially low prices.

Unsuccessful in either buying or producing uranium at prices that matched its contract sales prices, Westinghouse turned its efforts to renegotiating its sales contracts, hoping to get the utilities to pay for the loss that Westinghouse would otherwise face. John Mellor wrote on January 3, 1975:

> Contract renegotiation which removes or limits our liability without risk is so functional a strategy that it deserves the prestige and muscle that can only come from the highest levels of the corporation. All alternate options offer so much risk in corporate investment and can only offer potential limitation of liability that they should receive secondary consideration.

But Westinghouse met with little success in its efforts to renegotiate the sales contracts, and once more the blame was laid squarely on the shoulders of the company. David R. Smith, of the Nuclear Fuels Division, in a memo January 27, 1975, to J. M. Haley, who by this time had succeeded DeSalvo as head of Nuclear Materials and Services, wrote that it was "a time to face facts":

> Reflecting upon our . . . efforts to renegotiate the uranium contracts since initial review meeting in June 11, 1974,

leaves me as well as most others with a somewhat frustrated feeling.

It seems further that much of the frustration is a direct result of trying to avoid the facts, both within all levels of Westinghouse as well as in our trying to dream up strategy that we might be able to 'sell' to our customers. The facts are simply:

(1) Westinghouse sold uranium without having bought it.

(2) The potential cost to Westinghouse of obtaining that uranium either by buying it or producing it is now much higher than the Westinghouse committed sales price.

(3) Chances of the market prices coming down to the Westinghouse committed price levels again are negligible.

(4) The potential dollar exposure to Westinghouse if we were to fulfill these contracts at the committed sales prices is unacceptable for the future well being of Westinghouse as a corporation . . .

The probability that Westinghouse could convince any of our customers to renegotiate . . . would be partly dependent on the degree to which Westinghouse is willing to face the facts and admit the facts to our customers. So long as the customers are not told of the seriousness of the exposure to Westinghouse, they will be more likely to conclude that Westinghouse is only trying to make more profit on existing supplier arrangements or on planned or perceived 'low cost' production. We may, in fact, be hurting our chances of renegotiation of contracts by playing up our new technology approaches and painting glowing stories of lower cost production and broadcasting of 'low cost' reserves . . .

Albert Bethel, appointed vice-president in charge of uranium resources, testified at the Richmond trial on the Westinghouse efforts to renegotiate its uranium sales contracts. During the testimony, Judge Merhige interposed to ask: "By what logic did you reasonably expect them to accept any such renegotiations? . . . Is there any logic to it at all, Mr. Bethel?"

Bethel: "Well, I can't assert it's a highly persuasive logic. I agree, it's a very thin way to attempt to renegotiate, but we didn't find any real good ways to negotiate."

While the efforts to renegotiate the contracts with the utilities were unsuccessful, the uranium management section was just as unsuccessful in its efforts to buy uranium. By this time there was no hope that uranium could be purchased, except at prices higher than it had been sold. But purchasing at a loss would at least have the advantage of limiting the company's loss. Otherwise, there was no telling how much the loss might climb to.

Patrick Ducret, who became manager of uranium supply in 1974, wrote on February 5, 1975:

> Buying some amount of uranium now presents the additional advantage of hedging against the risks that no uranium could be bought precisely at the time we need it. This risk may not be great, but definitely exists . . . Therefore, it would seem that on short-term, at least, some amount of uranium should be purchased in the near future. This results in the certainty of a loss, the amount of which is known . . .

Again on March 6, Ducret almost pleaded: "The uncertainty of uranium prices suggests that Westinghouse reduce the risk by purchasing some fraction of this quantity now."

But right to the end, Westinghouse followed its policy of trying to buy uranium "more cheaply than anyone else," as Stewart Early had phrased it in a memo. By letter dated March 10, 1975, the Atlas Corporation invited Westinghouse and 80 other firms to bid at an auction sale of 1,250,000 pounds of uranium. Raymond Witzke, formerly manager of Nuclear Materials and Services with Westinghouse but then a senior consultant, sought approval for a Westinghouse bid of $19.40 a pound. He was instructed to bid only $16 a pound. The Westinghouse offer was the lowest of all the bids received by Atlas, despite the fact that Westinghouse was then short more than 80 million pounds of uranium.

Possibly part of the problem was that so many memos were being produced within Westinghouse that no one was reading them all, or at least paying enough attention. On the stand in

Richmond, Kirby stated: "In a corporation with 165,000 people in it, we have a lot more writers than we have readers, and this trial has proven it to me."

Lewis Booker, lead counsel for the plaintiffs, asked: "Do you sometimes think you have more writers than thinkers?"

Kirby: "Sometimes."

Reports of Westinghouse's uranium problem were starting to leak out, but in early 1975 there were few outside of the company who realized the full extent of the problem. Kirby was asked about the problem during a presentation to financial analysts in New York on March 27. "We have some exposure at the present time for the period 1984 and 1985," Kirby responded, "but we're working on it quite hard to make sure we are not over-exposed."

The full impact of the problem was laid out to Westinghouse's senior management at a briefing for the major projects review committee on March 31. Walter Dollard, general manager of the Nuclear Fuel Division, told the committee that the loss facing the company could be "staggering."

The following month Westinghouse hired the Chicago law firm of Kirkland and Ellis to examine the legal alternatives that might be available to the company. In June, Kirkland and Ellis "recommended to us that we had full rights under . . . section 2-615, and that they believed we had a sound basis for invoking that," Kirby later testified.

On July 14, Westinghouse issued a news release in response "to inquiries concerning its requirements for delivery of uranium to its utility customers under long-term contracts extending through 1995." The releases said that Westinghouse's ability to meet its contract commitments after 1978 was "difficult to predict." It added that "since it is possible that all legal obligations will be fulfilled without significant impact on future earnings, no provision for loss has been made or is contemplated."

The way in which Westinghouse planned to fulfil "all legal obligations" was to default on the contracts with the argument that it was excused from performance under section 2-615.

There had been suggestions that Westinghouse's default on its sales contracts announced on September 8, and the offer to provide uranium at higher prices from Westinghouse's own production, was really part of a strategy to pressure the utilities into accepting renegotiation of the contracts. Bethel, in a later memo, referred to the "2-615 caper." Three months after Westinghouse had announced its default, George White Jr. of the Nuclear Exchange Corporation, talked to Bethel, and in a memo dated December 12, noted:

"Their announcement and the entire 'commercial impracticability thing' was, as we guessed, the ultimate in a price renegotiation ploy. Bethel hopes and expects to work it out on a commercial rather than legal basis. He said, 'However, we had to use a 2 × 4 between the eyes to get the mule's attention.' "

TRIALS WITH NO END

Neither the trial in Pittsburgh before Judge Wekselman, nor the trial in Richmond before Judge Merhige, produced any definitive findings as to whether or not Westinghouse was legally excused from its obligations, or whether an illegal conspiracy by uranium producers had contributed to the price rise and to Westinghouse's problems.

Rather than hand down firm findings, both judges preferred to see the parties reach settlements, and strenuously urged that such settlements be made.

But the two judges did express some conclusions, in the form of comments from the bench by Judge Wekselman, and a ruling by Judge Merhige without supporting findings of fact or law. Neither judge legally settled the issues, and the two held contradictory views.

Judge Wekselman commented that there was "persuasive evidence" of "a conspiracy among U.S. and foreign producers to fix prices, to allocate markets and to eliminate competition from intermediaries in the uranium market such as Westinghouse." He added that Westinghouse had "introduced extremely persuasive, competent evidence that a number of interrelated contigencies not foreseen by the parties . . . rendered the performance of the asserted contracts commercially impractical."

At the conclusion of the testimony, Judge Wekselman was blunt in suggesting that Westinghouse and the three utilities should settle matters between themselves:

This isn't a case that I or any other judge should have to consider. These so-called captains of industry have shirked their responsibility by failing to resolve their own differences. Consider this as a warning: I am tired of pussy footing and more than that, I am tired of talking to lawyers when other, more powerful men, who have the ultimate power of decision, haven't been here.

Westinghouse chairman Robert Kirby and Duquesne Light chairman John M. Arthur heard the judge's message, loud and clear. Within a matter of weeks, settlements were reached with the three utilities. In the settlements reached after the Pittsburgh trial, Westinghouse agreed to provide cash payments plus equipment, services, and uranium, with a total estimated value of $11.5 million. The actual cost to Westinghouse was estimated at $6 million – about a third as much as it would have cost to supply the uranium at the contracted prices. The settlements reached in the Pittsburgh cases represented only about 1 per cent of the entire volume of uranium in dispute, but they set the pattern for later settlements.

In his final decree approving the settlements, Judge Wekselman stated that: "[T]he fiscal well being and possibly even the survival of one of the world's corporate giants was in jeopardy . . . the future of thousands of jobs was in jeopardy." Wekselman added that he "did not feel it was overstating the seriousness of the case to say that the economy of the Pittsburgh area and even the nation's future energy policies were involved."

As Merhige saw it, there would be no winners in the Richmond case.

If the utilities win, according to the evidence before me, the taxpayers are going to pick up a good part of it. If Westinghouse wins, about 25 million citizens are going to pick up the tab. They are customers that are served by those utilities. So there can be no winners. There can only be losers, and it is going to be you and me and the rest of us.

Where Wekselman had suggested – but not ruled – that Westinghouse was probably legally excused from its contracts, Merhige ruled exactly the opposite on October 30, 1980.

> [T]he court feels constrained to state its decision that Westinghouse did not meet its burden of establishing that it is entitled to excuse from the contractual obligations which the Court finds exists with the plaintiffs, either by reason of section 2-615 of the Uniform Commercial Code or the force majeure clause in its contracts with the plaintiffs.

Merhige added that "there are sound reasons for not issuing . . . supporting findings of fact and conclusions of law at this time." He said it would be "more orderly to issue a single unified set at the close of the relief phase of the litigation," and if his findings were issued at that time "they may well result in standing in the way of these cases ending, as I think they ought to end, in settlement."

In a word, Westinghouse had lost. But for the utilities, it was not a complete victory. Merhige had previously warned that if anyone thought they would "win" in a absolute sense of the word, they were "plain damn fools." And he confirmed that warning:

> The plaintiffs should not be misled by today's holding to the effect that Westinghouse is not excused from its contractual obligations. If anything, the Court is disposed to believe that, just as Westinghouse is not entitled to excuse from its contractual obligations, the plaintiffs aren't entitled to anything near the full measure of their prayers for relief.

Merhige concluded by once more urging the parties to settle.

> . . . these are cases which I think everybody admits should be settled if at all possible, in the public interest, and they are really business problems, and should be settled as business problems by businessmen, as I have been urging from the very first.

After nearly six years and legal costs of probably more than one hundred million dollars, the last of the seventeen suits brought by the utilities against Westinghouse was settled early in 1981, on terms approved by the courts. The settlements cost Westinghouse more than $950 million, which would be reduced to about $500 million after allowing for the effect on income taxes payable by the company. This does not include Westinghouse's legal costs.

The most trenchant coment on the whole episode came from Bill Gilchrist, who had retired as president of Eldorado in 1975 to set up shop as a uranium consultant. One of his first clients was Westinghouse. Gilchrist was the only Canadian to testify in U.S. proceedings involving the cartel. His deposition, taken at Westinghouse's initiative, was made in Toronto six days before the government of Canada passed the law which made it illegal for any Canadian to publicly talk about the affairs of the cartel.

In his deposition, Gilchrist was highly critical of Westinghouse for allowing itself to get caught short, and even more critical of the utilities for relying on Westinghouse for their uranium supplies.

"Westinghouse has been completely stupid – and the utilities have been even more so," Gilchrist said. "It is the most stupid performance in the history of American commercial life."

CHAPTER ELEVEN

What
The Grand Jury
Discovered

THE TROUBLES OF THE TRUST BUSTERS

The investigators in the antitrust division of the U.S. Department of Justice who monitor the world of business for signs of collusion, appeared to be nearly the last to learn of the existence of the uranium cartel. The Department of State and the Atomic Energy Commission had been well informed about the cartel since its inception in 1972; the Central Intelligence Agency had reported on the plans to form a cartel; and there had been repeated news stories about the cartel in the *New York Times*, the *Wall Street Journal*, the Toronto *Globe and Mail*, *The Guardian* of London, and other papers. Apparently the first that the Justice investigators learned of the cartel was from an article in the January, 1975, issue of *Forbes* magazine, which ominously warned that U.S. power utilities soon "may be at the mercy of a uranium OPEC." Two months later, the staff attorneys obtained permission to start a preliminary investigation, and by June the Justice Department notified the State Department that it intended to send letters to three foreign uranium firms – Rio Algom Limited, Denison Mines, and Rio Tinto-Zinc – requesting information and documents on a voluntary basis.

A State Department memo, bearing the imprimatur of Henry Kissinger, was sent on June 12 to U.S. embassies in Ottawa, Canberra, Paris, London, and Pretoria, instructing the embassies to advise the governments of the pending investigation, and to relay to Washington any "significant reaction." A week later, the U.S. embassy in Ottawa cabled Washington that the reaction of the Canadian government was "rather strange";

that Ottawa would prefer the Justice Department to direct its inquiries to Canadian government officials and not contact the companies directly; and that it would prefer all further communication on this matter to be made orally. There were further discussions between Justice and State. The letters seeking information from the three companies were not sent.

The investigation dragged on. In November, the antitrust lawyers assigned to the case – headed by Forrest Bannon – sought approval to send civil investigative demands to all leading foreign uranium producers. These would not be voluntary requests for information but demands. The Justice Department's office of operations scotched that idea. By late February, 1976, a year after the inquiry started, Justice again notified State that it intended to send letters with voluntary information requests to Rio Algom, Denison, and RTZ.

A week later, Julius Katz, an Assistant Secretary in the State Department, in charge of the Bureau of Economic and Business Affairs, visited Assistant Attorney General Thomas Kauper to talk about the investigation. Four years later, a Justice Department lawyer wrote that at this meeting "Katz urged that we close the investigation." That State was opposed to the investigation, and that Justice Department was determined to proceed, was in any event, made clear in a Justice Department memo to Katz on March 26, 1976:

> On March 2 you met with Assistant Attorney General Thomas Kauper to discuss our concern over the intention of the Department of Justice to extend the reach of its antitrust investigation of the uranium industry to foreign producers. It was agreed at that meeting that Justice would gather further information on the imports into the U.S. before making a decision on the future conduct of this investigation.

The memo reported that the Justice Department had gathered the uranium import data, had decided to proceed with the investigation, did not feel that "any further consultation on this matter is necessary," and proposed to send letters to the three foreign firms on March 31.

On that date, another cable was sent by Kissinger to the U.S. embassies in Ottawa, Paris, and London for relay to the respective governments. The cable noted that the letters had not been sent the previous year "following a series of discussions," but this time they were going out.

"The Department has expressed its concern to Justice that the investigation of foreign producers is questionable," the cable continued. "This view is based on the U.S. embargo on uranium imports which exists through 1977 . . . raising the question as to what effect, if any, do activities of foreign producers have on U.S. commerce." Justice, however, had compiled information which "reveals a probable level of future imports which could affect U.S. commerce." The cable concluded: "Request advise of any significant reactions."

What the reactions of Canadian and British governments were can only be guessed, but the letters failed to produce any voluntary information from the companies. They simply forwarded the requests from the Justice Department to their governments, and the investigation was once more stalled.

The first break in the case apparently came a few weeks later, from Westinghouse.

A later summary of a 1,000 page "fact memorandum," which had been prepared by Justic Department lawyers, records this break:

> May 5, 1976. FM [fact memorandum] states this was a big break in investigation when Westinghouse counsel told Kauper that they had evidence of an international cartel. It was also alleged that while it would be extremely difficult to prove, the domestic uranium producers had formed a conspiracy either on their own, or in concert with the international cartel.

Armed with this big break, the Justice Department on June 16, issued subpoenas to forty-five firms in the United States and abroad, which were involved, one way or another, in the uranium business.

The subpoena arrived in Pittsburgh two days later, where Gulf Oil counsel Frank O'Hara reported in a memo:

> This subpoena requires production of all documents, memoranda, correspondence, tabulations and other records of any sort relating to the exploration, development, mining, milling or other production, sale, distribution or

trading of uranium in the United States and in foreign countries during the period of January 1, 1971 to June 16, 1976.

It would comprise the largest collection of paper related to uranium ever collected in one spot. The subpoenaed companies were given less than two months – until August 4 – to produce the material to the grand jury.

In Ottawa, the Canadian government apparently called a meeting with those firms in Canada that had been subpoenaed – Gulf Minerals Canada, Rio Algom, Denison Mines, Uranerz Canada, and Eldorado Nuclear. The only reference to this meeting is a memo from Gulf Minerals counsel Roger Allen in Denver to Andrew Janisch, who at the time had succeeded Nick Ediger as president of Gulf Minerals Canada. Allen wrote:

> While Gulf Oil Corporation may not have control or custody of all of the documents and files of all of its foreign subsidiaries, including GMCL, or joint ventures, and may in some instances be prohibited from producing documents not within the United States, all of which may be clarified to some extent after the meeting with the Minister of Energy, Mines and Resources, scheduled in Ottawa on July 13, 1976, it nevertheless seems advisable that you at least commence a search to determine what documents you may have in Toronto office which have not been previously sent to either Denver or Pittsburgh office.

Whether or not the meeting on July 13 was actually held is not known. At a pre-trial hearing of the Westinghouse suit against the uranium producers at Chicago in 1980, Gulf counsel Max Gillam told the court he had been unable to find any indication that the meeting had been held. "I cannot talk to Mr. Janisch," Gillam said; "he is no longer employed by GMCL. He is a Canadian citizen employed by someone else. And his lawyer states he does not wish to talk to me." Janisch was then, in fact, employed by the government of Canada, as president of Canada's national oil company, Petro-Canada.

The Canadian companies never did respond to the subpoenas issued by the U.S. Department of Justice, but the government of Canada did – many times. The first response was a lengthy note entitled "Background paper on the Canadian uranium industry's activities in international uranium marketing," handed by Ottawa to the Department of Justice early in August. In essence, Ottawa said that the "uranium marketing arrangements" resulted from discriminatory U.S. policies, and in any event had not effected U.S. commerce.

The Canadian government "encouraged development of the Canadian uranium industry to meet the needs of the United States Atomic Energy Commission," the note said. Then, it claimed the Canadian industry suffered as the result of policies of the U.S. Atomic Energy Commission, including: the AEC withdrawal from further purchases of Canadian uranium in 1959; the import embargo in 1964; the "split tails" operation of the AEC enrichment plants, which allowed it to sell government stockpiles at a price of $10.50 to $12.00 a pound while non-U.S. uranium was selling for $5.00, and which further reduced the available market.

The note said that Ottawa "approved the marketing arrangements negotiated by Canadian uranium producers and legalized the arrangement" by a regulation under the Atomic Energy Control Act to "regulate export contract approvals in line with the informal marketing arrangments." It claimed that the cartel

> had been overtaken by market forces beginning in early 1974. Consequently since early 1974 the informal arrangements have been ineffective although meetings continued until October, 1975.
>
> A comparison of the directed minimum price and the U.S. price [shows that] the directed price is equal to or less than the U.S. price except for the months of February and March 1974. Even here the directed price [i.e. the cartel price] is much below the October, 1973 bids obtained by the Tennessee Valley Authority.
>
> In response to these actions, which weakened the uranium market, the Canadian government, after its repeated endeavours to have restrictions removed and having been rebuffed in its attempts to develop producer/consumer arrangements on a government to government basis, requested Canadian uranium pro-

ducers to participate in an informal marketing arrangement with international uranium producers.

The marketing arrangements . . . did not interfere with Commerce within the United States since [the U.S. market was specifically excluded, and the embargo] is not due to be relaxed until 1977 and will not be completely removed until 1984.

The same basic message was to be repeated by Ottawa, both publicly and in private discussions with Amercian authorities, over and over again during the next three years.

Not all of the companies subpoenaed by the grand jury were able to complete the search of all their files and produce all of the required documents by the August 4 deadline. Among them was Gulf Oil. A month after the subpoena had been issued, Gulf requested an extension of the deadline to September 30, stating that an Ontario statute blocked production of the Gulf Minerals Canada papers located in Toronto. As it turned out, the Ontario statute did not prevent Gulf from producing the Canadian documents, but before the requested extension to September 30, two other things happened. On August 29, officials of the California Energy Commission in Sacramento released the cartel documents stolen from the files of Mary Kathleen Uranium in Australia, revealing a fair amount about the operations of the cartel. Then on September 22, Ottawa passed the Uranium Securities Information Regulations, which made it illegal for anyone in Canada to reveal any of the cartel documents, or even talk about them, under penalty of up to five years in jail.

"The action was taken in light of the sweeping demand for such information by U.S. subpoenas, which, while served upon officers of United States companies, call for the presentation of information in the possession of subsidiary or affiliated companies 'wherever located,' " Alastair Gillespie, who succeeded Macdonald as Energy Minister, said in a prepared statement announcing the regulations. "Clearly this must be regarded as an issue of sovereignty. The government has therefore moved to prevent the removal of such documents from Canada." Gillespie provided reporters with another background paper, which set out basically the same facts and arguments contained in the paper handed to Justice Department the previous month.

Gulf's action in requesting extra time to respond to the grand jury subpoena and the intervening regulations passed by Ottawa, have resulted in allegations that Gulf requested the Canadian government to pass the regulation so that it would not have to produce copies of the cartel documents it held in Canada. The accusation that Gulf sought this protection from the Canadian government was to become an important issue in the suits by Westinghouse and the Tennessee Valley Authority against Gulf and the other uranium producers. However, Ottawa's response, more than a year before, to the first proposals of the Justice Department to obtain documents from Canada on a voluntary basis, clearly indicated that the Canadian government did not want the documents disclosed. Beyond doubt, Gulf was keenly aware that it was caught between the demands of the U.S. Justice Department to produce the documents, and pressure from Ottawa not to produce the documents.

That pressure increased, as new subpoenas requiring production of the documents were issued as a result of the private lawsuits in the United States. As a result of these fresh pressures, Gillespie, on November 8, wrote to the Canadian uranium producers, requesting that, "in light of recent developments in the United States," they deliver all copies of the documents to his office within four days. Gulf Minerals Canada did not turn over the documents to Gillespie as requested, but instead turned them over to a Toronto law firm, which has kept them locked in a vault.

It was possibly because of increased pressure from the Justice Department that Gulf declined to turn over its Toronto documents to Gillespie. Gillespie's action in requesting the documents brought added pressures from the Justice Department, and led to another discussion between Canadian and U.S. government officials on December 3. An internal State Department memo to Julius Katz gives the background of this meeting.

The State Department memo referred to "our substantive objections to the investigation as a whole," and the fact that Ottawa "has objected strenuously to the investigation." The memo added:

> The immediate issue is the issuance of a subpoena to Gulf Oil Corporation which has subsidiary producers of ura-

nium in the U.S. and Canada . . . The information request relates to data in Canada and occasioned a sharp response about two weeks ago from Gillespie, who directed that any and all documents located in Canada which related to the uranium investigation be deposited with the GOC [government of Canada]. Justice in turn threatened to seek an injunction from the Court which would enjoin Gulf from complying with the GOC directive. While both sides have agreed to withhold these actions, it was this issue which gave rise to the present consultation.

The U.S. courts, where the uranium litigation cases were being heard, pressed as hard as the Department of Justice for the release of the cartel documents. Judge Merhige, of the U.S. District Court in Richmond, on behalf of Westinghouse issued letters rogatory – a request from the courts of one country to the courts of another country for assistance in obtaining evidence – to the Supreme Court of Ontario. After hearings, the Ontario court rejected the letters rogatory from Judge Merhige, upholding the government's new uranium information security regulations. Justice Sydney Robins of the Ontario Supreme Court ruled:

> This case constitutes a rare occasion, certainly in relations with the United States, in which in my opinion legal assistance should be denied on the ground that to grant it would run counter to the public policy of this country. . . . In this very special factual situation letters rogatory should not, in my opinion, be enforced against officers of Canadian corporations whose actions during this pertinent period had received the stamp of approval of the Canadian government.

Newly elected U.S. President Jimmy Carter had been in the White House less than a month before he entertained the Prime Minister of Canada on an official visit for two days of discussions of bilateral issues, on February 22 and 23, 1977. The Canadian visitors were greeted on the lawn of the White House with a twenty-one-gun salute, and the following day Trudeau became the first Prime Minister of Canada to address a joint session of the U.S. Congress. It was a warm affirmation of the spirit of friendship that has long existed between the two countries that Trudeau brought to the Congress. "A Canadian in the United States is among friends," he assured the American legislators. "My message today is . . . an enthusiastic pledge of the spirited Canadian support in pursuit of those causes in which we both believe."

The nitty-gritty of the private discussions, however, focused on the type of irritants that can disturb the relations of the best of friends. Among these was Canada's long-standing complaint of attempted extra-territorial application of American laws, the issue of whether American companies operating in Canada comply with American laws or Canadian laws, an issue raised once again by the uranium affair.

A later State Department memo noted that during this visit,

> Prime Minister Trudeau raised long-standing Canadian concerns about the extra-territorial application of U.S. laws. The President responded by proposing that Attorney General Bell meet with his Canadian counterpart to try to alleviate the problem, particularly in the antitrust field. A positive atmosphere for future exchanges was generated at a meeting in June between the Attorney General and the Canadian Minister of Justice . . .

In fact, however, when Attorney General Griffin Bell visited Ottawa in June, he was treated to an explosion of angry words, and the atmosphere seemed anything but positive.

Bell's visit to Ottawa on June 16 and 17 coincided with two days of public hearings in Washington, held jointly by a Congressional sub-committee headed by a Democrat Congressman John E. Moss of California, and a committee of the New York State Legislature. The Moss committee had, with some difficulty, subpoenaed documents introduced in the suits against Westinghouse at Pittsburgh, which shed more light on the cartel activities. These documents, from Gulf Oil files in the United States, had been ruled confidential by Judge Wekselman, and had not been publicly disclosed during the trial at Pittsburgh. The Moss committee proposed to make them public at its Washington hearings, and Ottawa was upset.

Two days before Bell's arrival in Ottawa, Alastair Gillespie publicly criticized Gulf for having released the documents to the Moss committee. (At the same time Gulf was being strongly attacked by the Moss committee for trying to block disclosure of the documents.) Gillespie said Gulf's action caused him to "wonder about how good a Canadian citizen" Gulf Minerals Canada was, and suggested that the matter might be raised with Judge Bell when he arrived in Ottawa. Gillespie's remarks produced a prompt telegram from Gulf Oil chairman Jerry McAfee, assuring Gillespie that "at no time did Gulf voluntarily transfer these documents to any third party, including the U.S. Congress, Westinghouse or others."

In his prepared statement, Gillespie touched upon President Carter's recently announced decision to indefinitely defer development of a plutonium fast breeder reactor and reprocessing of spent nuclear fuel, as measures to curb the risks of nuclear arms proliferation. Deferring the fast breeders and reprocessing also had the effect of increasing the demand for uranium. A fast breeder reactor, for example, could produce about fifty times as much electricity from a pound of uranium as a conventional nuclear power reactor.

Gillespie noted that since the U.S. is not in a position to be a significant exporter of uranium, the increased demand resulting from the non-proliferation policies

> will fall upon the producing nations who banded together in an attempt to survive when access to the large U.S. market . . . was denied between 1964 and 1974 . . . The current calls for increased production from Canada can't help but appear incongruous in light of the protectionist actions of the U.S. policies of the past and the extra-territorial nature of the current U.S. antitrust investigation. Without the actions of the Canadian government we would not have been in a position to respond to the rapid increase in demand following the oil crisis of 1973 and the inability of one large U.S. supplier [Westinghouse] to meet earlier contracted U.S. and overseas markets.

Whether this constituted a threat is perhaps a matter of interpretation.

Bell held discussions on the problem of the extra-territorial application of U.S. antitrust laws with Justice Minister Ron Basford, External Affairs Minister Don Jamieson, and Trade Minister Jean Chrétien. The talks produced agreement on a reported "early warning system" intended to raise problems for discussion at an early stage. These talks may have produced a "positive atmosphere," but the U.S. Attorney General could not have been oblivious to angry words that were buzzing in the air.

On the evening that Bell had arrived in Ottawa, Donald Macdonald, then Finance Minister, had appeared on a television interview, where he accused the United States of using a "big stick" in its uranium investigation.

> They have an ambassador here in Ottawa. [Macdonald said.] Maybe he had better take a message back to Washington that there is not one law for the United States and a different one for everybody else . . . The U.S. was engaging in predatory pricing policies driving . . . Canadian and other producers out of the world markets . . . At the same time, companies like Westinghouse, with the American administration supporting them, were engaging in loss-leader tactics around the world . . . we acted to protect ourselves from these predatory American tactics and now they are saying 'you are maintaining a cartel.' We don't think the Americans should use a big stick against a Canadian policy which . . . was basically one to protect ourselves from predatory policies followed by the American government.

The next day, Bell was sitting in the visitor's gallery in the House of Commons where he heard Macdonald protest that "the United States would seek to apply its laws in Canada, against the laws of the government of Canada, and I do not regard that as a friendly act." Bell later told reporters: "I got the message."

Whether or not Griffin Bell was upset by what he had heard in Ottawa, there is no doubt that Ottawa was upset by what it heard Griffin Bell say in Chicago two months later. Bell was addressing a meeting of the American Bar Association on the topic of international comity, the principle that when the laws of two countries are in conflict, the country that has the least at stake should defer to the country that has the most at stake.

> Comity should work both ways. I see no excuse for deliberately enacting 'blocking' legislation solely to frus-

trate U.S. antitrust laws, without regard to the seriousness of the case or the national interest at stake . . . Let me make clear to you that I deem our criminal investigation of the international uranium cartel and our civil investigation of the international oil industry matters of fundamental United States interest.

We are obligated to do all that we reasonably can to prosecute foreign private cartels which have the purpose and effect of causing significant economic harm in the United States in violation of antitrust laws. To my mind there is a fundamental United States interest in not having our citizens pay substantially higher prices for imports because private firms get together and rig international markets. There is also a fundamental United States interest at stake when private businesses, although foreign, get together to injure and perhaps destroy an American competitor.

Bell did not name Westinghouse, but there is no doubt about which Amercian firm he thought foreign business had sought to destroy.

Trudeau brought up the Bell speech when he met with Carter in Washington a second time, in September, 1977, when the two leaders again discussed the uranium problem. "The Prime Minister and President Carter agreed every effort should be made to resolve this problem and the SSEA [Secretary of State for External Affairs] and Secretary Vance agreed the two sides should 'talk it out,' " a Canadian government memo later reported.

Subsequently Ministers agreed officials should seek to 'talk out' the problem in a way that would: take account of economic and political as well as legal considerations . . . obtain U.S. recognition that Canadian policies should not be challenged by the extra-territorial application of USA antitrust laws . . . obtain USA recognition that Canadian uranium marketing policy was valid and reasonable . . . and establish limits on the exercise of US extra-territorial jurisdiction affecting Canada and arrange agreed procedures to ensure USA would respect these limits.

The U.S. version of this second Trudeau-Carter meeting was outlined in a State Department memo:

> [W]ith respect to the uranium marketing question, we have indicated our understanding that the Canadian government took action in pursuit of what it perceived to be an important national interest. Similarly, we would expect Canada to recognize our fundamental interest in protecting U.S. citizens from the anti-competitive activities of uranium mining companies impacting on the American market which allegedly went beyond directions from the Canadian government.

At times, the protests from Canada were couched in the stifled language of international diplomacy, as in a note from Bud Cullen, acting Secretary of State for External Affairs, to American Ambassador Thomas Enders:

> I have the honour to refer to investigations, hearings and actions concerned with international uranium marketing arrangements. I have the honour to inform you that the policy of the Canadian government was to support and participate in international uranium marketing arrangements from 1972 to 1975 to ensure the survival of the Canadian uranium industry which was being damaged by the restrictive uranium trade practices of the United States . . . The Canadian government finds it objectionable that this Canadian government policy should be questioned under United States law.

THE BRITISH PLEAD THE FIFTH AMENDMENT

Canada was not the only area where the U.S. courts and the Department of Justice were finding difficulty in securing evidence and testimony concerning the affairs of the cartel. In London more than a year was spent in a frustrated effort to compel testimony before an American judge by seven top officers of the Rio Tinto-Zinc Corporation Ltd.

Judge Merhige sent letters rogatory addressed to the "High Court of Justice" in England, and after an English appeal court held that the RTZ officials must testify, Merhige travelled to

London to hold court in the American Embassy. The newspapers could hardly resist having some fun with this historic event. The *Washington Post* reported:

> It is a bit cheeky of those American lawyer chaps, coming to London and setting up court to ask questions about a uranium cartel.
>
> That wasn't the worst of it. Those Yankee lawyers brought their own judge, Robert H. Merhige, a fellow from somewhere called the eastern district of Virginia.
>
> This federal judge, as they call him, held forth, not in any proper British court of law, but over at the U.S. Embassy on Grosvenor Square. And the Americans put their questions to some very proper British businessmen.
>
> Well, one thing led to another, and Sir Mark Turner and Lord Shackleton of Burley, the heads of the Honours Committee, the one that selects knights and all that, and five other executives of Rio Tinto-Zinc, declined to answer . . .
>
> [A]s the Americans put it so inelegantly, Sir Mark and Lord Shackleton and the others 'took the fifth.' The fifth seems to be an amendment in their constitution which protects citizens against self-incrimination.
>
> Now, imagine – British citizens compelled to invoke the U.S. constitution to avoid testifying before an American judge who is holding court in London. A bit daunting.
>
> But that's not the end of it. Judge Merhige accepted their plea, but straight way the American lawyers started talking about something called the Omnibus Crime Control and Safe Streets Act. It seems this law allows the U.S. Attorney General to arrange criminal immunity for persons who plead the fifth – promising them not to prosecute them in any U.S. court, then compelling them to testify.

Judge Merhige had gone to London to get evidence for the case before his court – the suits by the utilities against Westinghouse – but Attorney General Griffin Bell wanted the same material for the grand jury investigation. Bell wrote to Merhige, directing him to grant the immunity in order to compel the testimony of the RTZ officials. "As you know, the Department of Justice has a firm policy against seeking such orders in private litigation except in the most extraordinary circumstances," the Attorney General had written to Merhige. This was one of those exceptional cases. "In my judgment, the testimony of the individuals for whom orders are to be sought is necessary to the public interest," Bell wrote. "The testimony these persons give may well be indispensable to the work of the grand jury, and the subject matter of this grand jury is of particular importance."

The RTZ officials still declined to answer any questions, and launched an appeal – supported by the UK government – to the Law Lords of the British House of Lords, the highest court in the United Kingdom.

In December, 1977, more than a year after Judge Merhige had sent his letters rogatory to London, the House of Lords ruled that the RTZ officials were not obliged to give evidence at a U.S. court. "[T]he evidence is sought for the purpose of an antitrust investigation into the activities of companies not subject to the jurisdiction of the United Kingdom," Lord Wilberforce declared in his decision. "[T]he attempt to extend the Grand Jury investigation extra-territorially into the activities of the RTZ companies was an infringement of United Kingdom sovereignty." Clearly, Canada was not the only country sensitive about this issue.

The *Financial Times* commented:

> This ruling is an important new episode in a continuing struggle by other countries to resist the attempt of U.S. courts and federal regulatory agencies to enforce their authority on foreign nationals transacting business outside of the U.S.

JERRY McAFEE IN THE HOT SEAT

Dr. Jerry McAfee, the avuncular chemical engineer from Port Arthur, Texas, chairman and chief executive officer of the Gulf Oil Corporation, was not really on trial that sweltering June day in 1977 as he sat beneath the glaring lights in room 2322 of the Rayburn House Office Building in Washington. It just seemed that he was on trial.

Jerry McAfee and S. A. Zagnoli, executive vice-president of Gulf Mineral Resources Corporation, were there to testify before the joint hearings of the House of Representatives, Subcommittee on Oversight and Investigations, Committee on Interstate and Foreign Commerce; and the New York State Assembly's committee on corporations.

Nineteen months before – on January 14, 1976 – when McAfee had taken on the job as chairman of Gulf, he knew he faced a monumental task in cleaning up some devastating problems that confronted the seventh largest corporation in the United States. What he had not counted on was that Gulf would soon be the principal target of a federal grand jury investigation, and involved in a series of suits where the company stood to lose hundreds of millions of dollars.

In the nine months before McAfee took over at Gulf, the company's earnings had plunged by 40 per cent. The company's enormous oil reserves in the Middle East, a principal source of Gulf's earnings in the postwar period, were in the process of being lost by government expropriation. But these were almost trifling matters in comparison with the job of cleaning up Gulf's image and re-establishing shattered employee morale in the aftermath of a scandal involving millions of dollars in illegal political bribes that had forced the resignation of Gulf's previous chairman and three other top officers.

Gulf's political slush fund had first come to light in a Watergate-related investment that had borne "Rose Mary's baby," a secret list of political donations kept by Richard Nixon's secretary, Rose Mary Woods. Included on the list was an illegal contribution of $100,000 from Gulf.

The full extent of Gulf's political payments was not brought to light until nearly three years later, in a report from a committee headed by two Gulf outside directors, John J. McCloy, a retired U.S. lawyer and a former distinguished public servant, and Toronto lawyer Beverley Matthews. The McCloy-Matthews report disclosed that during a 12-year period Gulf had made political contributions around the world totalling some $12 million, most of them illegal. Some $4 million of this had been funnelled through Gulf's Washington representative, Claude Wilde.

The report concluded that those who received Gulf's illegal political contributions were also to share in the blame. In addition to Richard Nixon, these included President Lyndon Johnson and Senators Henry Jackson, Hubert Humphrey, Howard Baker, and Russell Long. The McCloy-Matthews report stated: "It is hard to escape the conclusion that a sort of 'shut-eye sentry' attitude prevailed upon the part of both the responsible corporate officials and the recipients as well as on the part of those charged with enforcement responsibilities." The shut-eye sentry is the man in the Kipling poem:

> But I'd shut my eyes in the sentry-box
> So I didn't see nothin' wrong.

Gulf's board accepted the resignations of chairman Bob Dorsey, and other top officers, on January 13, 1976, and the next day selected McAfee, then fifty-nine to fill the top slot. McAfee, had barely time to tackle the urgent rehabilitation tasks awaiting him at Pittsburgh before the uranium affair exploded, requiring more of his working time and attention than any other single facet of Gulf's far-flung and varied operations.

The Moss committee, meanwhile, had set an elaborate national stage for its hearings in Washington on June 16 and 17, with Gulf and McAfee cast in the role as the villains in the drama.

Congressman John Moss had been quick to spring his committee into action, and establish a top billing on television and in the newspapers. Barely two months after the Mary Kathleen documents had been disclosed in his home state of California, Moss held his first hearing at Sacramento, where he declared:

> the right of the people of the United States to know and identify the economic forces affecting their daily lives is constitutionally second to none. So, too, is the power of the Congress of the United States, so that it may intelligently and adequately deal with the energy policies that will affect all of us for decades to come.

It was clear that Moss was determined that the big corporations would not escape the glare of his exposure by hiding behind foreign disclosure laws.

Months of painstaking examination of mountains of papers

followed the Sacramento hearing, most of the work falling to two young lawyers, the sub-committee's staff counsel Patrick McLain, and special counsel for the hearings, John Atkisson.

In addition to the Mary Kathleen documents, the key papers were in the evidence at the Pittsburgh trial, where much of the material had been sealed confidential by Judge Wekselman. The committee subpoenaed Westinghouse for

> copies of all documents in your possession . . . which were introduced or offered into evidence by Westinghouse in the matter of Duquesne Light Company vs. Westinghouse Electric Corporation in the court of Common Pleas of Allegheny County, State of Pennsylvania . . . relating to any allegations of any conspiracy existing among U.S. and foreign uranium producers to fix prices, to allocate markets, and to eliminate competition and competitors, including intermediaries in the uranium market . . . and copies of any testimony in your action relating to any introductions or offers of such service.

Westinghouse was all set to deliver the subpoenaed material to the committee on May 2, when, at 10:00 a.m. that day, Gulf obtained a temporary restraining order in a hearing before Federal District Judge G. L. Hart, restraining Westinghouse from delivering the documents pending a hearing on a preliminary injunction to be held two days later. When Westinghouse counsel James Johnston and vice-president Frank Cotter appeared before the committee hours after Judge Hart had issued the temporary restraining order, they were in a box: hand over the documents and be cited for contempt by a federal court, or hold onto the documents and be cited for contempt by a Congressional committee.

Congressman Henry Waxman of California, who chaired the committee hearing that day, held that the committee had precedent over any court. "It is the opinion of the chair that all of you and the corporation are in contempt of the Congress of the United States," Waxman told Johnston and Cotter, who continued to hang onto the documents.

Congressman Albert Gore of Tennessee revealed the type of reception that McAfee would soon face when he appeared before the committee.

I think it is absolutely incredible, the action Gulf has taken in trying to prevent this from coming out. Here we have one of the major corporations in this country allegedly sneaking around attending secret meetings to fix the price of uranium around the world. We find out about it. We ask for the information. They stonewall.

We got a proposal from the President of the United States today, stating . . . 'The United States must continue to count on nuclear power to meet its share of the energy deficit.'

We are dealing with one of the most serious crisis that this country has ever faced. The Congress of the United States is attempting to design an energy policy to meet this crisis. We are confronted with information that indicates the existence of a world-wide uranium cartel which could subject us to the same kind of extortion that we now have with oil. We are attempting to get the information to formulate wise policies on behalf of the people of this country, just let them look at the record of this case.

After two days, the temporary restraining order was lifted, and Westinghouse was free to deliver the material to the committee. The next question was whether or not the committee would make the material public, a matter dealt with at yet another session. Gulf counsel Irwin Coleman argued that the material should be kept confidential because it contained privileged attorney-client information, in deference to a request of the committee from the government of Canada, and because "the committee can completely fulfill its functions while at the same time granting confidential treatment to this material."

Staff counsel Patrick McLain argued that "the interests of the Congress are compelling at this time to put before the full Congress and the public the facts as they are contained in these documents." As for the request from Ottawa, McLain suggested that Gulf "took a knowing and active interest in the promulgation of these Canadian statutes and regulations which they are now trying to seek protection from." Coleman denied the allegation: "I am aware of absolutely no involvement on our part. I don't know what Mr. McLain is referring to."

The decision was up to the committee. There was little doubt about how they would vote. The Congressmen wanted the public to get the facts. And the news media coverage that these hearings could command would certainly be no political disadvantage to the committee and its members. The committee voted 11-0 to disclose the documents and hold its hearings in public.

Before the committee met to obtain testimony from the people at Gulf, the hearing was expanded to include three delegates from the New York State Assembly.

William F. Haddad, director of the New York State Legislature's office of oversight and analysis, had already started his own investigation of the uranium cartel. Haddad, son-in-law of New York millionaire John Hay Whitney and a former aide to Robert F. Kennedy, already had a flamboyant career, encompassing service with the Peace Corps and the Office of Economic Opportunity, state and city politics, publicizing, investigate journalism, and private business consulting. His New York State Assembly committee had delved into such matters as police harassment of political dissidents and alleged ties between a major sports conglomerate and the underworld.

Haddad was already starting to attract attention with his state investigation of the uranium cartel. He claimed that the government of Canada was threatening to thwart construction of a proposed multi-billion dollar natural gas pipeline from the north slope of Alaska, across Canada, unless the United States dropped the grand jury inquiry. In a report to the State Assembly, Haddad wrote that there was "little doubt" that the cartel "was, in large measure, responsible for the 700 per cent increase in the cost of uranium, resulting in higher energy costs to New York residents, and posing serious legislative and policy questions for the future development of nuclear power in the state."

Haddad also seemed to want to reach beyond the officers of Gulf to the company's major shareholder, the Mellon family of Pittsburgh.

> This is not the first time the Gulf Oil company has been in trouble. If the charges of this report [about the uranium cartel] are sustained, there could be other high level changes at Gulf. Yet the real power of the Gulf Oil Cor-

poration lies outside its official Board of Directors and its corporate executives. The real power . . . is with the Mellon family . . . yet, whenever there are charges proven against the corporation, true ownership remains untouched. If corporate corruption is to be effectively curtailed . . . it can only be done by legislation which reaches beyond existing corporate law and into actual control.

(The Mellon family, which at one time, owned 70 per cent of Gulf, held about 20 per cent ownership at the time, and by 1980, this had been further reduced to 11 per cent.)

Two weeks before the Moss committee was due to hear testimony from Gulf, Haddad phoned Patrick McLain and said that his State committee had obtained copies of the Duquesne documents, the key documents which the Moss committee itself had so much trouble getting. The thought that a New York State committee might upstage a committee of the United States Congress was not an attractive idea at the Rayburn Building in Washington. McLain and John Atkisson flew to Albany that day to talk to Haddad about the idea of joining forces.

As a result of the Albany meeting, Moss wrote to New York Assemblyman Irwin J. Landes, a former official with the Atomic Energy Commission and the chairman of the state's committee on corporations:

> Because of the mutual interest we share in this topic and due to the fact that we have developed much the same information on this subject, we are most pleased to invite you . . . to join us and participate in public hearings which the subcommittee will hold, with Gulf Oil Corp. as one of the principal witnesses.

New York sent Haddad, Landes, and Assemblyman Lloyd Riford to sit in on the Congressional committee. It was the first time that State and Congressional committees had joined forces to conduct an investigation.

"We weren't sure whether Haddad was bluffing, or whether he really did have the Duquesne documents," McLain later recalled. "We never did find out."

The final step to set the stage for Gulf's appearance before the committee was to brief the media. Copies of the Duquesne documents were provided to some fifty news people twenty-four hours in advance, and McLain and Atkisson spent hours going over the more important aspects with the news people. When McAfee and Zagnoli turned up for their appearance, most of the people crowded into the small Congressional hearing room were news people. Four banks of blazing lights glared at McAfee and Zagnoli as they sat behind the curving, white-panelled dais. The harsh light glinted off McAfee's gold rimmed glasses as he wiped the sweat from his brow with a rumpled, white handkerchief.

"For Americans with long memories, the episode smelled of the notorious and now-defunct House Un-American Activities Committee and of the late Joseph McCarthy's cynical red-baiting," was the opinion of *Forbes* magazine. "This time the victim was not an academician or intellectual. He was a businessman."

"Our hearings today and tomorrow will detail secret agreements between nations and companies to control the price and supply of uranium" Congress Moss said in opening the hearings. Whatever the reasons for the 700 per cent increase in the price of uranium, Moss said, "the timing of the cartel's formation and that of the price rise are one and the same. Whether that phenomenon is anything other than an astounding coincidence, we may learn today."

In his statement to the committee, McAfee argued that Gulf had participated "reluctantly" in the uranium marketing arrangement at the direction of the Canadian government; that the arrangement had no discernible affect on U.S uranium prices; and the price rise had been caused by a number of factors unrelated to the cartel, including the Westinghouse short sale.

McAfee quoted from a report prepared for the American Petroleum Institute by Kirkland and Ellis, the Chicago law firm which, on behalf of Westinghouse, had filed the suit in Chicago charging Gulf and the other uranium producers with conspiring to raise uranium prices. In the report for the American Petroleum Institute, Kirkland and Ellis had concluded that the price rise was not due to market conspiracy, and had written:

> Another reason for the price increase is Westinghouse's
> 1975 announcement that it would not fulfill most of its

long-term contractual commitments to 27 utilities to deliver 65 million pounds of uranium over the next 20 years, causing an influx of new demand.

McAfee had been under questioning by the Congressmen less than ten minutes, when Moss warned him to keep his responses "very, very direct, dealing only with the area of question and not going beyond that." To that point, McAfee's longest answer to any question had been exactly 136 words – far shorter than many of the questions.

The day's hearing was more than half over when the committee drew its most stunning testimony from the two Gulf witnesses on the stand.

Haddad was questioning Zagnoli. "Was the cartel successful overseas?" he asked.

> Zagnoli: 'In my view it did raise the price overseas . . .'
>
> Haddad: 'Was it effective in setting world quotas. Was it controlling on Gulf's markets?'
>
> Zagnoli: 'It was effective in allocating the market.'
>
> Haddad: 'Mr. Zagnoli, you are very vague. You were intimately involved in this. I have read the records in front of me. You have read them. I have read them. Please, please don't insult our intelligence. Was it effective in setting world quotas, yes or no?'
>
> Zagnoli: 'Yes.'

Thirty seconds later, Congressman Gore jumped to his feet.

> 'If counsel will yield briefly, you have elicited the admission from Mr. Zagnoli that the cartel was effective in raising the price. I would like to make an addendum. It was also effective in raising the prices to all U.S. utilities who purchased supplies of uranium in the foreign market during this period. Is that not correct. Mr. Zagnoli?'
>
> Zagnoli: 'I do not know.'
>
> Gore: 'Why don't you know? If the price was effectively raised by the cartel and the utilities purchased supplies of uranium in that market, it did raise the price that those utilities paid; correct?'
>
> Zagnoli: '[Y]ou can't be certain. This is hypothetical . . . It is my opinion that the prices would have been somewhat

lower so to the extent that the U.S. utilities bought overseas they probably paid a higher price.'

Gore: 'All right. Now, what you have said is that the cartel raised prices higher than they otherwise would have been. Gulf participated in the cartel. U.S. utilities bought uranium at a price that was fixed higher than it otherwise would have been . . . You have just conceded on the record before this committee that it did have an impact.'

Zagnoli: 'I would say the impact was insignificant.'

Gore: '[I]t was not insignificant to the purchasers of electricity in the TVA region . . . it is not insignificant for those who pay ever-increasing electric bills.'

McAfee attempted to get a work in. Moss banged his gavel. "Don't ever presume to do that in this committee," Moss commanded. "You will let the Congressman ask the question. When he has one for you, he will address it to you. Don't interrupt."

A few minutes later, Congressman Norman Lent of New York protested that the hearing had strayed beyond its proper realm. Whether or not Gulf violated antitrust laws "is beside the point," Lent said. That is a matter for the Department of Justice to determine, and one "which is not within our province to determine." Lent said the committee should focus on

whether or not the existence of this cartel did or did not, in any way, influence adversely the price American consumers have to pay for uranium . . . I am a little disappointed that it seems that the committee has – at least at this stage – not developed economic evidence to show this linkage and, instead, has concentrated on what I feel is a matter which is peculiarly within the ambit of the Justice Department.

That is not the way that Congressman Gore of Tennessee saw it.

I would submit as a matter of opinion, having covered trials as a newspaper reporter, that this appears to me, quite clearly, to be the kind of case that a jury would spend about 30 seconds on. I think it is that clear . . . Many, many U.S. consumers are paying more money and will pay even higher electric bills because Gulf and other companies fixed the price of uranium.

Later, Gore questioned McAfee about a memo written by former Gulf lawyer Roy Jackson. The memo discussed Gulf's plans – abandoned after the Canadian government set uranium export prices and allocation by regulation – to seek clearance from the Justice Department for its participation in the cartel, as well as discussions with other U.S. government officials, suggesting that the contacts be arranged by Claude Wilde.

> Gore: 'Now, this is the same Claude Wilde who was convicted on October 13, 1973, of making illegal corporate contributions to politicians in Washington, D.C. In March of 1976, he was indicted again on several counts on related charges. I am wondering if the suggestion that Claude Wilde will know who to contact in Washington D.C., was an indication that you are prepared to go outside of the normal channels of requesting a Justice Department memorandum on the propriety of your activities?'

McAfee bristled that the innuendo "is a bit of a cheap shot. The answer to your question, directly, is certainly no."

"I think that what you have done here is also a cheap shot at the American public; to fix the price and force them to pay something that they would otherwise not have to pay," Gore responded. "[I]f a group of corporations get together in secret and decide what they are going to charge the American public and eliminate competition it is taking wealth and property from American consumers under unjustified circumstances and in violation of the law."

Turning to the television cameras, Gore continued: "You have heard a lot of talk over the last decade about energy companies fixing the price of energy. It is usually some shadowy kind of thing, and it is difficult to get your hands on it. This is, in the parlance of Watergate, a smoking gun." Turning again to face McAfee: "You participated in a cartel. You fixed the price of uranium. It is astounding . . ."

As Gore wound up his accusations, the hearing was nearly over, and Moss turned to McAfee: "Would you like to respond? You may."

McAfee: "I disagree as thoroughly with most of what the gentleman has said as I can possibly disagree with anything. He is wrong, and I would hope that further consideration by the committee of the real facts, which have been presented to you today and which are available to you, will lead the majority of the committtee, Mr. Chairman, to understand that what the Congressman has said is completely wrong."

Gore was icy. He replied to McAfee: "Thank you for your response."

As the Moss committee continued to hold hearings sporadically throughout the following months, the fact that Gulf admitted that the cartel may have had some affect on some of the uranium purchased by U.S. utilities, was never lost sight of.

In Ottawa, however, the view of the matter was different. The mechanism uncovered by the Moss committee, by which American utilities may have paid a higher price for a small part of their uranium imports implied a double standard that infuriated people like Donald Macdonald. It implied that American buyers were injured if they were not permitted to buy uranium from foreign companies and countries at prices less than they paid for uranium from U.S. producers. As Justice Department officials later concluded, the cartel did result in higher prices for non-U.S. uranium during about an eighteen-month period, from mid-1972 to about the end of 1973, before other forces took over. Very little foreign uranium was purchased by U.S. utilities during this eighteen-month period, but the price was higher than it would have been without the cartel. The price for the foreign uranium during this period, however, was still no greater, and in most cases less, than prices for U.S. uranium.

If Congressman Gore had found a smoking gun, the first shot from it had been fired not by the cartel, but by the U.S. Atomic Energy Commission.

Two months after McAfee and Zagnoli had testified in Washington, Moss forwarded to Attorney General Griffin Bell copies of all the documents produced at the committee hearings, together with the testimony. "The Congress and the American people are keenly sensitive to the possible existence of a kind of domestic impunity for acts – otherwise illegal

– performed conveniently behind foreign corporate veils," Moss wrote to Bell. He was, he added, "very pleased indeed" to see Bell "put American multi-national corporations on notice that the Justice Department's scrutiny of antitrust violations will not in the future stop at U.S. borders."

On March 21, 1978, the lawyers in the Justice Department's antitrust division who had handled the investigation, presented their recommendations in a seven-chapter, one-thousand page document called the "fact memorandum." The investigation had started three years before. A grand jury had been empanelled nearly eighteen months before, to complete the investigation. If the department were to lay charges, it would have to be done before the term of the grand jury expired in early May. The final decision was up to Assistant Attorney General John Shenefield, in charge of the antitrust division.

The fact memorandum, on which Shenefield would base his decision, contained more than just the recommendations of the department's lawyers. It included an exhaustive summary of the evidence brought out by the grand jury; the views of senior officials in the department who had reviewed the staff's recommendations and the evidence; and a series of government inter-department memos.

Because it dealt with secret grand jury testimony, the fact memorandum has never been made public. A lawyer for the Senate Judiciary Committee, which later investigated the investigation of the Justice Department, was permitted, however, to examine, make notes, and take excerpts from this key document. A few copies of the summary report prepared by the lawyer for the Senate Judiciary Committee were later leaked to news reporters, and a copy found its way into the hands of the author. It provides the only available account of the basis for the final decision by the Department of Justice.

The Justice Department staff lawyers recommended that nine firms be indicted on felony charges of violating the Sherman Act as a result of an alleged price fixing conspiracy, plus misdemeanour violations of the Wilson Tariff Act as a result of alleged discrimination against uranium buyers and sellers – referred to in the fact memorandum as the "middleman case." They also recommended that thirteen other firms be named as co-conspirators.

The firms that the staff lawyers recommended be charged with felony acts were Gulf Oil Corporation; Gulf Minerals Canada Ltd.; Rio Tinto-Zinc of London; Rio Algom Ltd.; Rio Algom Corporation, U.S. subsidiary of Rio Algom Ltd.; Nuclear Fuels Corporation of South Africa; Uranex of France; Eldorado Nuclear Ltd.; and Uranerz Canada.

The staff lawyers in the Justice Department acknowledged that successful criminal prosecution would require proof that the conspiracies were not only intended to affect U.S. commerce, but actually did affect it. They claimed that the intent was clear both as to the price fixing case and the middleman case, but added that "we have only been able to identify actual impact on U.S. commerce within the context of the price fix case." Thus, in the case of price fixing, the nine firms would be charged with felony acts, while in the case of alleged discrimination against middlemen, only misdemeanour charges would be filed, the later carrying maximum penalties of up to $50,000 for each of the defendants.

"While the evidence is not overwhelming, we do feel that it is sufficient to support the conclusion that certain U.S. companies which purchased foreign uranium during the cartel's existence paid a price higher than they would have paid had the cartel not existed," the staff stated. They also argued that by increasing the price paid for foreign uranium, the cartel "may have" had an effect in increasing prices paid for U.S. uranium.

The memorandum reviewed the non-cartel factors, which it said contributed to the increase in uranium prices:

> nonetheless . . . the staff believes that it can sufficiently discredit the contention being advanced by some, notably Gulf, that these factors alone caused the increase in U.S. prices. In other words, we can prove that the cartel did have an impact on the U.S. market and its rising prices.

The staff warned that there would be an international ruckus.

> [W]e have no misapprehension as to the consequence of our bringing this case: there will be a diplomatic furor with the countries involved . . . On the other hand, failure to return these indictments will severely undermine our

credibility in the international area. Essentially, we will substantially reinforce the notion that a firm can ignore the U.S. antitrust laws and the U.S. government if it is willing to remain out of the United States for only eighteen months.

The findings and recommendations of the staff were passed up for review at higher levels within the Justice Department, and an eventual decision by Assistant Attorney General John Shenefield.

While the recommendations of the staff lawyers at the Justice Department were being reviewed, the Department of State anticipated that felony indictments would be handed down, an action which State clearly opposed.

"The antitrust division intends to make its recommendations for indictments to the Attorney General by approximately April 26," Julius Katz Advised Richard Cooper, Under Secretary for Economic Affairs in the department, by memo dated April 19. "Assistant Attorney General Shenefield has agreed to meet with you prior to that date. At that meeting, State will have the opportunity to express any concern it may have with respect to possible indictments of the members of the cartel."

The State Department did not agree with the conclusions reached by the staff lawyers at Justice. "[I]t is our view that the cartel had little or nothing to do with the uranium price increase," Katz wrote. "It was instead the result of the convergence of a number of factors, each of which was significant by itself and which collectively had an extraordinary impact on both the foreign and U.S. markets." The factors listed by Katz as having caused the price increase included a large increase in the amount of uranium contracted for purchase by U.S. utilities, rising from 6,000 tons in 1971, to 16,000 tons in 1972; 45,000 tons in 1973 and 48,000 tons in 1974; cut-backs in foreign uranium supplies from France, Australia, and South Africa; the Arab oil embargo; increased costs in mining uranium; and the Westinghouse default on its utility customers, which "sent these purchasers into the market in search of a huge amount of uranium."

"An equally important reason for not taking legal action

against members of the cartel is that indictments could materially affect the attainment of U.S. objectives in energy and non-proliferation policy," Katz wrote.

These depend on a secure and adequate supply of uranium as an energy source which is an alternative to both oil and plutonium. Indictments may have an unsettling effect on the uranium market by making it difficult for certain foreign producers to transact business with U.S. firms and could also lead to a further proliferation of civil litigation. The uncertainties caused by the potential liability or clouded access to the U.S. market conceivably could complicate the financing of much-needed expansion of production capacity. This same concern has been expressed by the Canadian government.

Whether or not it was because of pressure brought by the Department of State, or by the Canadian government, the Justice Department in the end did not accept the recommendations of the staff lawyers in the antitrust division.

The grand jury evidence and staff recommendations were first reviewed by four senior officials in the antitrust division, who in turn made their recommendations to Shenefield. None of the four recommended the filing of any felony charges.

Douglas Rosenthal, chief of the foreign commerce section, and Joel Davidow, chief of policy planning, recommended that misdemeanour charges be filed against three firms, under the so-called middleman case. Joe Sims, deputy assistant attorney general, and Richard Favaretto, deputy director of operations, recommended that no charges at all should be laid.

Davidow concluded that "the cartel committed classic antitrust violations;" that it had sufficient effect on U.S. commerce to warrant charges under normal circumstances; that there was no proof that the companies had been "compelled" by the governments to join the cartel, even though he felt the governments had clearly applied pressure. In fact, Davidow added, under international law, governments do not have the jurisdiction to order private companies to conspire to fix prices: "No nation has yet conceded to other countries that kind of 'act of state' diplomatic recognition," Davidow wrote. Despite all these factors, Davidow recommended only misdemeanour charges because, he said, the cartel arose out of the protectionist policies of the Atomic Energy Commission, and because its main effects were not directed at the United States.

Rosenthal similarly argued that there was no conclusive evidence that the cartel had any substantial impact on either U.S. uranium buyers or middlemen, and that the effectiveness of the cartel was overwhelmed by other events almost before it began. "To decide to bring a prosecution creates a possibility that we will have an interagency confrontation with other parts of government, including State," Sims wrote. "Given the merits here that is a fight that we might very well lose."

Favaretto concluded that the alleged conspiracy between the cartel and U.S. uranium producers "probably did not take place." He said that the best case for prosecution was "the case we did not discover." Even by a preponderance of the evidence, it would not be possible to prove that the cartel's price fixing activities actually impacted U.S. commerce in any directly substantial or even measurable way, according to Favaretto. While the cartel probably increased foreign uranium prices in the period mid-1972 to late 1973, it was not the cartel, but other events, which increased prices thereafter, in Favaretto's view. Even an intent to impact on U.S. commerce was questionable, he argued, because U.S. prices were above foreign prices throughout the relevant period.

Favaretto described the actions by the foreign governments in establishing the cartel as a "a rather measured response to a problem which the United States caused" with the uranium import embargo, which he described as a "devastatingly anti-competitive act."

As for charges of a boycott against middlemen, Favaretto said this "makes me very uncomfortable because it leaves us with Westinghouse people, who appear not to have dealt with us in good faith and with candor. They are clearly more interested in fostering their stance in the private litigation than in assisting us to reach a balanced conclusion."

The Justice Department filed an "information" suit on May 9 in Pittsburgh against Gulf Oil, charging it with participation in a plot to fix prices of uranium sold to middlemen and refusing to sell to Westinghouse. Gulf pleaded *nolo contendere* because, it said, "a successful defence would have been many times more costly than the maximum penalty provided by the law." The plea means that Gulf has been found neither guilty nor innocent. Judge Gerald Webber, despite the pleading of Forrest Bannon, even declined to impose the maximum penalty, fining Gulf only $40,000. A Department of State cable sent to various embassies noted that the preliminary reaction of the Canadian government "to Department of Justice's decision to charge Gulf with misdemeanour was one of satisfaction and relief." The cable quoted a Canadian official as having stated that "intensive consultations on this issue had been successful in avoiding a serious policy clash."

Others were less than delighted at the treatment accorded Gulf.

John Atkisson, special counsel to the Moss committee, later visited with a State Department official, who summarized the conversation in a memo:

> [H]e said that Moss was outraged by the action taken by Justice . . . They felt that both the charge and penalty levied on Gulf Oil in the face of overwhelming evidence of Gulf's participation in the cartel represents a mere 'parking ticket.' Moss surmised that political pressures must have been brought to bear by foreign governments.

Syndicated columnist Jack Anderson was even more blunt.

"The international oil cartel is despised around the world," Anderson wrote in his column. "But their pre-eminence in greed is challenged by another, less publicized group of international ripoff artists – the uranium cartel."

Anderson charged that "the Carter administration, despite clear evidence of the cartel's illegal gouging, refused to take action and then tried to keep Congress from finding out why. We have obtained documentary proof – which was denied to Senators and sealed by a federal court judge – that the Justice Department blew a strong case against the uranium cartel rather than embarrass foreign governments that were members of the price-fixing conspiracy.

"Internal Justice Department documents make clear Canada's role as ring-leader in the uranium price gouge and the incredible lengths to which the State Department went to cover up this role." Anderson promised more revelations about this "outrageous cover-up," but never provided them.

Senator Howard Metzenbaum, chairman of the Senate Judiciary sub-committee on monopolies, grilled John Shenefield at committee hearings about the Justice Department decision to not indict any members of the cartel. After some protracted debate, a staff member of the Metzenbaum committee was permitted to examine the Justice Department fact memorandum and other material, while the State Department released excised versions of other documents related to the uranium affair.

At Shenefield's final appearance before the Metzenbaum committee, in January, 1980, he again protested that his decision not to prosecute the cartel was not the result of any pressure, but because there was not enough evidence to win a prosecution.

Shenefield said that the investigation had uncovered only one sale, to Carolina Power and Light, where the cartel might have had an effect on the price that was paid. The staff attorneys he said, "came to the conclusion that it might well be possible, although it was going to be very difficult to do, to isolate out something like a dollar" of the $7 per pound paid for uranium from France by Carolina Light "as being attributable to cartel effects . . . The problem was from the prosecutorial point of view that the French government insisted thereafter that the entire contract be renegotiated. The sale actually occurred, as I am informed, at the level of about $45. Thus, as nearly as anyone can tell, there was something like $35 to $36 of increase attributable to some other factors, and maybe, if we were very lucky and all the evidence worked out exactly right, one dollar of influence of the cartel."

Metzenbaum grudgingly admitted that Shenefield's decision was not the result of pressure. "I have not found that his decision is not so clearly wrong that it was a product of undue pressure from external sources," Metzenbaum said. Although there was "a good deal of pressure," he concluded that there was no indication "that such pressure was effective."

Metzenbaum even concurred that there was valid reason for not prosecuting the non-American firms in the cartel.

A major factor militating against criminal prosecution of the foreign firms and individuals is that the cartel was a foreign reaction to an anti-competitive strategy of our own government, [the Senator said.] The evidence is clear that the cartel was not intended to, and did not have its primary effects on U.S. commerce. The basic price fixing and production allocation provisions were designed primarily to stabilize foreign markets. The anti-competitive action by our own government creates a strong argument in terms of the international laws of comity against criminal prosecution of the foreign nationals involved here.

Gulf Oil was another matter. "I do disagree strongly with Mr. Shenefield's decision to merely charge Gulf Oil Corporation with a misdemeanor charge," Metzenbaum said. ". . . Gulf Oil Corporation's posture as a proposed defendant is quite different from foreign firms. It is, after all, an American company and should obey American laws."

"[T]he interest of Canada and other foreign nations in avoiding having their uranium policies put on trial in the United States are relatively small, when compared with the United States' interest in prosecuting Gulf, an American firm which knowingly and wilfully violated American antitrust laws."

That is not quite the way it would be seen in Ottawa, London, Paris, Canberra, and other capitals. There, the question remains: when American companies operate abroad, whose laws do they obey?

.

CHAPTER TWELVE

The War
of Litigation

Amicus curiae. Friend of the court.

The courts in the United States dealing with a spateful of uranium law suits have had some powerful *amici curiae*. These friends included the governments of Canada, Great Britain, Australia, France, and South Africa. They produced innumerable *amicus curiae* briefs. Only they did not sound too friendly.

In the eyes of the American judges, actions by the five governments to block information on the activities of the cartel were perceived as efforts to shield the uranium producers and wilfully frustrate the administration of justice within U.S. courts. In the eyes of the governments, though, the American courts had no business in trying to apply U.S. laws to the activities of companies conducted outside of the United States.

Trapped in this litigation war were dozens of uranium producing companies who faced the prospect of enormous penalties if they failed to obey the orders of American courts to tell all about the cartel, and equally tough penalties from the other governments if they did.

Aside from the suits that the power utilities had brought against Westinghouse for failure to deliver contracted volumes of uranium, two other types of uranium suits dragged their way through the courts for years.

The first of these were suits in a Federal District Court in Chicago brought by Westinghouse and the Tennessee Valley Authority against both U.S. and foreign uranium producers for allegedly conspiring to raise the price of uranium.

At issue in the remaining suits was the question of whether

or not a number of other producers would have to deliver some 50 million pounds of uranium to General Atomic Company, an affiliate of Gulf Oil, at contracted prices of around $10 per pound, or whether they were free to sell it at prices ranging from $25 to $44 per pound.

The suits and counter-suits between General Atomic and its suppliers involved nearly half a dozen companies: United Nuclear Corporation, Reserve Oil and Minerals, Ranchers Exploration and Development, Houston Natural Gas, and Exxon Nuclear Corporation.

Largest of the suits brought against General Atomic was that by United Nuclear. In terms of the amount of money at stake, it was also the largest court case ever held in New Mexico.

United Nuclear is one of the pioneer uranium producers in New Mexico, tracing its history back to the feverish stampede of prospectors and promoters unleashed by the rewards offered by the U.S. Atomic Energy Commission starting in the late 1940's. The greatest rush in the history of U.S. mining had already started when Dick Bokum, a shrewd and flamboyant promoter, arrived on the scene. Bokum bought out a number of small miners and put together a series of partnerships that eventually evolved into United Nuclear. In addition to mining uranium, United Nuclear operates one of seven U.S. plants that frabricate enriched uranium into the form used as fuel in nuclear reactors. The United Nuclear plant supplies rods for the reactors of U.S. Navy nuclear submarines, as well as test reactors.

Between 1966 and 1971, United Nuclear signed contracts to supply some 29 million pounds of uranium to a number of power utilities. In 1971, Gulf Oil and United Nuclear went into partnership to organize a company called Gulf United Nuclear, owned 57 per cent by Gulf and 43 per cent by United Nuclear. The new firm was in business to produce and sell uranium, and expand the modest nuclear fuel fabrication services that had been established by United Nuclear. It turned out to be a money loser. In 1973, Gulf bought out United Nuclear's interest in the partnership, and continued the business under the name of General Atomic Company. General Atomic contracted to purchase from United Nuclear the uranium that had been committed to the power utilities. At about the same time, Gulf went into partnership in General Atomic with Scallop Nuclear, a subsidiary of the Royal Dutch Shell group of companies, to succeed the ill-fated partnership with United Nuclear. Shell's interest in the partnership, however, did not include the uranium that General Atomic had contracted to buy from United Nuclear, and thus Shell was not involved in the litigation.

On August 8, 1975, United Nuclear advised General Atomic that it would not continue to deliver uranium under the terms of the contract, and on the same day filed suit in Federal Court against both General Atomic and Gulf, seeking to void the contract. Later, this action was dropped and on December 31, 1975, United Nuclear filed a new suit against only General Atomic in the New Mexico State District Court of Santa Fe County, where it was assigned to Judge Edwin Felter.

In its suit, United Nuclear claimed that it was absolved from any obligations to General Atomic or Gulf because of their alleged illegal activities. Among other things, United Nuclear alleged that Gulf had coerced it into the partnership arrangement; had managed the partnership to the detriment of United Nuclear; had engaged in predatory efforts to control New Mexico uranium supplies, attempting to tie up huge quantities when the price was low and keep uranium out of competition with the cartel; had purchased UNC's uranium at low prices while secretly conspiring within the cartel to raise the price later; and had violated New Mexico antitrust laws.

United Nuclear's argument, in effect, was that Gulf was keeping its own uranium in the ground in anticipation of higher prices that would be arranged by the cartel, while trying to buy up as much low-cost uranium from United Nuclear and others as possible. The problem with this theory is that even the president of United Nuclear did not appear to believe it.

In a memorandum to the company's board of directors, United Nuclear president Keith A. Cunningham wrote: "The public impression . . . would suggest that uranium prices are not economic but rather are the direct result of cartel activities. This, as we all know, is not true . . . uranium prices are the direct result of economic forces coming to bear in a somewhat belated fashion."

The most controversial issue in this case involved the

release of cartel documents housed in Canada. It was an issue that would later bring the government of Canada into this New Mexico court case.

When United Nuclear filed its suit in the New Mexico court on December 31, 1975, it also issued interrogatories demanding, among other things, that both General Atomic and Gulf produce all information in their possession on uranium marketing and sales, which would embrace Gulf's cartel documents in Canada.

This was nine months before Ottawa issued the Uranium Information Security Regulations which made it a criminal offence to release any cartel documents located in Canada. Although there was then no law to prevent Gulf from producing these documents, one may speculate that the Canadian government might have applied pressure on Gulf to keep the information under wraps. The U.S. Department of Justice had started its investigation of the uranium cartel well before United Nuclear launched its suit in Judge Felter's court. In repeated representations to Washington, the Canadian government had strenuously objected to this investigation by U.S. law officials into activities that Ottawa considered to be in accord with Canadian law and national policies, and claimed did not affect U.S. commercial interests. Ottawa was clearly trying to keep the cartel documents out of the hands of the U.S. Department of Justice. Its efforts would be entirely futile if Gulf were to produce the documents in Santa Fe. It is inconceivable that Ottawa would have been unaware of the Santa Fe action, and the implications. Ottawa thus had every reason to try to dissuade Gulf from releasing the cartel documents in Judge Felter's court. What steps it may have taken, if any, to keep Gulf from spilling the beans can only be speculated.

Four months after United Nuclear had issued the interrogatories, General Atomic provided its responses. Judge Felter described them as "wholly inadequate and evasive answers."

Armed with a court order from Judge Felter, United Nuclear's counsel Harry L. Bigbee, a Santa Fe lawyer whose firm had also acted for Gulf Oil, then swooped down on General Atomic's offices in San Diego, California, with three microfilm crews to plough through General Atomic's files. Bigbee's team captured 180,000 pages of General Atomic and Gulf Oil documents on microfilm for use in evidence, including internal corporate documents related to the cartel.

The pre-trial legal procedures over the production of information dragged on and on, so long in fact that the whole case threatened to interfere with Judge Felter's plans to campaign for re-election in 1978.

Three lawyers involved in the case later, in sworn affidavits, related a discussion they had with the judge in his chambers in early August, 1977. No court reporter was present. According to the affidavits: "Toward the end of the proceedings, Judge Felter stated that the trial of this case would be over before the end of year, because he intended to run for re-election the following year and did not want this case to interfere with the election campaign."

The case was far from over by the end of the year, but Judge Felter was re-elected anyway. In fact, the publicity he got from handling New Mexico's largest court case did more to help than hinder his re-election. According to the *San Diego Daily Union*, as a result of the case Judge Felter had "acquired the image of a hometown hero able to punish meddling 'outsiders.' "

In August, 1976, United Nuclear issued its second set of interrogatories, this time directed more specifically at the cartel documents in Canada. The following month, Canada issued the Uranium Information Security Regulations.

As the battle over discovery dragged on, Ottawa protested efforts to secure information in defiance of Canadian law. In a diplomatic note issued in March, 1977, concerning the Santa Fe case, Ottawa protested to Washington that the matter

> raises questions directly bearing upon the acts and policies of the government of Canada [and] the consideration to be given by courts in the United States to the application in Canada of valid Canadian laws and regulations . . . it would be contrary to the national interest of Canada for the propriety or legality of actions of Canadian uranium producers taken outside the United States and which were required by Canada law or taken in implementation of Canadian government policy to be called into question before the United States courts and tribunals.

After nearly two years of procedural battles, the case finally came to trial on October 31, 1977.

An editorial in the *Daily Santa Fe New Mexican* on the day that the trial opened made it clear that a victory for United Nuclear would be a victory for the State of New Mexico. If United Nuclear won, New Mexico uranium would be sold for much higher prices, and the state would collect greater severance taxes. "All New Mexico residents have a direct stake in the outcome of a multi-billion dollar uranium lawsuit which will be heard in District Court beginning today," the newspaper stated. "[T]he state stands to gain huge severance tax windfall if the higher price is imposed."

No matter how scrupulous the judge might be, an implication in the editorial that a decision in favour of United Nuclear might enhance his prospects of re-election in 1978 was all too apparent.

The trial had been underway less than a fortnight before Judge Felter angrily accused General Atomic of hiding behind the Canadian regulations. General Atomic, he said, was attempting to "bring about cover-ups and stonewalling information," and to "hide behind procedural and other rules in order to play a game of hide-and-go seek with this court, and I am getting sick of it . . . I don't think that you are acting in good faith at all in this regard, and I think you are trying to suppress information that could be brought to light and aid this court, which you could voluntarily produce. I see no valid reason why you shouldn't do that, even though you may have a trial procedural shield that you can hide behind here."

On November 18, 1977, Judge Felter issued an order requiring General Atomic to "identify, clearly and definitively, all documents housed in Canada . . ." He also ruled that "all facts provable from documents housed in Canada which are not produced . . . are found against General Atomic Company, and said defendant is precluded from offering evidence herein in opposition to such findings of fact . . ."

What this meant in plain language was that if General Atomic did not produce the Canadian cartel documents, Judge Felter would accept as proven the allegations United Nuclear claimed could be proven if the documents were produced. Thus, failure to produce the documents in defiance of Canadian law could result in General Atomic losing the law suit in a default judgment – without any trial on the merits of the case – which is exactly what happened.

Judge Felter had ordered General Atomic and Gulf to break Canadian law or suffer the consequences. In justifying this order, Judge Felter wrote:

> Deference to the sovereignty and national interest of Canada or its provinces cannot be accomplished through sacrifice of the sovereignty of New Mexico and of due process of law and equal application and protection of law afforded by the laws of New Mexico. [New Mexico's laws] must govern over the national interest or policy of a foreign country. . . No rule of comity would require a sovereign state of the United States to so abdicate the protection of fundamental rights under its general laws that are necessary to a fair trial in favor of special foreign laws that are not concerned with any aspect or requirement of fair trial.

Judge Felter's ruling promptly brought another diplomatic note, December 9, from Ottawa to the U.S. Secretary of State:

> The Canadian government is deeply concerned that an order has been issued by a United States court, the effect of which would be to compel the identification and production of documents in Canada contrary to Canada law, a result that would be inconsistent with international comity.

On the same day, Energy Minister Alastair Gillespie wrote to Gulf Minerals Canada president R. N. Taylor, warning him not to release the documents:

> I am sure you are aware that the government of Canada is very concerned about attempts by courts in the United States to extend their jurisdiction into Canada. . . . In view of the decision of the District Court in New Mexico, I take this opportunity to point out to you that the provisions of the Regulations effectively prohibit Gulf Minerals Canada Limited from assisting General Atomic Company in complying with the Order of the District Court in New

Mexico, by producing, or identifying, documents coming within the provisions of the regulations.

When General Atomic filed its responses to United Nuclear's second set of interrogatories, in February, 1978, it did not, as Felter had ordered, either identify or produce the cartel documents. Felter again found General Atomic's answers "unresponsive and evasive," and accused the company of "the utmost bad faith."

The stage was thus set for Judge Felter's default judgment, which came on March 2, freeing United Nuclear to reap more than a billion dollars in extra revenues, together with the "huge severance tax windfall" for the State of New Mexico. In his judgment, Judge Felter accused General Atomic of having "followed a conscious, wilful and deliberate policy . . . in cynical disregard and disdain of the rules of procedure relating to discovery and this court's discovery orders, of concealing rather than in good faith revealing the true facts concerning the international uranium cartel." He said that General Atomic had "covered up the fact of Gulf Oil Corporation's participation in an international uranium cartel" and "thereby deliberately concealed the existence of evidence which it knew to be highly relevant to the antitrust issues treated in UNC's complaint." The company, he ruled, was guilty of "obstruction of justice" and a "wilful, deliberate and flagrant scheme of delay, resistance, obfuscation and evasion."

Felter held that the cartel was effective; that it had artificially increased uranium prices; that Gulf withheld production with the "intent to monopolize New Mexico uranium reserves"; that it "locked up" United Nuclear's reserves with the intent of keeping them "out of competition with the cartel" and "eliminating middlemen as competitors."

The Canadian government intervened once more, with an *amicus curiae* brief to the U.S. Supreme Court on an appeal that had been launched against Judge Felter's order to compel production of the cartel documents in Canada.

Ottawa's brief argued against what it called Felter's "incorrect assumption that the needs of litigation in New Mexico 'must govern' and outweigh any interest of Canada," and accused the New Mexico court of having "conducted itself in a way calculated to enter into conflict with the interest of the government of Canada."

"The New Mexico courts committed grave error in failing to give proper consideration to Canada's laws and in imposing sanctions upon a party which was unable to produce documents without causing a contravention of these laws," the brief stated.

Perhaps the most crucial aspects was Ottawa's assertion that,

> by entering a default judgment and exposing a party to substantial damages, the court's decision poses a continuing problem to international relations in that it will encourage Canadian nationals and residents to violate Canadian laws in the future in order to avoid the severe consequences of non-compliance with U.S. judicial processes.

The U.S. Supreme Court did not squash Judge Felter's order to General Atomic and Gulf to produce the Canadian documents. And in August, 1980, the New Mexico Supreme Court upheld Judge Felter's default award to United Nuclear, and again rebuked both General Atomic and Gulf Oil for a "a course of misconduct in discovery which began at the very onset of the case."

"In discovery, as well as in other aspects of this litigation, General Atomic's efforts have been marked by an extraordinary lack of diligence that can't be characterized as accidental, unintentional or involuntary," the State Supreme Court ruled.

Two weeks after this ruling, an arbitration panel, proceeding under federal arbitration laws, reached totally different conclusions. The panel was headed by former Illinois Supreme Court Chief Justice Walter Schaefer.

The arbitration panel found that there had been no attempt to monopolize uranium supplies or eliminate competitors; that the cartel had no effect on U.S. uranium prices, and that there was no evidence that United Nuclear had been "coerced" into any arrangements with Gulf or General Atomic. United Nuclear, according to the arbitration panel, "decided to break its commitment so that it could sell its uranium at higher prices to other purchasers."

The arbitration panel ordered United Nuclear to provide General Atomic with cash payments and uranium supplies worth – on the basis of 1980 uranium prices of about $30 a pound – a total of some $750 million.

While the final outcome of the Santa Fe case has still to be determined, there was a certain irony in the position in which United Nuclear found itself in the litigation in Chicago. In this case, United Nuclear was accused of having conspired with none other than Gulf Oil, as well as others, in illegal antitrust activities to fix uranium prices and boycott middlemen.

THE TROUBLE WITH LAWYERS

And [Jesus] said, Woe unto you lawyers also!
for ye load men with burdens grievous to be borne,
and ye yourselves touch not the burdens
with one of your fingers.

Luke, 11:46

In the litigious atmosphere that blossomed into full flower in American society during the 1970's it became difficult for a major corporation to clear its throat without first consulting a lawyer. A problem arises in finding a law firm that does not have a conflict of interest from having advised competing firms on corporate throat clearing about related matters.

Between 1965 and 1980, the number of lawyers working in the United States doubled to exceed half a million, and legal costs soared to more than $30 billion a year. The number of lawyers in the United States was three times per capita the number in England, five times as many as in West Germany, and twenty times as many as in Japan.

The warning of U.S. Chief Justice Warren Burger seemed a dangerous prospect. "We may be well on our way to a society overrun by hordes of lawyers, hungry as locusts, and brigades of judges in numbers never before contemplated."

Largest by far of all the legal cases – in terms of length, legal costs, and the amount of money at stake – are those involving antitrust matters. Antitrust action by the Justice Department which forced El Paso Natural Gas Company to divest itself of a subsidiary, Pacific Northwest Pipeline Company, took fifteen years. The U.S. Justice Department antitrust suit against International Business Machines had been underway eleven years by 1981, and produced more than one hundred million documents – far more than any single person could ever read. In 1980, MCI Communications Corporation won $1.8 billion in a triple damage award from an antitrust suit against American Telephone and Telegraph, the largest legal award in history.

With $200 an hour not an uncommon fee for a big-name lawyer, the legal costs of litigation have become staggering. When Gulf Oil sued former officers of the company to recover illegal political payments, it collected $2 million, but paid $1.7 million in legal costs. The law firm that handled MCI's successful antitrust suits against AT&T was expected to collect $93 million.

However, for the complexity of issues, the number of suits involved, the amount of money at stake, and the international entanglements, the uranium case stands out as a landmark in litigation history.

With so many firms and so many lawyers involved, it was perhaps inevitable that conflict of interest problems would arise in the case of Westinghouse Electric Corporation vs. Rio Algom Limited *et al.* Three separate law firms were to be disqualified from participating in the case.

The Chicago law firm of Kirkland and Ellis is one of the largest in the United States. In 1976, it had 140 lawyers on its staff in Chicago, and another 40 lawyers working in its Washington offices. On October 15, 1976, the lawyers of Kirkland and Ellis filed the complaint on behalf of Westinghouse against the uranium producers in the Federal District Court in Chicago.

On the same day, the Washington lawyers of Kirkland and Ellis delivered a 230-page report they had prepared for the American Petroleum Institute. The Kirkland and Ellis report for the API argued that uranium price increases had been caused by competitive market factors, and by Westinghouse. That would lead to the first conflict of interest problem in the uranium litigation.

The complaint filed in Chicago by Kirkland and Ellis named twenty-nine defendants, including seventeen American and twelve foreign firms.

Eight of the defendants named were associated with the Rio Tinto-Zinc group: Rio Tinto-Zinc Corporation Limited and Rio Tinto-Zinc Services Ltd., in London; Conzinc Riotinto and Mary Kathleen Uranium Limited in Australia; Rio Tinto-Zinc Corporation of America (later dropped from the suit); Rio Algom Limited in Toronto; and two U.S. subsidiaries of Rio Algom Limited, Rio Algom Corporation (which operates a small uranium mine in Utah), and Atlas Alloys (which markets specialty steels in the United States).

Gulf Oil Corporation and its subsidiaries were to figure most prominently among all the defendants.

From Canada, in addition to Rio Algom and Gulf Minerals, Denison Mines, and its subsidiary, Denison Mines (U.S.) Inc., were named.

Three of the defendants were involved with South African uranium: the Anglo-American Corporation of South Africa Limited; Nuclear Fuels Corporation, and Engelhard Minerals and Chemical Corporation, partly owned by Anglo-American.

In addition to the RTZ interests, there were four other defendants with interests in Australian uranium: Pancontinental Mining Limited; Getty Oil Company (which has an interest in Pancontinental); Queensland Mines Limited; and Noranda Mines Ltd. of Toronto.

Ten U.S. uranium producers were named: Kerr-McGee Corporation; the Anaconda Company; United Nuclear; Utah International Inc. (owned by General Electric); Phelps Dodge Corporation; Western Nuclear Inc. (owned by Phelps Dodge); Homestake Mining Company (Westinghouse's former partner in uranium exploration and development plans); Reserve Oil and Mineral Corporation; Federal Resources Corporation; and Pioneer Nuclear Inc.

Several firms that had been active in the cartel were not included among those Westinghouse accused of having rigged uranium prices. Those omitted from the Westinghouse action were Eldorado Nuclear, owned by the Canadian government; Uranex, partly owned by the government of France; Urangesellschaft of West Germany, and its Canadian subsidiary, Uranerz Canada Limited. A year later, when the Tennessee Valley Authority filed suits on similar grounds against thirteen uranium producers, Uranex, Urangesellschaft, and Uranerz Canada were among those charged.

The suits filed by the TVA were later consolidated, at least for purposes of discovery, with the Westinghouse action, to be heard by U.S. District Court Judge Prentice Marshall in Chicago.

Four of the defendants filed motions with Judge Marshall to disqualify the Kirkland and Ellis firm, claiming that as members of the American Petroleum Institute, they had provided the law firm with confidential information on their uranium operations, privileged information that could be relevant to the Westinghouse litigation.

The Kirkland and Ellis report had been prepared for the API for use in opposing proposed legislation in Congress to break up the large American oil companies by separating their control over production, refining, transportation, and marketing activities, as well as ownership in other forms of energy, principally coal and uranium. The Kirkland and Ellis study claimed that participation of the oil companies in the uranium business had actually increased production and competition and that, like other energy industries, the uranium business was highly competitive. The large increases in uranium prices, the report said, were largely attributable to increased demand and a lack of supplies. "Another reason for the recent price increase is Westinghouse's 1975 announcement that it would not fulfil most of its long-term contractual commitments to 27 utilities to deliver 65 million pounds of uranium over the next 20 years, causing an influx of new demand," the report had stated.

In ruling against the motions to disqualify Kirkland and Ellis from the case, Judge Marshall noted that a comparison of the report for the API and the Westinghouse complaint "reveals a basic conflict." He found, however, that there was no evidence that information obtained by the law firm's Washington office for the API report had been made available to the Chicago office for the Westinghouse action. "With the modern-day proliferation of large law firms representing multi-billion dollar corporations in all segments of the economy and the governmental process," Judge Marshall ruled, "it is becoming increasingly difficult to insist upon absolute fidelity to rules prohibiting attorneys from representing overlapping legal interests."

Judge Marshall seemed surprised to learn a few days later that his rejection of motions to disqualify Kirkland and Ellis might be appealed.

Glenn McGee, counsel for Kerr-McGee, commented in court that the judge's ruling was "certainly very thorough, a very careful memorandum. I only find one problem with it, and that is that it reached the wrong conclusion."

"Are orders which refuse to disqualify counsel appealable in this circuit?" Judge Marshall asked.

"They are, Your Honour," replied Kirkland and Ellis lawyer Fred Bartlet.

Marshall: "Are they?"

Bartlet: "Yes, sir."

Marshall: "Without a certification or any such step on my part?"

Bartlet: "Yes, sir."

The U.S. Court of Appeals for the Seventh Circuit later ruled that Judge Marshall had "abused his discretion." Kirkland and Ellis was disqualified from the case. The big Chicago firm had handled Westinghouse's defence in the suits by the electric power utilities at Richmond, and had also by this time spent more than a year and a half working on the Chicago case. The Appeal Court estimated that the law firm had collected $2.5 million in fees for its work on the Chicago case. A group of Westinghouse shareholders was later to file a suit against Kirkland and Ellis, demanding that it return the fees to Westinghouse.

Even before the appeal court ruled on Kirkland and Ellis, another motion had been presented to Marshall by Gulf, this time asking him to disqualify the Santa Fe firm of Bigbee, Stephenson, Carpenter and Crout, the firm that had acted for United Nuclear in its suit against Gulf before Judge Felter in New Mexico. Harry Bigbee's firm was again acting for United Nuclear, which was now, like Gulf, being sued by Westinghouse. If that were not bad enough, the Bigbee firm had also acted for Gulf in its uranium business in New Mexico during the five-year period to 1976. Nine of the twelve lawyers in the Bigbee firm had worked for Gulf. Gulf's uranium activities were tied up in the issues involved in the Westinghouse suit. Nevertheless, Marshall rejected Gulf's motion to disqualify the New Mexico firm. There was another appeal. Again Judge Marshall was over-ruled and the Bigbee firm was disqualified.

Westinghouse, meanwhile, was having difficulty finding a

replacement for Kirkland and Ellis. It had hired a Chicago firm, Freeman, Rothe, Freeman and Salzman, but also wanted another firm to work on the case as well.

A request by Westinghouse for an order from Judge Marshall authorizing the appearance of Jones, Day, Reavis and Pogue brought swift objections from half a dozen of the defendants, most of whom had been clients of the Jones firm. They said that the Jones firm had been given privileged information that could have a bearing on the litigation. Another problem was with two lawyers who had recently joined the Jones firm from the antitrust division of Department of Justice. Donald Baker and Jonathon Rose had both been involved in the grand jury investigation of the uranium cartel, and had been involved in discussions about the investigation with the Department of State and with Canadian government officials.

"I think Westinghouse has to ask itself whether in the circumstances of this case they . . . want this law firm that comes . . . with a lot of barnacles on it as far as this law suit is concerned," Judge Marshall commented from the bench.

Westinghouse withdrew its request to use the Jones firm, and later hired the big New York firm of Donovan, Leisure, Newton and Irvine as its lead counsel.

The troubles with the law firms added at least a year to the lengthy discovery process, before the trial could get underway. Discovery in this case would be a lengthy process, under the best of circumstances. Files would have to be examined in offices around the world. Millions of pages of documents would have to be produced and carefully examined for any light they might shed in either helping the plaintiffs to prove their charges, or the defendants to disprove them. Testimony would be taken from scores of people in deposition proceedings. The deposition hearings for each witness might last anywhere from one day to as long as two weeks.

Reading of depositions by lawyers during the trial can be a boring process that drags on for weeks. During the pre-trial hearings, consideration was given to videotaping the statements so that the videotapes could be played back in court, eliminating the play acting involved in reading the statements.

"I had occasion recently to try a very, very interesting civil action," Judge Marshall commented from the bench. "It lasted nine days. A substantial portion of the evidence was adduced by deposition, and three out of eight jurors slept during most of the deposition reading."

The deposition readings, said Marshall, can become "ludicrous . . . We had a young woman playing the role of a fifty-eight-year-old-man, and we had a man playing the role of a woman who, according to the transcript, was going through the menopause."

Another approach suggested by Marshall was to hire actors to read the deposition statements. "[T]here are a lot of them in town here who would love the part-time work," he commented.

As the discovery process and pre-trial hearings dragged on and on Judge Marshall displayed his impatience at the snail-like progress. By late 1979, when one of the counsel asked for additional time to prepare a brief, Judge Marshall was, figuratively speaking, ready to lay down the law.

"This law suit is now three years old," the judge commented from the bench. "Do you know how long it took the United States of America to fight World War Two on two continental fronts? Three years and eight months. Now, let's get about it. How much time do you need, Mr. Goodrich? You are in a war."

Before even the discovery stage was completed, verbal shots fired from around the world would make it seem like Judge Marshall was, indeed, in the middle of a war.

TENNESSEE VALLEY ENTERS THE FRAY

On Monday, August 15, 1977, the sub-committee on Oversight and Investigations of the U.S. House of Representatives' Committee on Interstate and Foreign Commerce resumed public hearings after a two-month lapse, and came a-calling on Nashville, Tennessee, home town of the world's largest electric power producer, the U.S. government-owned Tennessee Valley Authority. Tennessee's own Albert Gore Jr. would chair the Moss committee's hearings in the state legislative buildings on this particular, hot summer's day.

The Westinghouse suit against the members of the uranium cartel and the U.S. producers that had allegedly conspired with the cartel to raise U.S. uranium prices had been filed ten months before. No one had purchased as much uranium from the cartel members as the TVA. In August, 1974, it had contracted to buy 400,000 pounds of uranium from Uranerz Canada at a base price of $10.75 a pound, although this price was later raised by the Canadian government. It had also contracted to purchase 17 million pounds from Rio Algom Limited, for delivery over a 22-year period starting in 1979, the largest commercial uranium purchase that had ever been made. Under the contract with Rio Algom, the price was to be the greater of an amount based on the cost of production, or a market-related price to be negotiated two years prior to delivery.

If Congressman Gore was right that the cartel had increased uranium prices 700 per cent, no one would be stung more than the Tennessee Valley Authority and its electric power consumers. Yet the TVA had not taken any action against the cartel, and Congressman Gore wanted to know why.

Possibly one reason was that the TVA was among those utilities then suing Westinghouse in Richmond, Virginia, for failure to deliver contracted uranium supplies. In that suit, TVA and the other plaintiffs had brought out evidence seeking to show that there had been no boycott of uranium supplies by the cartel, that the cartel members had offered large supplies of foreign uranium to U.S. buyers, that the cartel prices for foreign uranium were no higher than the prices paid for U.S. uranium. Moreover, TVA's own uranium marketing expert had testified that it was not the cartel that had increased U.S. uranium prices.

But that was not the way that Congressman Gore saw it. "[T]his subcommittee has painstakingly assembled cold, hard facts which describe in detail the formation and operation of a secret, sophisticated, and powerful international uranium producer's club, as it came to be known, which has raised the price of uranium by secretly rigging bids and fixing prices," Gore said in opening the hearings at Nashville.

The principal witnesses at the hearing that day were four TVA representatives: Aubrey Wagner, chairman of the board; Erik Kraven, assistant chief, nuclear procurement branch; Jack Gilleland, assistant manager of power; Allan Mullins, chief of the nuclear raw materials branch.

"I know this committee is interested in the effects the producers' international marketing arrangement may have had on TVA's ratepayers," Wagner stated. He added that TVA's legal staff was investigating "the impact of the cartel on TVA . . . and any possible course of action TVA might have."

The TVA position was not aggressive enough to suit Gore. He accused the TVA officials of "bending over backwards to be doubly cautious not to in any way upset" Rio Algom, the utility's big uranium supplier. "I would hope that instead TVA would redouble its efforts to represent the consumers and institute antitrust actions . . . when evidence of a cartel is received," he added.

The testimony of the TVA officials, however, did not seem to suggest a strong case for launching an antitrust action.

Kraven told Gore that the contract with Uranerz "was considerably less than the prices being quoted as a cartel. If there was a cartel, whatever information we had in hand at that point in time was that it either was not very effective or they were not all hanging together."

"[A]ll of the evidence that we could see ourselves from our own experience of talking with individual producers indicated that if a cartel were operating, the effects of it were so small that we could not see them," Mullins testified. "We just could not see any effects of it."

Gilleland said that it was "extremely difficult for TVA to determine the effect, if any, that the cartel had on either the foreign or domestic price of uranium at any point in time. Other factors, such as the way Westinghouse conducted their uranium business, obviously had a large effect."

Gilleland also stressed the importance to TVA of the uranium contracted for purchase from Rio Algom. "Considering the possibility of substantial uranium shortages in the 1980's being able to obtain a 17 million pound commitment in this period was very attractive," he said. "These 17 million pounds represented some 15 to 20 per cent of TVA's projected requirements over the 1979-90 period and were an attractive hedge against future shortages. The Rio contract is still very important in assuring TVA an adequate supply of uranium in future years."

TVA's legal staff must have been sharper at discerning the

cartel effects than the company officials who had testified at the hearings that day in Nashville. In any event, three months after Congressman Gore had urged the TVA to "institute antitrust actions," the big utility did just that. In its suit against 12 uranium companies, TVA claimed that it had been boycotted in its efforts to contract for the purchase of 86 million pounds of uranium, and the 20 million pounds that it had been able to secure were at artificial and non-competitive prices.

The contract for the 17 million pounds of uranium that Gilleland had said was so advantageous to TVA later appeared to be far less advantageous. Under the terms of their contract, TVA and Rio Algom began negotiations on the price to be paid for the first year's deliveries, to be made in 1979. Unable to reach a negotiated price, the matter was sent to arbitration, as provided for in the contract. The arbitrator set a price of $45.52 a pound for 1979 deliveries. In 1978, negotiations led to a tentative price of $47.56 for 1980 deliveries. TVA decided that this was too much, and again sent the matter to the arbitrator. But the arbitrator set the price for 1980 deliveries even higher, at $51.50 a pound.

Between the time that the prices were set and the start of scheduled deliveries two years later, uranium prices began once more to decline. By 1980 they had fallen to as low as $30 a pound, far less than TVA would have to pay under its contract with Rio Algom.

In July, 1979, Rio Algom made its first uranium delivery under the TVA contract, amounting to 500,000 pounds. It was delivered to the Port Hope refinery of Eldorado Nuclear for conversion into uranium hexafluoride, the first step, after mining and milling, in the final fabrication into the form used as fuel in nuclear power plants. TVA was scheduled to make payment of $22.7 million by July 22. Three days before that, Westinghouse – with the concurrence of TVA – obtained a preliminary injunction from Judge Marshall restraining TVA from making payment to Rio Algom because of the litigation then underway. The injunction required TVA to pay the $22.7 million into an escrow account under the jurisdiction of a U.S. court. Rio Algom then launched suits in a Toronto court, seeking $2.2 billion in damages from Westinghouse and TVA, claiming that the injunction restraining payment had been obtained by "conspiracy" between the two companies, and "with the malicious purpose" of damaging Rio Algom.

WORDS OF WORLD WAR THREE

"Far be it from me to start World War Three," quipped a judge sitting on the U.S. Court of Appeals for the Seventh Circuit, which was hearing an appeal from a ruling issued by Federal District Court Judge Prentice Marshall in the case of Westinghouse Electric Corporation vs. Rio Algom *et al.*

It was perhaps a measure of the international tensions surrounding the uranium litigation that no one in the crowded Chicago court room laughed at the judge's little joke.

Two principal aspects of the suits brought by Westinghouse and the TVA against the uranium producers pitted the U.S. courts in a heated conflict with the five governments involved in the uranium cartel, threatening to rock international relations.

The first aspect involved the refusal by nine of the foreign defendants to appear before Judge Marshall to answer the charges in the Westinghouse and TVA complaints, and to submit themselves to the jurisdiction of the Chicago court.

The second aspect involved ten other defendants who appeared before Judge Marshall to defend themselves, but refused to comply with court orders to produce cartel documents, which they could do only by breaking foreign non-disclosure laws. Extensive hearings were held before Judge Marshall on the question of whether these defendants acted in good faith, or whether sanctions ought to be applied for their failure to produce the documents as ordered. As with the default judgment, the sanctions sought against those that refused to produce the cartel documents potentially involved billions of dollars.

Four months after the Westinghouse complaint had been filed, Judge Marshall, in February, 1977, held the non-appearing foreign defendants in default. They were Anglo-American, Conzinc Riotinto, Mary Kathleen Uranium, Nufcor, Pancontinental, Queensland Mines, Rio Algom, Rio Tinto-Zinc and Rio Tinto-Zinc Services. Later, when TVA included Uranex among its defendants, the French firm also declined to submit itself to the jurisdiction of the American court. While Rio

Algom Limited did not appear before Judge Marshall to defend itself, its two U.S. subsidiaries – Rio Algom Corporation and Atlas Alloys – did.

Court procedures on what to do about the defaulting defendants dragged on for years.

In January, 1979, Judge Marshall issued a "Final judgment order on issues of liability" concerning the non-appearing defaulters, ruling that hearings might proceed on the amount of damages to be applied. He also acted to prevent the defaulters from moving assets out of the United States.

The failure of the defaulters to appear in court and answer the charges means, Marshall ruled, that they

> have confessed those allegations and have admitted the truth of all well pleaded factual allegations in plaintiff's complaint.
>
> A final decision upon the claims made against the non-defaulting defendants will surely not be rendered for several years. . . . In the interim, plaintiff faces the possibility that the defaulting defendants, which are all foreign corporations, may conceal or transfer their assets which are subject to execution by United States courts. Without a final default judgment entered against these defendants . . . plaintiff will be unable to procure a writ of execution to begin the process of collecting any subsequent damage award.
>
> The defaults are not the result of inadvertence or excusable neglect . . . these defendants have chosen not to appear or answer the complaint in any manner whatsoever, despite ample opportunity to do so. Indeed, we are told that one of the defaulters directed its agent to destroy the copies of the summons and complaint by tearing up each page . . .

An appeal against Judge Marshall's order was launched, and meanwhile the discovery process and pre-trial hearings continued.

In March, Marshall heard a request by Atlas Alloys, asking for permission to make payment of $1.5 million which it owed to its parent company, Rio Algom Limited in Toronto. Marshall took the opportunity to again admonish the defaulters.

"[T]he likely recovery by the plaintiff against those defaulting defendants, unless at some future time they should appear and challenge the proof of damages, will clearly exceed half a billion dollars and could well approach two billion dollars," Marshall stated.

"This is a treble damage action, the consequence of which is the reasonable likely recovery by Westinghouse from the defaulting defendants will range, when trebled, from 1.5 billion to 6 billion dollars.

"The likelihood of plaintiff's ultimately prevailing on the merits" in respect to attaching the U.S. assets of the defaulters, "is overwhelming," the judge stated.

Judge Marshall made it clear that he was sorely vexed at what he perceived as deliberate attempts to obstruct justice in his court:

> I realize that courts and those who occupy courts, namely judges, are inclined at times to exaggerate their importance, but the history of this case with respect to the nine defaulting defendants demonstrates a pattern of calculated obduracy designed solely to frustrate the orderly processes of this court and the orderly administration of justice in this court. The public interest with respect to the administration of justice in this court can be served only by taking the firm position . . . that they respond to the orderly processes, the lawful processes, yes, the due process of this court.

The foreign governments flooded Marshall's court with a raft of protests against the entry of the default judgment.

France sent a diplomatic note to the Department of State. "To attack Uranex's conduct is in fact to attack the conduct of the government of France," the note stated. "The courts of another country cannot be permitted, in matters so sensitive, to inquire into the motivations or conduct of a sovereign nation – or those acting under their instructions."

France argued that where there is a conflict between the laws of different countries, it should be settled by government negotiations and not in the courts.

The French claimed that submission by Uranex to the jurisdiction of U.S. courts would be "an affront to French sovereignty." They protested "the fundamental unfairness of subjecting a defendant to antitrust liability under circumstances where a foreign government has encouraged, directed and otherwise participated in that defendant's activities."

The South African government wrote that the appearance in the court of Anglo-American and Nufcor

> could have involved acceptance of the extra-territorial jurisdiction of U.S. courts – a course of action which would not have been regarded favourably by the South African government.
>
> The South African government respectfully suggests . . . that such extra-territorial application to non-U.S. uranium producers, acting lawfully in terms of their own national laws and international law, would constitute a challenge to the sovereignty of nations and could disturb friendly relations with the United States . . . the legal and economic implications of such application would extend beyond the business activities and financial position of the South African companies concerned and the uranium industry.

Similar views were expressed in *amici curiae* briefs from Australia, Great Britain, and Canada.

The arguments of the defaulters and the five governments on the appeal against Judge Marshall's order were heard by three judges on U.S. Court of Appeals for the Seventh Circuit in the fall of 1979. One of the judges snapped that the arguments of the foreign governments amounted to "nice diplomatic language" which in effect says that the U.S. antitrust policy "is a stupid policy . . . That may be right . . . but we have to follow it." He also said it sounded as if the defaulters were trying "to get of scott-free [while] thumbing their noses at the jurisdiction of American courts."

It was then that one of the judges quipped, "Far be it from me to start World War Three."

When the appeal court handed down its decision, in February, 1980, it added further fire to fuel the conflict.

The appeal court over-ruled Judge Marshall on one aspect, ordering that the hearing on the amount of damages to be levied against the non-appearing defaulters be deferred until after the trial of the appearing defendants. Then if Westinghouse were successful, the amount of damages to be applied against both the appearing and the non-appearing defendants could be considered at a single hearing. If Westinghouse were unsuccessful against the appearing defendants, it would still be able to proceed on damages against the defaulters. But that could be years away.

The appeals court gave Westinghouse another option, however. It if dismissed its claims against the other defendants, it would then be allowed to proceed immediately with hearings on the damages to be applied against the defaulters. On the surface of it, this would allow Westinghouse to save years in litigation, while still collecting just as much money since, as the appeals court said, "Westinghouse could look to any one defendant for full satisfaction of the damage award." The catch is that the defaulting defendants did not have billions of dollars of assets in the United States for Westinghouse to seize, and seizing assets in foreign countries would be almost impossible. The defendant that Westinghouse would logically look to, more than any other, would be the one with the most assets in the United States, its Pittsburgh neighbour, Gulf Oil. So Westinghouse decided to continue with its case against all the defendants.

The appeals court had harsh words to say about efforts by Rio Algom to move assets out of the United States.

"The situation confronting the District Court was extraordinary," the decision declared.

> In order to avoid execution on the default judgment, Rio Algom Limited instructed its American subsidiaries to transfer their assets to Canada. The defaulting defendants circumvented and even ignored the District Court's restraining order in an effort to transfer funds out of the United States. Had the Court not exercised its injunctive powers the default judgment would have been rendered meaningless.

And harsh words were also said about the foreign governments, by the appeals court.

> [T]he defaulters have contumaciously refused to come into court and present evidence as to why the District

Court should not exercise its jurisdiction. They have chosen instead to present their case through surrogates. Wholly owned subsidiaries of several defaulters have challenged the appropriateness of the injunctions, and shockingly to us, the governments of the defaulters have subserviently presented for them their case against the exercise of jurisdiction.

This statement by the appeals court brought a prompt and strong protest from the Department of State.

Department of State legal adviser Robert Owens wrote to Associate Attorney General John Shenefield, requesting his "assistance in drawing to the attention of the court the concern of the United States government over the court's criticism of friendly governments for presenting their views to the court as *amici curiae.*" The court's language, said Owens, "has caused serious embarrassment to the United States in its relations with some of our closest allies."

The five governments, Owens wrote, "have substantial interest" in "certain broader issues" raised by the litigation, concerning "the propriety of the exercise of United States jurisdiction . . . over persons of foreign nationality for actions taken outside of the territorial jurisdiction of the United States." A further concern was that the involvement of these governments in uranium marketing is "now being challenged, not through diplomatic channels, but through private damage litigation in a U.S. court."

While the State Department did not share all of the views expressed by the governments ("and certainly does not condone the non-appearance of the nine defaulting defendants"), Owens said that the governments "should be afforded an opportunity to present their views to the court." In fact, wrote Owens, the State Department had encouraged them to do so. "It is important," he wrote, "that courts be made aware of the international implications of their decisions."

Shenefield forwarded Owens' letter to the appeals court, adding that the Department of Justice "fully concurs" with the views expressed by the Department of State.

But if the language of the appeals court upset the cartel governments and the Department of State, there were even more blunt words still to come from Judge Marshall, dealing with the second contentious aspect raised by the case, the non-disclosure laws.

THE CASE OF THE MISSING DOCUMENTS

While the question of the absent defendants continued, so too did the conflict between the orders of the U.S. courts to produce the foreign cartel documents, and the laws of the foreign governments that prohibited their disclosure.

The basic question before Judge Marshall was the same one that had been before Judge Felter: whose laws shall be obeyed? Repeated appeals were made, particularly to Ottawa, for permission to release the documents. There were letters, endless meetings, court action.

In another related proceeding, an appeals court came to a different conclusion than Judges Felter and Marshall, ruling that in this particular case, the foreign laws did prevail over a U.S. court order.

In 1977, Westinghouse had filed a suit in the Federal District Court in Utah against Rio Algom Corporation, and George Albino an American citizen, resident in Canada, who was also president of the parent Rio Algom Limited. An appeal by Rio Algom to Ottawa for permission to produce the documents was denied. Rio Algom and Albino failed to comply with the orders of the U.S. court. The court ruled that Rio Algom had not made a "good faith" effort to produce the documents. The company was fined $10,000 a day. The fine was appealed. Ottawa intervened with yet another *amicus curiae* brief. The appeals court found that in this case, the interests of Canada were greater than the interests of the United States, and the fine was squashed.

The Utah action had little impact on the proceedings in Chicago.

On November 7, 1979, Judge Marshall issued an order to the defendants to produce the foreign cartel documents by January 2, 1980, or face the consequences.

In Marshall's view, the non-disclosure laws had been adopted "for the express purpose of frustrating the jurisdiction of the United States courts over the activities of the alleged international uranium cartel." The judge was not prepared to be frustrated.

In his ruling ordering the production of the documents, Marshall wrote that he did not wish "to force any defendant to violate foreign laws" but sought "to make each defendant feel the full measure of each sovereign's conflicting demands."

Marshall concluded that a U.S. court has the authority to order documents located abroad "if the particular defendant is within the personal jurisdiction of [the] court and has control over the requested documents." The exercise of this authority, however, is discretionary, and "should not ignore" conflicting foreign laws. In Marshall's view, the factors to be considered were: "(1) the importance of the policies underlying the United States statute which forms the basis for the plaintiffs' claims; (2) the importance of the requested documents in illuminating key elements of the claims, and (3) the degree of flexibility in the foreign nation's application of its non-disclosure laws." Having considered these factors, he concluded that the documents should be ordered.

Marshall rejected requests by the defendants to apply the rule of comity. This would have required him to balance the interests of the United States in this case against the interests of the other countries. "It is simply impossible to judicially 'balance' totally contradictory" national interests, Marshall declared.

He also rejected the act of state doctrine, which holds that parties cannot be prosecuted for acts compelled by the laws of other countries. "The issue is not whether those laws are valid," Marshall writes, "but rather, conceding their validity, whether they excuse defendants from complying with a production order."

Ordering production of the documents, Marshall said, "will serve to declare Westinghouse's right to the discovery it seeks, thereby framing the competing interests of the United States and the foreign governments on a plane where the potential moderation of the exercise of their conflicting enforcement jurisdictions can be meaningfully considered."

On January 2, 1980, the defendants who had been ordered to produce the documents reported to Judge Marshall that they were unable to do so. Gulf Oil and Gulf Minerals Canada reported that they had withheld approximately 13,000 documents consisting of about 40,000 pages. They had also produced, from their U.S. and other offices, about 8,000 documents that would have been barred had they been located in Canada. Denison failed to produce 255 documents. (Denison president John Kostuik later testified that, "as a good Catholic," he had instructed his staff "under pain of mortal sin" not to keep anything in writing relating to the cartel activities, and that when he came across such written material, he tore it up.) Noranda Mines said it was withholding sixteen file drawers of documents in its Toronto office, and may have "many thousands" more in Australia. Getty Oil said it was withholding a "small number" of documents in Australia. Engelhard was withholding 245 documents in the files of its South Africa subsidiary.

Following the failure to comply with the orders to produce the documents, Westinghouse filed motions seeking sanctions against these defendants. If the sanctions were granted as requested, and sustained on appeals, Westinghouse and TVA would win their suits, and would stand to collect billions of dollars. Game over. No trial.

The defendants filed motions claiming that Judge Marshall lacked jurisdiction to apply the requested sanctions, and even if he did, he should not exercise it because of the consideration due to the interests of the foreign governments.

The pre-trial hearings on the motions for sanctions and the matter of jurisdiction continued throughout 1980.

March 26, 1980. Marshall was feeling increasingly frustrated. The appeals court had ruled that he could not proceed with hearings to fix the damages to be paid by the non-appearing defendants. The appearing defendants had refused to produce the documents. All appeals to the foreign governments to relax the non-disclosure laws had failed. The Supreme Court of Canada had just upheld the Canadian blocking law. A new government had been elected in Canada. The short-lived Conservative government of Joe Clark had been defeated, and Pierre Trudeau had been resurrected from announced retirement to lead the Liberals to another election victory.

Michael Freeborn, counsel for Noranda, was before Judge

Marshall, asking for additional time to respond to the motions for sanctions. He also wanted time for another meeting in Ottawa, planned for March 30, with the newly elected Canadian government, to "make them aware of the severity of the sanctions which Westinghouse and TVA are seeking."

Marshall declared from the bench:

> My friend, I want to tell you one thing, I am not going to change the scheduling of this case with the rise and fall of the Canadian government or any other commonwealth government. We have stayed our hands. We have deferred to them. And we are not going to do it any more.
>
> So from now on, if you want to make that argument, put it in writing and make it on the record, but don't take up my time with it. And you may transcribe these remarks, and you may transmit them to the governments of Canada, Australia, Great Britain and South Africa.

Freeborn started to respond, but did not complete his first sentence before Marshall interrupted again.

"I hope that Trudeau has more sense than Clark," Marshall said, "but I doubt it, because he was there before Clark."

In one sentence, a U.S. district court judge had questioned the sense of both the Prime Minister of Canada and the former Prime Minister of Canada. Marshall's outburst did not enhance the prospects of winning co-operation from the Canadian government at the meeting that was held four days later. Ottawa was more determined than ever to resist the U.S. courts.

On the morning of June 3, 1980, the walnut panelled courtroom on the 23rd floor of the Everett McKinley Dirksen federal building in downtown Chicago was crowded with close to 100 people, as Judge Prentice Marshall prepared to open a mini-trial in multi-district litigation number 342. Large cardboard boxes crammed with documents were piled high in the jury box. The documents would be introduced by the lawyers as exhibits and used for cross-examination. Some of the highest paid corporate lawyers in the United States crowded into the small courtroom. The legal costs ticked away at a rate approaching one hundred dollars every minute.

The pre-trial hearing was on the question of whether the

defendants had exercised "good faith" effort to comply with the court's order to produce the cartel documents or whether, as Westinghouse alleged, they had deliberately sought to hide behind the non-disclosure laws and frustrate the U.S. judicial process. The pre-trial hearing saw the first witness give evidence in the suits that had been brought by Westinghouse and TVA.

The first witness was Toronto lawyer Robert A. Smith, Q.C., who testified for Gulf on matters of Canadian law, specifically the Uranium Information Security Regulations. He had been retained by Gulf Oil, he said, to "find a way to obtain" the 13,300 non-disclosed cartel documents which were being held for Gulf Minerals Canada in the vaults of another Toronto law firm, McCarthy and McCarthy. He had not succeeded.

In the back of the courtroom sat Gulf Oil chairman Jerry McAfee, waiting his turn to testify. It did not come until the second day, and then he was on the stand for nearly two days.

Behind the bench, Judge Marshall was a bundle of barely contained energy. A tall, lean man with reddish, grey-streaked hair and rimless glasses, his jaunty bow tie peaked out from under his black robes. He leaned back in his chair, propped his feet against the bench, and stared pensively at the ceiling. He ran his fingers through his hair. He leaned forward, sprawling across the bench. As he interrupted to ask a question or issue a comment, he gesticulated with arms, his long fingers spread wide.

It was not the first antitrust case involving government actions in Canada to be heard by Judge Marshall. A few years earlier, eight American firms had been tried before Judge Marshall on antitrust charges involving the marketing of potash, in which officials of the government of Saskatchewan were named as co-conspirators. The provincial government had established a prorationing scheme for the sale of potash produced in the province. It was not unlike the state-run oil market prorationing schemes that have long governed the bulk of U.S. oil production. In the potash case, the American firms were charged with antitrust actions related to the Saskatchewan marketing plan and involving U.S. production. They were acquitted by a jury.

Samuel Murphy Jr., of the New York law firm of Donovan,

Leisure, Newton and Irvine, counsel for Westinghouse, paced the Chicago courtroom as he grilled McAfee with a penetrating, nasal voice. McAfee, his white hair combed straight back, responded in a quiet, but firm and gravelly voice.

"One of our fundamental business principles is that we observe to the best of our ability both the letter and the spirit of the laws of the land wherever we operate," McAfee declared. When there is a conflict in the demands of the laws of different countries, then "this is a matter that needs to be sorted out between the governments . . . a private company should not be put in the position of somehow sorting out the conflicting orders from two different governments."

Why, demanded Murphy, did Gulf chose to obey the laws of Canada, rather than the orders of a U.S. court?

"Mr. Murphy," replied McAfee, "I have difficulty believing that this court, or any court, would order Gulf, or me or any person to violate the laws of another country."

For a man whose company had lost a billion dollar judgment in a New Mexico court for failing to break Canadian law, Jerry McAfee seemed to be clinging to a tenacious faith.

Early in 1981, a lot of the pressure that had boiled up in the Chicago litigation cleared as rapidly as clouds after a summer storm, when most of the suits were settled out of court.

The settlements meant that the costs to the defendants would be only a fraction of the $2 billion to $6 billion figure that Judge Marshall had suggested was inevitable.

It also meant that questions about whose laws American companies must obey when they operate in other countries, would continue unresolved.

The first of the Chicago suits was settled in January, when Westinghouse reached an out-of-court agreement with Gulf Oil. By April, Westinghouse had settled all but six of the twenty-nine suits it had brought against the uranium producers. Under the terms of these settlements, Westinghouse was to receive $100 million in cash ($25 million of this from Gulf), plus favourable terms for the purchase of 23 million pounds of uranium. Westinghouse, in turn, was obligated to share these benefits with the power utilities that had earlier sued it.

The Tennessee Valley Authority, also in early 1981, settled

seven of the twelve suits that it had brought against the uranium producers, for $2 million, and dismissed its suit against France's Uranex. The TVA was also released from disputed contracts it had to purchase uranium, while Rio Algom dropped the multi-billion dollar counter suit it had filed in Canada against the TVA.

Most of the supply contract disputes involving General Atomic had also been settled, with the notable exception of the United Nuclear suit. Here the question remained whether the decision of Judge Felter in favour of United Nuclear, or the decision of the arbitration panel in favour of General Atomic, would ultimately prevail.

The Tennessee Valley Authority, however, continued to press its charges against four firms: Gulf Oil Corporation, Gulf Minerals Canada, Engelhard Minerals and Chemical Corporation, and Uranerz Canada Limited.

CHAPTER THIRTEEN

The Great
Canadian Cover-Up

The most bizarre aspect in the entire story of the cartel and its aftermath was the length to which the government of Canada went to protect the Canadian members from prosecution under U.S. law, only to turn around later and charge the same firms with criminal conspiracy under Canadian law.

The most extreme measure taken to protect Canadian firms from prosecution in the United States was the Uranium Information Security Regulations, enacted by means of an order-in-council under the Atomic Energy Control Act, and approved by the government of Canada on September 22, 1976.

As with similar measures in Australia, France, South Africa, and Great Britain to protect uranium producers in those countries, Ottawa's regulations were intended to prevent American antitrust laws from applying to the activities of companies operating outside the United States under the laws of other countries.

Or at least that was the reason given by the government of Canada. Opposition Members of Parliament – particularly in the Progressive Conservative party – had a different explanation. They claimed that the gag law was a gigantic cover-up of illegal activities in which the government itself participated. More than that, they argued, the gag law was an infringement on the rights of Parliament, an attack on freedom of the press, and a threat to the basic democratic rights of every Canadian.

"[T]his is the most damnable order-in-council ever passed in this country," thundered the late John Diefenbaker, the fiery prairie lawyer and former Prime Minister.

Whichever – protection against invasion of U.S. laws, or a

261

threat to Canadian democracy – the Uranium Information Security Regulations had some peculiar results.

For more than a year it was illegal, under the threat of up to five years in jail, for any Canadian to even discuss any documents related to the activities of the cartel, including those made public in the United States and splashed across the front pages of hundreds of newspapers.

Because of the privilege they enjoy to say things that are illegal for other people to say, Members of Parliament were not restricted, during debate in Parliament, in what they could say about the cartel or the cartel documents. Outside of Parliament, however, it would be illegal for them to have even read the cartel documents. How could they talk about them inside the House if they had not first read them outside the House?

A judge in the Ontario Supreme Court confirmed that it would be legal for Members of Parliament to talk about the cartel in Parliament, and release information to reporters. But if the reporters then published that information, they would be breaking the law, according to the judge. A literal interpretation of the judge's findings would have made even the publication of Hansard, the daily verbatim transcript of proceedings in the House of Commons, an illegal activity.

While the intent of the regulations was to prevent the release of information that could be used by the U.S. Department of Justice in criminal prosecution against members of the cartel, or by companies in private litigation, they did nothing to prevent the public release in the United States of thousands of pages of cartel documents. Some of the more revealing cartel documents, stolen from the files of Mary Kathleen Uranium, had been released and reported in the press even before the Canadian regulations were passed. Massive amounts of additional detail were disclosed in the courts and before the Moss committee after the regulations had been issued.

One effect of the regulations made it illegal for Canadians to read about the cartel activities that were broadcast on television and published in the United States.

There was probably not a single newspaper, radio station, or television station in Canada that did not break the gag law. Most of them published or broadcast the revelations of the cartel activities that had been disclosed before U.S. courts and the Moss committee. No one was prosecuted. Members of Parliament made no secret of the fact that they had, contrary to Canadian law, obtained copies of the documents that the Moss committee had released in the United States. No Member of Parliament was charged with breaking the law.

Despite the fact that the regulations have been more breached than observed, and despite the accusations that they infringe the rights of Canadians and violate the Canadian Bill of Rights, they have been upheld by three separate court rulings, including a ruling of the Supreme Court of Canada.

The regulations, however, have not been without some effect in keeping information under wraps. They may not have prevented the disclosure of cartel documents that were in the United States, but they have put a tight lid on documents located in Canada: so tight, that the failure to pry them loose threatened to cost some members of the cartel – particularly Gulf Oil – billions of dollars.

Whether or not the 13,000 or more cartel documents in Canada that have not been disclosed reveal any additional significant information about the cartel's activities is a matter of conjecture. Many of these undisclosed documents are bound to be duplicates of those already produced in the United States.

WHEN TORY TALK WAS CHEAP

For more than a year, Tory Members of Parliament mounted a major attack against the regulations; demanded their removal, both in Parliament and in an appeal to the courts; and demanded production of all the documents still locked up.

In May, 1979, when Joe Clark's Conservative party was elected to power, it was widely presumed that one of their first actions would be to repeal the Uranium Information Security Regulations. How could they do otherwise, in light of the sustained and vociferous demands they had made in Opposition? Yet the Conservative government not only failed to repeal the regulations, but acted as firmly as the former Liberal government in keeping the lid tightly clamped on.

No adequate explanation has been advanced to explain why, once in office, the Conservatives abandoned the views they expressed in Opposition. One suggestion has been that heavy pressure was applied by other governments involved in the cartel, particularly Margaret Thatcher's government of Great Britain. The inescapable inference, however, is that once in power, the Conservatives felt compelled to uphold the regulations for the same reasons that the Liberal government felt compelled to apply them in the first place.

The Uranium Information Security Regulations attracted little attention at first. They were short, succinct, and on the surface they seemed innocuous enough. They provided that:

> No person who has in his possession or under his control any note, document or other written or printed material in any way related to conversations, discussions or meetings that took place between January 1, 1972 and December 31, 1975 involving that person or any other person or any government, Crown corporation, agency or other organization in respect of the production, import, export, transportation, refining, possession, ownership, use or sale of uranium or its derivatives or compounds, shall
>
> (a) release any such note, document or material, or disclose or communicate the contents thereof to any person, government, Crown corporation, agency or their organization unless
>
>   (i) he is required to do so by or under a law of Canada, or
>
>   (ii) he does so with the consent of the Minister of Energy, Mines and Resources; or
>
> (b) fail to guard against or take reasonable care to prevent the unauthorized release of any such note, documents or material or the disclosure or communication of the contents thereof.

It was not until nearly a year later that the Conservative party tumbled to the political possibilities of what they would forever after call the gag law. Even then, it was a Canadian reporter based in Washington who triggered the Tories into an attack. When John Atkisson and Patrick McLain, counsel for the Moss committee, released copies of the committee's cartel documents to the news people in advance of the hearings in June, 1977, there was one member of the Canadian press corps in Washington so upset about what seemed to be nefarious dealings revealed in the documents, that he determined to take action. The reporter clearly was one of those people who had "in his possession or under his control" material proscribed by the regulations, which he shipped off in a bundle to Sinclair Stevens, former Toronto banker, Member of Parliament, and financial critic in the House for the Conservative party. Thus, right from the start of the Moss hearings, the combative Stevens was well armed with an initial set of cartel documents, which he later augmented with further material from proceedings before the Moss committee and U.S. courts.

Stevens was convinced that he had a political bomb, possibly powerful enough to blow the Liberal government out of office. The trouble was, how could he use it? Stevens now illegally had "in his possession or under his control" documents related to the cartel. He took the documents to a Toronto law firm, seeking advice as to whether they provided a basis to get legal action launched against the government and cartel member under the Combines Investigation Act. The lawyers refused to handle the case. Stevens later told the House that when he had brought the regulations to the attention of his lawyers "they said they could no longer continue to even review the documentation, or to advise me on the subject, as they themselves might be charged under the provisions of the Atomic Energy Control Act . . . Within one hour, the documents in their entirety were returned to my Toronto office."

Even had he obtained legal advice, Stevens would have still been stymied since the regulations specifically excluded releasing the documents to any agency of the government. And to get action launched, Stevens would have had to release the documents to the anti-combines Director of Investigation.

That left Parliament. Stevens opened the attack there in August, 1977, during a special summer session called to deal with a proposed natural gas pipeline across Canada from the arctic coast of Alaska. Like most Parliamentary debate, it proceeded in fits and starts, during a period that extended over several years.

Stevens charged that there had been "apparently illegal activities of a uranium cartel" in which "the Canadian government took an active part" and demanded an inquiry "as to whether the provisions of the Combines Investigation Act have been violated." According to Stevens, "Canadian consumers have been injured while international companies may gain billions in windfall gains."

Conservative Leader Joe Clark accused the government of having

> promulgated a most extraordinary order in council which in effect makes it illegal for me as Leader of the Opposition, any Member of this House, any member of the gallery, or any member of the public of Canada to carry, discuss, or have in his possession any of a wide range of documents which are public in other countries and would normally be public here.

Clark asked the government to "repeal the regulation in this most offensive order in council."

According to Gerald Baldwin,

> it may well be that we are free to discuss it in the House. But how do we get it there? . . . I am prohibited from finding and obtaining that information in a documentary form and bringing it to this House. I can use it once I get it here – but how can I get it here legally? I am prohibited from showing it to members of the public or the media.

"I would find it difficult to debate this issue from the cell, which might be occupied more properly by other people," Baldwin added at a later stage of the debate.

Baldwin moved that the House declare that the regulations are not binding on Members during Parliamentary debate, and that "all documents may be obtained, produced and used in connection with any inquiry into questions of privilege or into the legality and propriety of the actions of the government, ministers and others in the establishment of a uranium cartel." That would have taken the lid off all the cartel documents.

According to Prime Minister Trudeau,

> The precise and exact effect [of Baldwin's motion] would be to do exactly what Westinghouse wants to be done in order to get out from under this Canadian policy . . . The question put to you, Mr. Speaker, is the following: In order to debate this policy, do the Opposition have to get

secret facts of the group of producers, the effect of which will be to serve Westinghouse, USA?

That led to the odd spectacle of charges and counter charges about which party was serving the interests of which American corporation. At one point, Energy Minister Alastair Gillespie questioned whether Stevens was "acting as an agent of a foreign corporation . . . We are all aware that the issues which he has been promoting are the issues which Westinghouse of the United States have been promoting . . ." Stevens responded that Gillespie "seems to be stoutly defending Gulf U.S."

Elegant decorum has seldom characterized Parliamentary debate, either in Ottawa or in the mother of Parliaments at Westminster, and especially before M.P.s cleaned up their act to make it fit for family viewing on television. The debate on the uranium gag law was no exception, as the following exchange reveals. It also reveals the quick-temper of Donald Macdonald, former Energy Minister and then Finance Minister.

Trudeau pointed out that the infamous gag law had already been challenged in court and found valid, when Gerald Baldwin interjected: "We are talking about natural justice, not legality."

> Trudeau: 'If we are talking about natural justice, it seems to me – '
> Baldwin: 'You don't understand what natural justice is.'
> Trudeau: '[T]he first precept would be to hear the other side of the question.'
> John Fraser: 'You passed a law which says nobody can hear the other side of the question.'
> Donald Macdonald: 'Shut up, big mouth.'
> Steve Paproski: 'Listen to the red neck.'
> Macdonald: 'The animal is back. Welcome back animal.'

"[W]hat are you covering up?" the thundering Diefenbaker demanded to know. "I have looked over the records and there has not been one in all of Canada's history which I can find that denies Canadians in such a manner the right to have information on the question or to disclose what anyone may know concerning it."

Trudeau taunted the Tories several times to take their case to the courts. Referring to Gerald Baldwin, he told the Speaker that "if he feels that the order in council does not permit him to have due process in this country, then I think they should attack the order in council under the Bill Of Rights." A few minutes later, Trudeau added:

> When you go before the courts and you believe in your legal case, when you are not simply involved in political histrionics such as we have seen in the past couple of days, you don't fool around; you go to a lawyer, you take the government to the courts, and you prove your case and you have the courage to do it.

The Tories did go to court, but the finding that they got from the judge upset members of Parliament on both sides of the House.

The application brought to the Supreme Court of Ontario by Conservative Leader Joe Clark and five other Conservative Members of the House, sought a declaration that the uranium information security regulations were null and void. It also sought, in the likely event that the regulations were again found to be valid, declarations from the court that the cartel documents could be provided by the M.P.'s lawyers in order to obtain advice as to possible legal proceedings, and that they could be disclosed in the course of Parliamentary debate.

Shortly before the court ruled in the case, the government amended the regulations, on October 14, 1977. The amendment, in effect, limited the application of the regulations to those who had in any way been involved in the cartel arrangements. No longer was it illegal for Canadians to possess, read about, or talk about the cartel documents that had been made public in the United States – a futile aspect of the regulations, which in any event, had never been enforced. But it still kept the lid clamped on all the cartel documents in Canada that had not been disclosed.

"The regulations were passed because it became obvious, late in 1976, that the government would have to act to prevent documentation on the marketing arrangements from being released to U.S. courts," Gillespie said in announcing the amendment. "Failure to take such action would have placed the government in the untenable position of allowing evidence to be provided to a foreign court for use in the possible prosecution of Canadian nationals for acts that were in accordance with Canadian law and government policy."

Gillespie said the regulations "were drafted on an urgent basis," and acknowledged the criticisms that they had prohibited "full and frank discussion of the events of that time." The amendment, he said, will limit application of the regulations "to persons associated with uranium producers and the federal government. They will not preclude discussion by others of documents that are now in the public domain."

On the day that the Uranium Security Information Regulations were amended, Consumer and Corporate Affairs Minister Warren Allmand announced that he had ordered Robert Bertrand, Director of Research and Investigation in the Bureau of Competition Policy, to hold an investigation to determine whether the Combines Investigation Act had been violated as a result of the cartel marketing arrangements. An inquiry under this Act – like an inquiry by a U.S. grand jury – is not public. If the inquiry finds that there is no basis to lay charges, the evidence considered during the inquiry might never be made public. When the government's chief monopolies watchdog completed its inquiry in 1981, and the government declined to make it public, the storm was to once more erupt in Parliament.

Meanwhile, the findings of Chief Justice Gregory Evans of the Ontario Supreme Court on the application by Joe Clark and the other five Conservative M.P.s were made as though the regulations had not been changed, and thus in some respects were academic.

Justice Evans ruled, once again, that the regulations were valid, except for the clause permitting cartel documents to be released with the consent of the Minister of Energy, which he said was *ultra vires* of the Atomic Energy Control Act.

The judge also found that the regulations did not prevent Members of Parliament from disclosing cartel documents to their lawyers for the purpose of seeking legal advice, or "from releasing or disclosing any such documents in the course of Parliamentary debate or to the press."

What the press might be allowed to do with any cartel

documents provided by Members of Parliament was, in the judge's opinion, another matter.

"The privilege of the Member is finite and cannot be stretched indefinitely to cover any person along a chain of communication initiated by the Member," Justice Evans held. "The privilege stops at the press. Once the press have received the information, the onus falls on them to decide whether to publish. They cannot claim immunity from prosecution on the basis of parliamentary privilege which protects the Member from releasing the information."

In the House of Commons, the judge's findings were greeted with loud protests from all sides.

"I read that judgment with amazement," said John Diefenbaker. The rights and privileges of Members of Parliament, he asserted, "are not determined in the courts: those rights are determined in the House of Commons and are not subject to interpretation by any court outside the supreme court of Parliament."

"[O]ur freedom of speech in this place cannot be curtailed from the outside, and the people of Canada have the undoubted right to know what goes on in this place," echoed Stanley Knowles, the veteran New Democratic member from Winnipeg and a recognized authority on parliamentary procedure. "Is he [Justice Evans] trying to say to me that on a day when there has been a discussion on the uranium cartel in this House, I cannot send Hansard to my constituents?"

"I think judges have the right to make nonsensical obiter dictum," observed Andrew Brewin, "and this is precisely what this judge has done . . . I propose that we should disregard it entirely."

The Speaker of the House, James Jerome, was in agreement, when he handed down a ruling on the judge's findings, declaring that

> nothing which was said by the Chief Justice alters in any way the privileges, the power and rights possessed by members in the relationship with the press in respect of proceedings in the House . . . I say, again that this House remains the master of its own practice, particularly on the question of privilege, and this House will exercise its own judgment on our practices and precedents.

Diefenbaker, the father of the Canadian Bill of Rights and ever the defender of the supremacy of Parliament, applauded the Speaker's ruling.

> I tell you, sir, that the ruling you have just given shows a Solomonesque capacity. It will be read in future years as upholding the rights of Parliament, making it clearly understood that declarations outside of Parliament shall not in any way impede, interfere with or diminish the rights of Parliament or, indeed, the rights of the press, for those rights were determined under the Bill of Rights passed by this House in 1960.

The amendment to the gag law unshackled Stephen Roman, allowing him to enter the fray with a blistering attack on Sinclair Stevens, a former political ally. Roman had unsuccessfully campaigned for a seat in Parliament under the Conservative banner in two federal elections in a riding adjacent to Stevens's. In a letter sent to all shareholders of Denison Mines, and to every Member of Parliament, five days after the regulations were amended, Roman replied to the charges by Stevens that the cartel was illegal and resulted in higher electricity prices for Ontario consumers.

> If Mr. Stevens chooses to disregard the facts for his own political purposes, that is one thing, but when, in so doing he pillories the Canadian uranium industry unjustly and baselessly and thereby impugns the integrity of this company, its employees and, by association, its shareholders, the time has come to state the truth once more for the Canadian public.

The truth, as Stephen Roman reported it, involved another recapitulation of the events and reasons that led the government to organize the cartel, and the non-cartel factors responsible for the increase in uranium prices. The government, Mr. Roman said, "acted properly in encouraging and directing Canadian participation in the so-called cartel," while "the Canadian uranium producers acted properly in becoming participants." Refuting a "scandalous suggestion" by Stevens of a cosy relationship between Denison Mines and the Liberal party, Roman could not resist a final shot: "In the most recent

271

campaign for leadership of the Progressive Conservative party of Canada, Denison extended to Mr. Stevens the use of Denison's aircraft and as well made a contribution to the campaign." Presumably it was the last campaign contribution that Mr. Stevens received from Denison Mines.

The great cartel cover-up debate flared in Parliament again in May, 1978, as a result of earlier motions by Sinclair Stevens asking the government to produce some thirty-six cartel documents. The debate, by this time, seemed somewhat pointless. All the documents that Stevens had requested had already been made public in the United States. Stevens had copies of the documents that he was asking the government to produce. It was no longer illegal for him to have them, to talk about them, or even to give them to the press – except that the press already had many of them. The government knew that Stevens had the documents, which he had requested be produced. Still, the government declined to produce them, and the final angry words on the subject were exchanged, in a debate that seemed to have little meaning but lots of rhetoric.

Even though the regulations had been amended, Stevens charged,

> anyone who knows anything about the cartel is still forbidden to shed any light on the matter. . . . it is ludicrous that we in this House, and the Canadian people in general, should have to turn to United States tribunals for information about the activities of our own government, information which should rightly come from Ottawa . . . most of these documents are already in hands of those foreign tribunals. They are there now. They were there when we asked for them last August. The only thing this administration accomplishes by denying them to Canadians is to humiliate this House and the Canadian people . . .

Stevens accused the government of a cover-up comparable to the attempts of former U.S. President Richard Nixon to hide the Watergate scandal:

> It is a sordid tale, Mr. Speaker, a tale of a government more concerned with cover-up and hiding the facts than of levelling with the Canadian people. Perhaps the worst ex-

ample of a government conspiracy to break the laws of Canada has been this instance of the uranium cartel fiasco. . . .

In this country we would not have a Watergate in-vestigation, because basically if Mr. Nixon had been the Prime Minister of this country, his consent would have had to be sought for an investigation. If Mr. Nixon were then to act in the way our emperor, the Prime Minister, acts in respect of the uranium cartel, the investigation would never have taken place.

Government members responded with a lengthy and familar defence of the cartel marketing arrangements. Gillespie advanced two reasons why the cartel documents should not be disclosed: in order to block extension of American laws into Canada; and because Canada, he said, was obliged under its agreements with other cartel governments, not to disclose the information.

Gillespie also defended the legality of the government's action:

so far as the activities of an industry are effectively regulated, they cannot be in violation of the Combines Investigation Act. The regulation did not operate so as to ex-empt the producers from any activity which might unduly lessen competition in the domestic market . . . While we have no reason to believe that the arrangement did violate the Combines Investigation Act, it was because of the need to resolve allegations that it had done so that my colleague, the Minister of Consumer and Corporate Affairs, directed the director of investigation and research to conduct a formal inquiry under the Combines Investigation Act. That inquiry is now well underway and has had full access to documents and other material in respect of the marketing arrangement.

One year and four days later the Conservative Party was elected to power. The government of Prime Minister Joe Clark may have been among the shortest in Canada's history, lasting only seven months from the date of the election in May, 1979, until it was defeated in the House, but it had ample time to repeal the gag law it had so bitterly attacked. No action was taken.

On December 13, 1979, Jerry McAfee wrote to Prime Minister Clark, seeking help to resolve a difficult problem confronting Gulf. Courts in the United States had ordered Gulf to produce the cartel documents Gulf Minerals Canada held in Toronto. Failure to comply with the orders of the U.S. courts could cost Gulf hundreds of millions of dollars, perhaps even billions. But if Gulf did produce the documents in violation of Canadian law, officers of the Gulf companies in Canada could wind up in jail for as long as five years.

Following the election of the Conservative government, it seemed reasonable to expect that chances of obtaining Ottawa's approval to release the documents might be better. Gulf had appealed to Canada's new Energy Minister, Ray Hnatyshyn, three months before McAfee wrote to the Prime Minister, but had obtained no response. Then McAfee took his appeal to the top. Writing to Joe Clark, McAfee said:

> we understand that the Canadian government may well be re-considering its policy on this matter and that an ultimate decision may be forthcoming shortly. If there is any way Gulf Minerals Canada Limited or Gulf Oil Corporation can disclose in the United States court proceedings the documents or information subject to the uranium information security regulations, we very much want to do so, and I respectfully solicit your co-operation in making such disclosure possible.

McAfee said he thought the disclosure would be "appropriate" since the marketing arrangement had been long since terminated; since "much of the information contained in the documents has undoubtedly been made public already"; and "perhaps most importantly, if the documents are not disclosed Gulf Oil Corporation and other Canadian uranium producer defendants may suffer significant economic hardship . . . including enormous judgments levied against them by default."

McAfee's letter was delivered to the Prime Minister the day after it was written – on the same day that the Conservative government was defeated in the House.

Walter Baker, at the time Acting Prime Minister, responded a week later to Gulf's request: "This is to inform you that the government is not prepared to allow the disclosure of documents and information covered by the uranium information security regulations."

Only one final possibility of obtaining disclosure of the cartel documents in Canada now remained: an appeal to the Supreme Court of Canada.

Five days after Walter Baker wrote to McAfee, Gulf obtained letters rogatory from U.S. District Federal Judge Prentice Marshall in Chicago, addressed to "the Appropriate Judicial Authority in Canada," seeking release of the cartel documents. With the letters rogatory, Gulf was able to obtain a hearing before the Supreme Court, involving what must have been one of the more unusual requests to be heard by the court. Gulf Oil Corporation of Pittsburgh was seeking an order from the Supreme Court of Canada to compel its two Canadian subsidiaries, Gulf Canada Limited and Gulf Minerals Canada Limited, to produce the documents. The net effect, though, was to seek a declaration that the uranium information security regulations were invalid.

Five Justices of the Supreme Court, led by Chief Justice Bora Laskin, spent two days hearing the case. Bud Estey, the former counsel for Gulf Minerals and by then a Justice of the Supreme Court, was obviously not among those who heard the case. Gulf's request to the court was opposed by the Attorney General.

On March 18, 1980, the Supreme Court handed down its decision. For a third time, the regulations were upheld by a court; Gulf's request was denied.

Chief Justice Bora Laskin's language was muted, but he made it clear that the court was resisting the application of U.S. laws in Canada. In his judgment, Laskin wrote:

> The participation of the government of Canada in the cartel arrangement was made known to the public, and it seems to me that the resistance to disclosure was not so much a matter of the maintenance of secrecy as it was of an assertion of Canadian sovereignty to resist the extraterritorial application of United States law.

"UNLAWFULLY CONSPIRED"

On May 16, 1981, the man who for seven years had been the chief civil servant in charge of policing Canada's monopoly laws was assigned by the federal cabinet to a new job. Robert J. Bertrand, formerly Assistant Deputy Minister in the Bureau of Competition Policy, Department of Consumer and Corporate Affairs, and Director of Research and Investigation under the Combines Investigation Act, was appointed chairman of the Anti-Dumping Tribunal.

One of Bertrand's final acts as Director of Investigations was to report that participation by Canadian firms in the uranium cartel, mandated by the government of Canada, had led to violations of Canada's monopolies laws.

Bertrand's report on his four-year inquiry into the affairs of the cartel was in the final editing stages when his transfer to the Anti-Dumping Tribunal was announced. A week later, Bertrand's report, together with some 75,000 documents, were in the hands of Jean Chrétien, Minister of Justice and Attorney General.

The task then before Chrétien and his officials was to determine whether or not there was sufficient evidence to prosecute the companies, individuals, or even government officials, alleged to have violated the law. Under normal circumstances, if charges were laid, all of the evidence accumulated during the four years of Bertrand's inquiry would be brought out in the resulting trial. If no charges were laid by the Attorney General, the results of Bertrand's inquiry would normally never be made public.

But the circumstances were far from normal. For one thing, Parliament had twice been assured by cabinet ministers that the results of the inquiry would be made public. More important, a refusal to make Bertrand's report public would inevitably lead to suspicions that the government was trying to cover up its own activities.

In the House of Commons, the Opposition parties, led by the pugnacious Sinclair Stevens, were again voicing demands that the government tell all. Trudeau and his ministers were equally as adamant that they would tell nothing.

In Chrétien's view there were two separate issues: Canada's participation in an international uranium marketing agreement, which was okay; and whether or not the cartel had an effect on prices paid by Canadian consumers, which was maybe not okay.

"[T]he question of having an agreement with other nations involving the matter of uranium . . . according to international law is completely legal," Chrétien told the House. "The Canadian companies subject to this international agreement acted in accordance with international law and, in my opinion, in their dealings with other countries, they fully complied with Canadian law. As for the offences committed within Canada, these companies must abide by the antitrust legislation of Canada."

"When does the minister intend to make the inquiry public?" Stevens demanded of Consumer and Corporate Affairs Minister André Ouellet. He reminded the Minister that when the inquiry had been ordered in 1977 the then Minister, Warren Allmand, had promised that the results would be made public. As recently as March 4, 1981, Ouellet had told House that Bertrand's inquiry had not been completed, but "when it has been completed, his findings will be made public."

As far as Ouellet was concerned, the findings of the Director of Investigations had been "known and made public. This has been done since the document has been referred to the Department of Justice for review. I can therefore say the findings of the Director have certainly been made public . . . The whole affair is now in the hands of the Department of Justice."

"[T]hat is absolutely fantastic," Stevens responded. "On March 4, the minister told us that the findings of the Director would be made public. Now we are told that the conclusions have been made public in that since that there has been a reference to the Minister of Justice."

No matter what the Minister of Consumer and Corporate Affairs may have said, Chrétien held firmly to the position that the inquiry report would never be made public unless charges were made in court.

"[W]hen the Attorney General of Canada receives a report from the Director of Investigation and Research, he must, after due consideration, decide whether or not to prosecute. If he does, then the report is naturally made public before the courts. If, on the other hand, he decides not to prosecute, then the report stays as it is . . . the report I have received remains a privileged document between the Director and the Attorney General, pursuant to the Combines Investigation Act. I know of no other precedent where a report was made public other than through a court proceeding and never was a report made public when the Attorney General ruled against prosecuting the companies or the individuals involved."

Meanwhile, Chrétien still faced the task of deciding whether or not to prosecute. "[I]t is my duty to look at the nature of the report and see if there is cause to prosecute companies or individuals, and to proceed if I am satisfied as Attorney General of Canada that there is sufficient evidence to warrant prosecution," Chrétien told the House. "It is a very voluminous piece of work involving 75,000 documents; there is evidence to look into, and the report which I am studying at this time, and in due course as Attorney General of Canada I will face my responsibilities."

As far as Stevens was concerned that was "like asking suspects in a group of suspects to pass judgment as to whether other members of the group shall be charged with certain illegalities."

The government was clearly in a bind. It would either have to press charges against persons involved in the cartel, which it had been instrumental in establishing, or risk continuing accusations of a cover-up.

The answer to that problem came on July 8, when summonses were issued, alleging that all six Canadian firms involved in the cartel – Rio Algom, Denison Mines, Gulf Minerals Canada, Uranerz Canada, Eldorado, and Uranium Canada – had "unlawfully conspired with other named persons to lessen unduly competition in the production, manufacture, sale or supply in Canada of uranium, uranium oxide and other uranium substance."

Note the key phrase that limits the area said to be affected by the alleged conspiracy.

Only in Canada, you say? Pity.

CHAPTER FOURTEEN

A Few Cartel Issues

"People of the same trade seldom meet together, even for merriment and diversion but the conversation ends in a conspiracy against the public or in some contrivance to raise prices."

Adam Smith, in *Wealth of Nations*

The American attitude toward business still seems firmly rooted in the writing, more than 200 years ago, of that Scottish professor of moral philosophy, Adam Smith. The rule seems to be that there is nothing wrong with capitalism except the capitalists. They'll form a cartel every time they get the chance, Adam Smith had warned.

No other economy has ever been as predicated on Smith's principles of competitive trade as an ideal than the American economy; and no country has adopted such extensive and stringent measures to outlaw efforts to avoid that competition.

The centrepiece of this far-reaching police effort to ensure competition is the 1890 Sherman Antitrust Act. The U.S. Supreme Court has called it "The Magna Carta of free enterprise."

Donald Baker, former U.S. Assistant Attorney General in charge of the Justice Department's antitrust division, claimed once that U.S. antitrust laws reflect America's "frontier" values:

> a strong sense of the worth of individual effort and the value of individual liberty . . . a solid distrust of government, a deep lack of respect for those in authority . . . a feeling that the consumer will be better served if businesses have to hustle to survive.

No other country in the world has a more open society than the United States – in respect to its governmental processes, its economic processes, its judicial processes. It can surely be no accident that the United States has not only the most open society, but also the most affluent.

Yet despite this openness, there is an American double standard when it comes to competition abroad.

There, not even the United States fully lives up to the ideals of competition. Billions of dollars are spent every year by the Department of Justice, by the regulatory agencies, and by the courts to stamp out every act that is perceived to illegally limit competition, even if the perception is not always perfect. At the same time, legislators and regulators implement measures to legally limit domestic competition with the regularity of clockwork. Other measures limit competition where it counts most, in international trade.

Competition, noted a 1980 editorial in the *Wall Street Journal*, has few friends.

> Corporate executives pay lip service to it, but seldom refuse a little federal protection . . . successive administrations and Congresses have piled up a great mass of market constricting legislation in the form of regulations, subsidies and penalties.

The editorial quoted a study by the Council for a Competitive Economy which found that in 1979, Members of Congress supported economic competition only 42 per cent of the time: "Senators voted against the free market 55 per cent of the time and Representatives 59 per cent, and majorities in both houses favored anti-competitive measures more than half of the time."

Nowhere is competition more vital than in international trade. "It is as foolish for a nation as for an individual to make what can be bought cheaper," Adam Smith wrote in 1776. Two hundred years later another champion of competition, economist Milton Friedman, wrote that no measures such as the Sherman Antitrust Act or the Interstate Commerce Commission "could do as much to assure effective competition as the elimination of all barriers to international trade."

That the United States can at times be as guilty as any other nation in reducing competition is amply demonstrated by an eighteen-year program to limit oil imports – by far the largest commodity in world trade – and a twenty-year program first to prohibit and then to limit uranium imports.

It is not, however, the lapses of the Americans from their own ideals of competition that enrage its trading partners, for they are just as guilty, and sometimes more so. What infuriates America's trading partners are U.S. attempts to apply U.S. laws to other countries, to force compliance with competition concepts that the United States preaches, but does not always practise. It is a case of "do as I say, not as I do," and those charged with offenses against U.S. laws are tried in U.S. courts.

Concern by other countries about the long arm of U.S. law has existed for decades, but never to the extent reached in the late 1970's, and climaxing in the uranium affair.

For the most part, the concerns have been couched in the polite language of international diplomacy. But diplomacy has seldom restrained former Energy Minister Donald Macdonald. In a speech delivered to a Calgary energy conference in 1979, Donald Macdonald, by then no longer a government official but a practising lawyer again, issued the harshest criticism of U.S. policies related to the uranium affair.

> In no other commodity have we witnessed such narrow and predatory United States government action as was followed with respect to the absolute embargo [of uranium imports] and the simultaneous abuse by the United States of its enrichment facilities to drive Canadian exporters and others out of the remaining foreign markets. . . . If, at most times, the United States has been a good friend and a good neighbour, her policies with respect to uranium have been about the shabbiest hypocrisy that we have seen in international commerce. One hopes that the departure from honest dealing by the Americans will turn out to be an aberration in our commercial and political relations with them.

One bad turn, it seemed, deserved another, and the result has been a sort of uncontrolled nuclear chain reaction.

The first bad turn that triggered this chain reaction was, of course, the U.S. uranium import embargo. It fully deserved the second bad turn, the uranium cartel. And no matter how great the provocation nor how justified the objectives, it was not a good turn, for any arrangement that seeks to carve up markets by means of rigged bids is inherently odious. That led to the worst turn of all, the American efforts to apply American law to punish other uranium producers for trying to charge prices as high as American producers charged. Because it had already established its own monopoly and monopoly prices, the United States was the one uranium consuming nation in least danger of being hurt by any foreign uranium monopoly, and the only nation to claim that it had suffered damage. The final events in this chain reaction are a series of measures by Great Britain, Canada, and others to repel the invasion of U.S. laws, another bad turn that suppresses information, increases government intervention, and threatens to further inhibit free trade and competition. Yet the countries involved had little choice but to resist the invasion of U.S. laws.

THE LONG ARM OF U.S. LAW

"If someone fires a gun into the United States, that is clearly of concern to our government," says Douglas Rosenthal, former deputy chief of foreign commerce in the antitrust division of the U.S. Department of Justice. "If a foreign company is doing the equivalent of aiming a gun at U.S. consumers, that is our concern too."

To stop foreign companies firing at American consumers, U.S. law enforcers and regulatory agencies have tried to pin on the badges of the policemen of world business. They seek to force foreign companies to obey American laws, even if it means breaking foreign laws. U.S. courts have assumed the mantle of world courts, taking it upon themselves to decide whose laws a company or a citizen of another country must obey.

At the heart of the issue is the question of how conflicts of business laws should be resolved. Unilateral decisions made by American bureaucracy and tribunals? Or negotiations between the governments involved? Increasingly, the United States and its law enforcement agencies have tried to take these matters into their own hands.

"No other nation has been able to assert successfully the right to enforce its legal process outside its own territory." wrote Charles Maechling, Jr., a Washington lawyer and former State Department official, in the American Bar Association Journal in 1977. According to Maechling, no other country "has sought so vigorously to bring overseas activity within its ambit."

Antitrust is not the only area where the United States has extended the long reach of its legal arm.

In the 1960's, there were strong protests in Canada over U.S. laws that prevented Canadian subsidiaries of American companies from exporting goods to certain countries, such as Cuba and China. American firms were later tripping over each other in a rush to do business with China, and meanwhile the United States was seeking to regulate how its foreign-based subsidiaries conduct business in the Middle East. U.S. claims that foreign-based companies controlled 25 per cent or more by American shareholders are subject to American law, even if they do no business in the United States, are objected to everywhere. Equally unwelcome are the efforts of such regulatory agencies as the Securities Exchange Commission and the Commodities Futures Trading Commission to regulate banking, accounting, trading, and information disclosure in other countries.

Perhaps the most wide-ranging has been the efforts of the U.S. Federal Maritime Commission to regulate all shipping, including connecting links, that involves any U.S. commerce. In one ruling, the FMC declared that foreign flag vessels operating between Thailand and Singapore and between ports of Indonesia were common carriers in United States commerce. In the eyes of the FMC, even overland transportation systems in Europe, such as nationalized railways, are theoretically subject to U.S. regulation.

The ultimate folly of this unilateral approach to regulating international trade has been unwittingly described by former Justice Department official Donald Baker.

"Where a foreign country wants to send its ships or planes to our ports, we can quite rightly insist that they be subject to U.S. antitrust and regulatory jurisdiction – just as the foreign country can insist that our ships and planes be subjected to their antitrust and regulatory jurisdiction," Baker wrote in *The National Law Journal* in 1980. "If, of course, the two sovereigns issue flatly conflicting commands, then trade between the two nations may be impossible."

That could be the ultimate effect of trying to regulate world trade by judges and lawyers through litigation in the courts, rather than by negotiations between governments. The judges could make trade impossible. Just think what that would do to competition!

But it is the reach of U.S. antitrust laws that has caused the most concern.

The United States at one time refrained from extending its antitrust laws to other countries. In a 1909 ruling, the U.S. Supreme Court held that it would be contrary to the comity of nations for a nation to apply its own laws to acts done outside its jurisdiction. The situation had changed by 1945, however, when the U.S. courts held that an agreement by five European and one Canadian aluminium producer to allocate the amount of aluminium to be produced had an effect on U.S. prices. The court declared that "any state may impose liabilities, even upon persons not within its allegiance, for conduct outside its borders that has consequences within its borders which the State reprehends." Thus was borne the U.S. "effects doctrine" under which the reach of U.S. antitrust law has steadily expanded ever since.

U.S. courts are expected to exercise restraint in extending the reach of U.S. antitrust laws by considering which country or countries have the greatest interest at stake in a particular case. If the interest of foreign countries is judged greater than the affect on American interests, the U.S. courts are expected to defer to the foreign interest, under this rule of international comity. But according to Charles Maechling, the application of this rule has "been notably deficient in American courts and regulatory agencies for the last few decades."

Non-American firms were brought further within the grasp of U.S. antitrust law by a Supreme Court ruling that they must comply with the discovery process of U.S. courts, by far the most extensive and expensive discovery process in the world. The Supreme Court held that foreign firms must make a "good faith" effort to comply with the discovery orders of American courts, even if compliance is illegal under the laws of their home nations.

This, of course, was exactly one of the key issues at stake in the Westinghouse suit in Chicago.

Another leap forward for American antitrust law was the "Antitrust Guide for International Operations," issued by the Department of Justice, in January, 1977. It gave clear notice of intent to invoke U.S. antitrust law against activities outside the United States undertaken in compliance with the laws of foreign countries, or even encouraged by foreign governments in accordance with national policies. Foreign defendants in a U.S. antitrust action cannot argue that what they did was legal where they did it; they must prove that what they did was compelled by foreign law.

This "sovereign compulsion doctrine," according to J. S. Sanford of Canada's Department of External Affairs, in the summer 1978 issue of the *Cornell International Law Journal*, inhibits the ability of foreign governments to secure voluntary compliance by companies to national policies, and may lead to increased government intervention in business affairs:

> the government and the private sector may prefer to avoid the formality and rigidity of legislation, and compliance with policy may instead be secured through discussion and voluntary action permitted, but not compelled, by domestic law.
>
> [However,] application of the foreign compulsion defence would induce foreign governments to adopt less permissive and more mandatory and inflexible forms of intervention in the private sector, including direct intervention in the affairs of U.S. multi-nationals of a kind to which U.S. government representatives have objected in other contexts. . . . This kind of intervention would not be attractive to the private sector . . . Intervention and coercion may become the lesser of two evils, however, if the alternative is abdication of the government's power to guide the Canadian economy in accordance with Canadian interests.

By leaning on the foreign compulsion doctrine, the Americans appear to look askance at the practice of governments in seeking to persuade corporations to undertake certain actions, rather than passing a law to compel them. Yet the practice is so American that it is known by an American term. It is called "jaw-boning." The U.S. program which had a greater effect than any other in limiting competition – the policy to limit oil imports – was first implemented without any laws or regulations to compel compliance.

The central issue, in Sanford's view, was whether the private sector in Canada will be

> more responsive to Canadian or to foreign law and policy directions . . . the Canadian government must be able to retain the ability to determine resource and industrial development policies for Canada. The government will lose this ability if the multi-nationals that play a major role in the Canadian resource and industrial sectors are more responsive in their Canadian activities to U.S. law than to Canadian policies and national interest.

This factor, according to Sanford, compelled the Canadian government to block the uranium documents from the U.S. courts, and assert Canadian sovereignty. But Sanford also hinted that blocking legislation may not be enough, and that stronger action might be required:

> If the threat of antitrust liability in the United States is a significant disincentive to compliance with Canadian policy then the Canadian government may also have to consider providing the necessary 'cover' through legislation or other forms of direct intervention, to confer immunity from antitrust liability. The degree of intervention required for this purpose will be largely a function of the evolution of the U.S. doctrine of foreign compulsion. The more restrictively that doctrine is applied, the more foreign governments will feel obliged – whether they like it or not – to subject the private sector to mandatory rather than flexible controls.

Sanford argues – like so many others – that the solution is to take matters of international trade dispute out of the hands of the courts.

In such conflicts, writes Sanford,

it is inappropriate for one of the governments involved in the policy conflict to seek to impose its desired solution by invoking its domestic law before its tribunals to adjudicate the legality of conduct in another jurisdiction. The difference should be resolved, as are other intergovernmental differences, by consultation and negotiation.

The trouble with the American "effects doctrine", according to former British Trade Secretary Edmund Dell, is that if the United States wants to regulate whatever affects its domestic commerce, it might as well regulate everything everywhere. "The U.S. is such a significant element in the world economy that there is almost nothing you can do that doesn't affect the U.S.," Dell said in 1977.

And Dell would have none of it. "We will not allow other countries to determine the law in this country," he said. "We will do that ourselves."

Two antitrust cases – the uranium case and the shipping case – finally goaded the British into erecting a strong island barrier to American antitrust laws in 1980.

In the shipping case, a U.S. grand jury in 1979 indicted several European shipping lines for alleged violation of U.S. antitrust laws. Rather than face the formidable costs of fighting the charges in court, the firms involved worked out a settlement with the U.S. Justice Department, and pleaded *nolo contendere*. Thirteen individuals were fined $50,000 and seven companies were fined $1 million each. But that was not the end of the matter. A total of thirty-four private suits were brought against the companies, and if successful, the treble damages could amount to several billions of dollars.

The British were not happy. In the first place, argued British Trade Secretary John Nott, the alleged activities were not illegal under any European laws. More importantly, Nott argued, shipping is a multi-national activity involving the interests of many countries, and should thus be a multi-jurisdictional activity, not an activity subject to the exclusive jurisdiction of the United States. "If problems arise," Nott said, "they should be the subject of mutual discussion and agreement, rather than for one country to take unilateral action with no regard for the legitimate shipping and trading interests of others."

In a tough speech delivered in Los Angeles in September, 1979, Nott warned that the British were about to take defensive measures: "good relations between our countries are being impaired" by the long arm of U.S. law, especially "in the complex field of antitrust law," he told his American audience.

Nott said that "a company which is registered, situated, operating and employing people in the United Kingdom is subject to the laws of the United Kingdom . . . and not of the United States . . . even if it is American controlled."

The following month, Nott introduced in Parliament the Protection of Trading Interest Bill. The measure, he said,

> is primarily a reaction to the accumulation of attempts by the United States, since the 1950's, to impose its own economic and other domestic policies on individuals and companies outside its territorial jurisdiction, without regard for the trading interests of other countries. . . .
>
> We have tried over the years to deal with a worsening situation through negotiation but with little success. We are still firmly of the view that matters affecting international trade should be dealt with by consultation between governments. However, where this does not work we must be prepared to take a stand.

The bill was passed by Parliament in 1980 with the strong support of both Conservative and Labour Members.

The act provides for several things. It allows the British Secretary of Trade to prohibit compliance with orders issued by foreign courts for the production of documents and information, and also allows him to prohibit the enforcement in Britain of certain types of damages awarded by foreign courts. The most sweeping aspect, however, would permit a British company to recover two thirds of any loss it might sustain as a result of a triple damage award in a U.S. antitrust action.

The effect of this will, for example, severely limit the amount that Westinghouse might collect from Rio Tinto-Zinc in the uranium case. Judge Marshall has already found Rio Tinto-Zinc guilty, by default, of the charges brought against it by Westinghouse, and – other than appeals – has only to determine the amount of the damages to be applied. To illustrate what could happen, assume that Westinghouse were awarded, say, $500 million in actual damages against Rio Tinto-Zinc and another $1 billion in penalties under the treble damage action. Westinghouse could then seize $1.5 billion of Rio Tinto assets located in the United States to satisfy that award. But if it did, then under the new British Act, Rio Tinto could sue to seize $1 billion of Westinghouse's assets located in Britain.

The net effect is that neither Westinghouse, nor any of the firms that have sued the British shipping companies, will stand to collect very much from any damages they may be awarded under U.S. antitrust laws.

In Ottawa, a similar bill, called the Foreign Proceedings and Judgments bill, was introduced in the Canadian Parliament in the summer of 1980. The bill was not passed before Parliament was recessed, but could be re-introduced.

Meanwhile, even in the United States, there appeared to be some recognition that American antitrust laws had reached too far.

A bill introduced in the U.S. Senate in 1980 by Senators Jacob Javits and Charles Mathias called for the establishment of a special year-long commission to consider "the international application of U.S. antitrust laws." Among other things, the proposed commission was to have examined "the effect of the application of U.S. antitrust laws on U.S. relations with other countries" and the scope and application of U.S. antitrust laws "to foreign conduct and foreign parties."

The bill was opposed by the Department of Justice, and was not passed before the 1980 U.S. elections. Whether or not a similar measure will be proposed in the future remains to be seen.

But the *Washington Post*, for one, has argued that it is time to take international trade disputes out of the hands of the courts. In an editorial in late 1979, the *Post* stated:

> Especially in Europe, it is common for governments to promote industrial policies requiring mergers, division of product lines and markets, and pricing agreements. This is frequently done to create industries capable of competing with bigger and better established U.S. companies. Americans have worked out their rules of competition at

home, and are now trying to extend them into international commerce as sort of an afterthought. But to most Europeans and Canadians, competition mainly means international competition, with industry at home organized above all to meet the pressure of that unforgiving environment.

The Sherman Antitrust Act is not a suitable instrument for the regulation of world trade. Maintaining international competition is the proper business of diplomats and negotiation, not federal judges and litigation.

In the end, competition itself is the victim of the uncontrolled chain reaction that was triggered by the U.S. uranium import embargo. The international conflict it has created is but one more barrier to free trade and competition, at a time when many fear the spectre of a renewed era of mercantilism.

Perhaps the concept of free trade and its twin sister, competition, is an ideal that will never be fully realized. Even that first great champion of free trade and opponent of mercantilism, Adam Smith, was never confident of success. "To expect . . . that freedom of trade should ever be entirely restored in Great Britain," he wrote, "is as absurd as to expect that an Oceana or Utopia should ever be established in it." Smith blamed this on the fact that, according to him, "the sophistry of merchants inspired by the spirit of monopoly has confounded the common sense of mankind."

Smith was speaking of the kind of monopolies that are not attacked by the U.S. Department of Justice, the kind that are, from time to time, sponsored by the policies and laws of the United States itself. Just how much these can confound common sense is demonstrated not only by the U.S. uranium embargo, but also by an earlier program of U.S. import restrictions that strikingly parallels the disastrous U.S. effort to restrict oil imports.

COMMON SENSE CONFOUNDED

. . . I am just wondering if you are not advocating the same policy that the oil companies advocated for many years. That was, keep out the import of oil so that they can have no competition in the field of prices here for their domestic oil, and they would have the whole market, you might say.

Now whether we did wisely or not, that is what we did. Today with depleted oil and gas supplies in this country we are now at the mercy of imported oil, price-wise at least, and maybe quantity-wise.

Now, if we forgo our opportunities today to buy foreign [uranium] ore, aren't we just doing something that is expedient for the next decade or more, and will we not live to rue the day that we didn't conserve our domestic supplies? This kind of bothers me, I will admit.

> Representative Chet Holifield,
> Member of the U.S. Congressional
> Joint Committee on Atomic Energy,
> October 4, 1973.

Congressman Holifield was to be deeply bothered, indeed, by events that were taking shape even as he spoke.

He made these remarks at a hearing of the Joint Committee on Atomic Energy in response to yet another request from the U.S. uranium producers for protection from imports.

J. C. Stephenson, chairman of the uranium advisory committee of the American Mining Congress, had just urged a "uranium import policy designed to maximize the utilization of the domestic resource base." Stephenson said that this was "particularly important in view of the danger of our becoming dependent upon foreign sources for another of our energy raw materials."

It was exactly the same argument that had been used as the basis to limit oil imports: keep out imports in order to sustain a viable domestic industry and thus avoid dependence on foreign sources of supply.

It was an utter failure.

Four days after Holifield had admitted that this approach "kind of bothers me," the Arab members of the Organization of Petroleum Exporting Countries embargoed oil supplies to the United States and certain other western nations, setting off the price spiral that would see the world price of oil increase nearly 2,000 per cent in 8 years. The former U.S. oil import control program did nothing to cushion Americans from the shock of higher oil prices, the threat of shortages, nor the steadily increasing dependence on imported oil, which grew to half of the total oil supplies used in the United States.

Not only did the oil imports controls fail to meet their objective, they also carried a hefty price.

During the 18 years that the program was in effect, Americans paid as much as 80 per cent more than other countries for their oil supplies, the principal source of energy.

And blocking out the world's largest market to foreign producers provided a good deal of the impetus for the formation of the OPEC, the oil producers cartel, in the same way that the uranium import embargo later led to the uranium cartel.

Finally, if the program had been intended to benefit American oil producers, even in that regard it was a dismal failure. Because of the import limitations, U.S. oil producers wound up selling at comparatively low prices oil which they could otherwise have later sold for more than ten times as much.

It could be said that the U.S. oil imports control program was as big a flop as the later international uranium cartel. And that, perhaps, is sufficient commentary on the effects of government intervention in a competitive market economy.

Until after the Second World War, the United States was the largest oil consumer, producer, and exporter in the world. But the United States could not keep pace with enormous supplies of low cost oil developing in other areas, particularly the Middle East. In 1948 the United States became a net importer of oil for the first time, and the volume of low-cost oil imports was growing at a rate of about 15 per cent a year. In 1954, President Eisenhower called on the oil companies to honour a voluntary program to limit oil imports to 12 per cent of total U.S. petroleum consumption. In 1959, mandatory oil import controls were imposed, again seeking to limit imports to 12 per cent of total supplies. In 1972, with oil imports rising, with domestic supplies declining, and with a threat of shortages looming, President Nixon finally scrapped the oil imports program.

The quarter of a century that followed the Second World War was the era of cheapest energy supplies that the world has ever known. Oil prices were remarkably steady during this period, and in relative terms, the cost of energy dropped sharply.

But thanks to the import controls, it was Japan, western Europe, and other oil consuming nations that reaped the biggest benefits from this low cost energy.

Over a twenty-five-year period to 1970, the average price for U.S. oil production increased only 68 per cent, to $3.18 a barrel. During the same years, the price for Saudi Arabia crude, the benchmark for world oil prices, increased only 12 per cent to $1.80 per barrel.

Denying the U.S. market to other producers, contributed to the glut of oil supplies that prevailed throughout most of the postwar period, and thus to lower prices. Throughout the period of the U.S. import controls, other nations were able to purchase oil at prices $1 to $1.50 per barrel less than American oil prices. This provided a significant advantage for the industrial competitive ability of countries like Japan. Petroleum consultant Peter R. Odell, writing in *Oil and World Power*, claimed that the importance of this lower cost of energy to oil consuming countries may have been as "great as the effects of the Marshall plan for European recovery."

But if the oil consuming nations were pleased with the benefits of low-cost energy, the oil producing nations clearly were not. Because of their concern about selling their natural resources at distress prices, and because they had been precluded from competing in the world's largest market, the governments of oil-producing countries in South America, the Middle East, and elsewhere met in Baghdad on September 5, 1960 – one year after the imposition of the U.S. mandatory oil import controls – to form the Organization of Petroleum Exporting Countries.

It has been estimated that without the import controls, U.S. oil production would have been reduced by one-third to one-half during the 1960's. As a result of the controls, American oil producers sold at least an additional 10 billion barrels of oil during this decade, for a price of about $30 billion. But had that same 10 billion barrels of oil been produced during the 1980's instead of the 1960's, the price would have been not $30 billion, but at least $400 billion.

By restraining competition in the market, the effects of the U.S. oil import controls included: higher energy prices for American consumers; a competitive advantage for the economies of other oil-consuming countries; the formation of the most powerful producer's cartel in history; an impaired ability to counter the power and effects of that cartel; an added force to the upward spiral of prices.

If the United States should once again turn to similar protective measures, in order to maintain a viable domestic uranium producing industry so as to reduce reliance on imported energy, the ultimate effects would inevitably be of the same character.

Yet in times of difficulty, the pleas for protection are seldom stilled.

The boom in uranium prices that started in 1974 was short lived. After reaching a peak of about $43 a pound, by 1980 uranium prices had dropped to $30 a pound. In real terms, discounting inflation, the price of uranium had been cut nearly in half. Uranium was again in surplus supply. Inventories were overflowing. Exploration for new uranium deposits had virtually ceased. Some mines were shut. And in 1980, U.S. uranium producers were once again seeking measures to limit imports in order, they claimed, to maintain a viable domestic producing industry.

Was Adam Smith right? Will common sense forever be confounded? Will we never learn?

SOME NOTES
ON THE BIBLIOGRAPHY

I have not read everything that is available on the international uranium cartel. No one has. No one ever will.

Even U.S. Federal District Court Judge Prentice Marshall, who has spent years in hearings on the suit brought by Westinghouse Electric Corporation against twenty-nine uranium producers in Chicago, is quoted as stating that he does not intend to read the entire record. He could not.

The record of all the litigation related to the uranium cartel has been estimated to total well in excess of 10 million pages. That includes transcripts of the trials and pre-trial hearings, hundreds of deposition statements, an even greater number of briefs and motions, which have been filed with the courts, and mountains of exhibits. In addition, there is the record of hearings before various legislative and administrative bodies.

A full decade devoted to nothing else but reading this record would not be long enough to complete the task.

Yet the record of the litigation proceedings is a primary source of information on the cartel, and its background.

This complete litigation record was made available to me through the generous offices of Dr. Jerry McAfee, chairman of the Gulf Oil Corporation, at Gulf's head offices in Pittsburgh. I had requested, from Mr. McAfee, Gulf's assistance in making available to me only information that was a matter of public record. That is all that I received from Gulf, and that is all I wanted.

Gulf generously provided me with office space in which to work, while I read as much of this documentation as I could. Large cartons of transcripts, deposition proceedings, and other court documents I had requested were wheeled in on freight dollies.

My approach, generally, was to read as much of the transcripts as I could, focusing on who I considered to be the key witnesses, and from this identifying key exhibits and other documents. The court cases are identified in the bibliography. I have not attempted to list all the individual documents in these proceedings that I have drawn upon. Those that I have quoted from are identified in the text. An exception is the *amici curiae* briefs of foreign governments to the U.S. courts, which I have listed because they seem particularly relevant.

In addition to the court documents of public record obtained from Gulf, a very few leaked documents obtained from other sources have proven useful. These were documents from a subcommittee of the U.S. Department of Justice in Washington, and a very few cabinet documents from the Canadian government in Ottawa. These are identified in the text, although the sources of these, of course, are not. The assistance of those who volunteered these records to me is gratefully, if anonymously, acknowledged.

More than a score of interviews with industry and government officials in the United States, Canada, and Great Britain, provided another important source of information. Because of the sensitivities related to the various litigation, most of those to whom I talked chose to speak to me on an off-the-record basis. Their assistance is, again, anonymously acknowledged. Two notable exceptions who did not hesitate for a moment to grant me on-the-record interviews were former Canadian cabinet minister Donald Macdonald, and Jerry McAfee.

I should hasten to add that no one provided me with any information which, to my knowledge, was in violation of Canada's Uranium Information Security Regulations, or the laws of any other country that continues to put a clamp on some of the cartel documents, a relatively small number in relation to those that have been made public. Whether access to this proscribed material would have contributed any significant additional information is a moot question. In any event, it was with a feeling of some relief that I was spared the need to decide whether or not to break the laws proscribing the publication of this material, because the opportunity never came my way.

More than 400 articles in newspapers, magazines, and learned journals, as well as numerous books and monographs, were perused for source material. Only the more relevant ones are listed in the bibliography.

In tracking down this material, I had efficient assistance from librarians in the Library of Congress in Washington, the Toronto and Ottawa public libraries, and the University of Toronto, who thus willingly, if unwittingly, have contributed to this book. Jim Weller of the Canadian Nuclear Association also provided helpful material from that association's library. Mary Jane Jones provided helpful assistance for some of my research in Ottawa.

In researching documents related to the Manhattan Project to build the atomic bomb during the Second World War, I received splendid assistance from Mr. Charles Dewing of the U.S. National Archives in Washington, in a visit to that centre which was all too brief.

Despite all this generous assistance, the end result remains a book that has been approved and sanctioned by no one, and for which the author must take all the blame for any errors. It would be incorrect to state that the book reflects the opinions of only the author, for I have quoted the views and opinions of many others; and these in turn have, in many cases, helped inform and influence my own views. Nevertheless, any views not specifically attributed to someone else, are simply one man's opinion.

Bibliography

JUDICIAL PROCEEDINGS

American Arbitration Association. In the matter of an arbitration between General Atomic Company and United Nuclear Corporation. Final award. San Diego, California, December 12, 1980.

Canada, Supreme Court. Judgment re Gulf Oil Corporation v. Gulf Oil Canada Limited, C. D. Shepard, Gulf Minerals Canada Ltd., and R. Niel Taylor, March 12, 1980.

United Kingdom, House of Lords. In re Westinghouse Electric Corporation uranium contract litigation, multi-district litigation docket 235, appeals. London, December 1, 1977.

United States:

District Court for the eastern District of Virginia, Richmond. Westinghouse Electric Corporation, uranium contracts litigation, multi-district litigation docket 235.

District Court for the northeastern District of Illinois, eastern division, Chicago. In re uranium antitrust litigation, multi-district litigation docket 342.

New Mexico. District Court of the First Judicial District, County of Santa Fe. United Nuclear Corporation v. General Atomic Company *et al.*, case no. 50827.

Amici Curiae **Briefs of Foreign Governments to U.S. Courts re Uranium Litigation:**

Australia, to U.S. District Court, Chicago, May 29, 1980; September 17, 1979.

Canada, to U.S. District Court, Chicago, May 21, 1979; May 21, 1980; July 1, 1980.

Canada, to U.S. Supreme Court, re appeal on ruling of New Mexico State Judge Edwin Felter, April 17, 1978.

Republic of South Africa to U.S. District Court, Chicago, August 16, 1979.

United Kingdom of Great Britain to U.S. District Court, Chicago, September 27, 1979.

DIPLOMATIC NOTES OF FOREIGN GOVERNMENTS TO UNITED STATES RE URANIUM

Australia. Aide memoire, July 23, 1970. Diplomatic note, March 23, 1978.

Canada. Diplomatic note no. 210, August 4, 1968. Aid memoire, July 23, 1970. Diplomatic note no. EPC-25, November 8, 1978.

France. Statement to U.S. Department of State, October 27, 1978. Memorandum, September 26, 1979.

LEGISLATIVE PROCEEDINGS

Canada, Parliament, House of Commons, debates, Hansard. 1965 – June 3 and 4: 1970 – March 2, 3, 19, and 20: 1971 – May 13: 1974 – December 20: 1976 – June 9 and 17; July 9: 1977 – June 17; August 4, 5, and 9; October 25; November 14, 16, 21, and 24.

United Kingdom, Parliament, House of Commons, Hansard (debate on Protection of Trading Interest Bill), November 15, 1979.

United States, Congress, House of Representatives, Subcommittee on Oversight and Investigations of the Committee on Interstate and Foreign Commerce. Hearings re uranium cartel, November 4, 1976; June, 16 and 17, 1977; August 15, 1977; December 8, 1977.

United States, Congress, Joint Committee on Atomic Energy. 1957 – February 21; 1958 – February 19, 24, 25, and 26: 1959 – February 23 to 26; 1960 – January 27; February 19: 1963 – April 3; July 30 and 31; August 1: 1964 – June 9, 10, 11, 15, and 25.

United States, Congress, Senate Judiciary Committee. 1979 – December 7: 1980 – January 24.

BOOKS

Avery, David. *Not On Queen Victoria's Birthday* (a history of Rio-Tinto Zinc). Wm. Collins Sons and Co., London, 1974.

Bertrand, Goldschmidt. *The Atomic Adventure*, Macmillan, New York, 1962.

Carrington, John. *Risk Taking in Canadian Mining*. Pitt Publishing, Toronto, 1980.

Cave Brown, Anthony, and MacDonald, Charles B., editors. *The Secret History of The Atomic Bomb*. (An edited version of the multi-volume official Manhattan Engineering District history). The Dial Press/James Wade, New York, 1977.

Compton, Arthur H. *Atomic Quest*. Oxford University Press, New York, 1956.

Eggleston, Wilfrid. *Canada's Nuclear Story*. Clarke, Irwin and Company, Toronto, 1965.

Eldorado Mining and Refining Limited. *Uranium in Canada*. Eldorado, Ottawa, 1964.

Gowing, Margaret. *Britain and Atomic Energy*. Macmillan, London, 1964.

Griffith, J. W. *The Uranium Industry – Its History, Technology and Prospects*. Department of Energy, Mines and Resources, Ottawa, 1967.

Groves, Lt. General Leslie R. *Now It Can Be Told*. Harper, New York, 1962.

Hayes, Denis, *et al. Red Light For Yellowcake*. Friends of the Earth, Australia, 1977.

Hewlett, Richard G., and Anderson Jr., Oscar E. *The New World*, volume one of the history of the U.S. Atomic Energy Commission. AEC, 1972.

Hyams, Barry. *Hirshhorn: Medici From Brooklyn*. E. P. Dutton, New York, 1972.

LeBourdais, D. M. *Canada and the Atomic Revolution*. McClelland and Stewart, Toronto, 1959.

Lewis, Richard S. *The Nuclear Power Rebellion*. Viking Press, New York, 1978.

Metzger, H. Peter. *The Atomic Establishment*. Simon and Schuster, New York, 1978.

Morrison, Robert W., and Wonder, Edward F. *Canada's Nuclear Export Policy*. The Norman Patterson School of International Affairs, Carleton University, Ottawa.

Sherwin, Martin J. *A World Destroyed: The Atomic Bomb and The Grand Alliance*. Alfred A. Knopf, New York, 1975.

Taylor, June H., and Yokel, Michael D. *Yellowcake: The International Uranium Cartel*. Pergamon Press, New York, 1980.

ARTICLES, PAPERS, MONOGRAPHS, AND OTHER MATERIAL

Anderson, Jack. "Justice Department. Blew Uranium Cartel Case." *Washington Post*, Washington, September 17, 1979.

Baker, Donald I. "Antitrust conflicts between friends: Canada and the United States in the mid-1970s." *Cornell International Law Journal*, Summer, 1978.

Bell, Griffin B. "Address to the American Bar Association," Chicago, August 8, 1977.

Brown, Carson L. "Elliot Lake: the world's uranium capital." *Canadian Geographical Journal*, Ottawa, March 2, 1972.

Business Week. "The uranium dilemma: why prices mushroomed." November 1, 1976.

Business Week. "Creeping cartelization." May 9, 1977.

Business Week. "Anglo American's golden windfall." March 17, 1980.

Canadian Nuclear Association. "Proceedings of the first Canadian conference on uranium and atomic energy." Toronto, January 11-13, 1960.

Cheeseright, Paul, *et al.* "Pushing back the boundary of U.S. jurisdiction." *Financial Times*, London, November 29, 1979.

Cira Jr., Carl A. "Current developments in antitrust and foreign trade." Address to the Westchester-Fairfield Corporate Counsel Association, May 23, 1979.

Financial Post. "U.S. urges no uranium for de Gaulle." Toronto, January 18, 1964.

Financial Post. "Big on-off again talk of uranium sale." Toronto, January 25, 1964.

Forbes. "Steve Roman's waiting game." New York, October 1, 1970.

Forbes. "Blacks, whites and Harry Oppenheimer." New York, June 15, 1973.

Forbes. "It worked for the Arabs." New York, July 15, 1975.

Forbes. "Westinghouse: the waiting period." New York, December 1, 1975.

Forbes. "Bureaucractic imperialism." New York, November 15, 1977.

Gibson, Paul. "DeBeers: can a cartel be forever?" *Forbes*, New York, May 28, 1979.

Greider, William. "Proper Britains invoke 'fifth': Yanks want them to sing." *Washington Post*, Washington, July 13, 1977.

Griffin, Joseph P. "American antitrust law and foreign governments." *Journal of International Law and Economics*, volume 12.

Heise, Horst. Various reports in Oilweek magazine, Calgary, On Gulf's uranium exploration and Rabbit Lake discovery in Saskatchewan. August 12, 1968; April 29, 1968; August 14, 1967; December 9, 1976; December 16, 1967.

Hermann, A. H. "The long arm of U.S. antitrust." *Financial Times*, London, June 15, 1977.

Hughes, Emmet John. "Joe Hirshhorn, the Brooklyn uranium king." *Fortune*, New York, 1956.

Joskow, Paul L. "Commercial impossibility, the uranium market, and the Westinghouse case." *The Journal of Legal Studies*, University of Chicago, January 1977.

Kelly, Paul. "The uranium men discover they've got a lousy image." *The National Times*, Melbourne, August 16, 1976.

Kohlmeier, Louis. "The uranium affair." *Journal of international law and economics*, volume 12.

Lang, Herbert H. "Uranium mining and the Atomic Energy Commission." *Harvard Business History Review*, Harvard University, 1962.

Le Craw, D. J. "The uranium cartel: an interim report." *The Business Quarterly*, University of Western Ontario, Winter, 1977.

Lee, John M. "Uranium town in search of a boom (Elliot Lake)." *New York Times*, December 23, 1964.

Lellouche, Pierre. "International nuclear politics." *Foreign Affairs*, New York, Winter, 1979/80.

Maechling Jr., Charles. "Uncle Sam's long arm." *American Bar Association Journal*, March, 1977.

Marks, Lee R. "State Department perspectives on antitrust enforcement abroad." *Journal of International Law and Economics*, volume 12.

McIntyre, Hugh C. "Uranium, nuclear power and Canada – U.S. energy relations." C. D. Howe Research Institute, Montreal, 1978.

Meyers, Harold B. "The great uranium glut." *Fortune*, February, 1964.

Middleton, Drew. "Canada offers to sell uranium for French atomic force." *New York Times*, January 17, 1964.

Morgenthaler, Eric. "Yellowcake caper: Westinghouse's woes over uranium supplies affect entire industry." *Wall Street Journal*, September 30, 1976.

Mulholland, Joseph P. *et al.* "An analysis of the competitive structure in the uranium supply industry." U.S. Federal Trade Commission, Washington, 1977.

Nucleonics Week, New York. Various items on Canadian, Australian, and Japanese uranium negotiations. April 29, June 10, and July 15, 1971.

Perrin, Stryker. "The Great Uranium Rush." *Fortune*, August, 1954.

Phillips, Alan. "Our wild atomic city (Elliot Lake)." *Maclean's*, Toronto, May 25, 1957.

Probyn, Stephen and Anthony, Michael. "The cartel that Ottawa built." *Canadian Business*, Toronto, November, 1977.

Roberts, Leslie. "The Algom Story." Rio Algom Limited, Toronto, 1955.

Robertson, David S. "Uranium price movement and the reasons therefor." David S. Robertson & Associates Limited, Toronto, February 6, 1978.

Runnalls, O. J. C. "The uranium industry in Canada: A brief submitted to the Cluff Lake Board of Inquiry," Regina, Saskatchewan. Department of Energy Mines and Resources, Ottawa, April, 1977.

Smith, Richard Austin. "The incredible electrical conspiracy." *Fortune*, April and May, 1961.

Time magazine. "The uranium cartel's fallout: billion-dollar lawsuits are popping up everywhere." November 21, 1977.

United States, Atomic Energy Commission. Development of the Atomic Energy Industry. Report to the President of the United States, November, 1962.

United States, National Archives, Washington. Record Group 227, records of the Office of Scientific Research and Development, S-1 Committee, Bush-Conant correspondence. (Documents related to the development of the atomic bomb.)

Watkins, Lynden. "Unidentified firm bids for control of Denison Mines." Toronto *Globe and Mail*, February 27, 1970.

Wood, Jefrey L., and Carrea, Victor M. "The International uranium cartel: litigation and legal implications." *Texas International Law Journal*, volume 14:59.